RETHINKING
CLASSROOM
MANAGEMENT

RETHINKING
CLASSROOM
MANAGEMENT

Strategies for Prevention, Intervention, and Problem Solving

Patricia Sequeira Belvel ▪ Maya Marcia Jordan

CORWIN PRESS, INC.
A Sage Publications Company
Thousand Oaks, California

For information:

Corwin Press, Inc.
A Sage Publications Company
2455 Teller Road
Thousand Oaks, California 91320
www.corwinpress.com

Sage Publications Ltd.
6 Bonhill Street
London EC2A 4PU
United Kingdom

Sage Publications India Pvt. Ltd.
M-32 Market
Greater Kailash I
New Delhi 110 048 India

Printed in the United States of America

Library of Congress Cataloging-in-Publication Data

Belvel, Patricia.
 Rethinking classroom management: Strategies for prevention,
intervention, and problem solving / Patricia Belvel, Marcia Jordan.
    p. cm.
Includes bibliographical references and index.
 ISBN 0-7619-4522-9 (c) — ISBN 0-7619-4523-7 (p)
 1. Classroom management. 2. Classroom environment. 3. Conflict
management. I. Jordan, Marcia. II. Title.
 LB3013 .B394 2002
 371.102′4—dc21   2002005182

This book is printed on acid-free paper.

  04 05 06 10 9 8 7 6 5 4 3

Acquisitions Editor:	Rachel Livsey
Editorial Assistant:	Phyllis Cappello
Developmental Editor:	Elisabeth Magnus
Production Editor:	Diane S. Foster
Typesetter:	Bramble Books
Proofreader:	Andrea Martin
Indexer:	Teri Greenberg
Cover Designer:	Michael Dubowe
Production Designer:	Sandra Ng

Contents

Foreword

In *Rethinking Classroom Management*, Pat Belvel and Maya Jordan offer teachers an exciting and dynamic opportunity to rethink current classroom management practices. This book invites teachers to become engaged in examining their beliefs, practices, interactions, and outcomes with students in order to increase student achievement. Providing a compelling structure of ideas, procedures, and examples by which a teacher can develop exemplary classroom practices, this interactive text gives a clear and concise framework for establishing strategies that work. Preservice through veteran teachers who read this book will gain a strong sense of what excellent classroom management practices should be and how to attain them. I have never seen a more comprehensive and concise book that takes classroom management theory to practice. The classroom leadership framework introduced in the book causes all of us as educators to rethink our teacher role in the classroom.

Belvel and Jordan know from years of experience in the classroom as teachers the importance of classroom management as a foundation for the student learning environment. It is their ability to share this rich teaching experience, including that of thousands of teachers they have worked with over the years, that makes this book so meaningful for daily practice in the classroom. By engaging the reader in the reality of the classroom, the authors set the stage for the reader to assess what they know and create a meaningful avenue for connection to relevant experience to the set for new learning. Any teacher who reads this book will be able to develop strategies that are personally defined and owned by them to use in their daily interactions with students. No teacher's class will be the same after experiencing and practicing these crucial classroom management beliefs and practices. We know from research and best practices that if classroom management practices are not in place, students will have an ineffective learning environment. *Rethinking Classroom Management* provides every teacher with a comprehensive way of creating classrooms where students are self-managing and learning takes place.

The strength of this book comes from the linkages made in the three major sections of *Rethinking Classroom Management*: rethinking beliefs and roles, prevention strategies, temporary interventions, and problem-solving strategies. The authors never lose sight of the need for teachers to be effective classroom managers and keep an unwavering focus on student learning. I invite you to read, interact, practice within your classroom, and critique the effective classroom management strategies presented here. Otherwise I pose the question: Can we continue to condemn our students to classroom management practices that are not effective and fail to provide all of our students with the best learning environment in which they can achieve their best? Belvel and Jordan challenge us to rethink our practices so that we challenge ourselves—and rise to the occasion. As educators who want the best for our students, we can expect no less.

Marsha Speck, EdD
Professor, Educational Leadership
Director of the Urban High School Leadership Program
San Jose State University, San Jose, California

Preface

Welcome all teachers, from preservice to veteran educators. *Rethinking Classroom Management* is an exciting opportunity to rethink your classroom management practices. This book presents an interactive process where every chapter begins with an authentic classroom scenario for you to create your own personal connection to your experiences as a student and teacher. *Rethinking Classroom Management* is a work that has been in process for over 20 years. It evolved from a behavior management workbook to a self-esteem workbook, to a classroom management workbook, and most recently a classroom leadership workbook. Now it has arrived as this rich teacher-driven, integrative framework of research-based strategies that will invite responsibility, resourcefulness, and mutual respect for both teachers and students. Successful teachers have used the strategies presented here for years. They were formally documented and labeled after observing and annotating what excellent teachers do when they are orchestrating instruction. Teaching has a minimum amount of agreed-upon professional language to describe what is done in the classroom. Physicians can talk to each other from other countries about a patient and speak using the same terms. Lawyers can communicate from one continent to another using common language. We want to provide teachers with the same ability to share successes and be consciously competent about their leadership skills.

These strategies will provide you with initiative and increased flexibility in being congruent with your beliefs about students and teacher needs. The framework and techniques presented come from real live classrooms, both our own and those of the teachers we've worked with for the past 20 years. Their richness developed as we learned more and more about how effective teachers use their leadership skills to create classrooms where students are self-managing. Teachers who model and teach the students these strategies are able to accommodate individual and cultural differences.

During our process as teachers, we evolved through rethinking our classroom management and made our last years the easiest and best. We both experienced a shift in students' intrinsic motivation and our own need to "control" as benevolent dictators. Our shift created a more positive environment for both our students and ourselves. As our stress level decreased, we shared leadership in the classroom. Our hope for you is that you can learn and use these same strategies sooner than later and make your first years among your easiest and best.

■ OVERVIEW OF THE BOOK

Rethinking Classroom Management begins with Part I, "Rethinking Our Roles in the Classroom." You are empowered and encouraged to take the time to shift your thinking and discover your beliefs and values as educators. The leadership framework is built upon this shift and provides a structure for *Rethinking Classroom Management*.

Parts II and III present three sets of strategies: prevention, intervention, and problem solving (Figure I.1). Part II focuses on prevention strategies, since we all know that "an ounce of prevention is worth a pound of cure." These strategies are at the heart of classroom management and provide the foundation for you to be an effective and influential leader in your classroom. In 80% to 85% of your interactions with any group you are leading, whether in the classroom or in any other leadership role, these preventions will foster success. By the end of the Part II you will be able to build the relationships that are the foundation for cooperation and establish a positive classroom climate using more than 10 prevention strategies. These strategies are designed to create a caring community of learners, inviting students to become citizens rather than tourists in your classroom.

Part III addresses temporary intervention techniques (Chapter 7) and solution-focused problem-solving strategies (Chapter 8). Temporary interventions are for use when learning ceases and a classroom upset has caused the brains of both teachers and students to "downshift" and prevent clear thinking. We will differentiate between discipline and punishment and clarify the leader's role in teaching and modeling respectful behavior in honoring each other's needs. These interventions will eliminate the most common disruptive student behaviors seen in most classrooms. Remember that the preventions eliminated 80% to 85%. By the end of Chapter 7, you will be able to effectively manage classroom disruptions in ways that are congruent with beliefs about mutual respect. You will be able to apply the "principles of positive intervention" that are embedded in all of the techniques that help shape students toward more appropriate behaviors. The goal here is to have interventions constitute less than 3% to 5% of your leadership interactions in the classroom as preventions increase.

Chapter 8 explores problem-solving strategies for solving repetitive problems and finding solution-focused outcomes using a "no-blame" model in which one thinks about "the problem as the problem" rather than "the person as the problem." The remaining 5% to 15% of classroom problems will require problem solving. By the end of this chapter, you will be

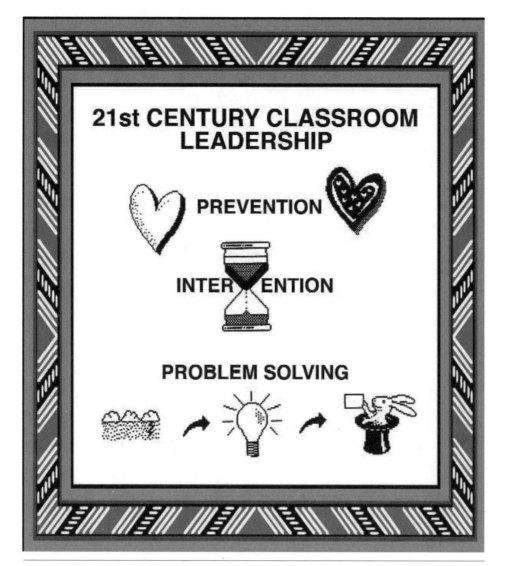

Figure I.1.   Three Sets of Teaching Strategies for Leadership

able to use solution-focused problem-solving strategies with individual students and with groups. These strategies will invite them to take responsibility and to become involved in creating constructive solutions that are "win-win" for everyone in the group.

The original concept of a framework approach to classroom management was developed by Jeanne Horan Herrick in 1980. It has been adapted, expanded, and revised on the basis of the latest research of Alfie Kohn, Frank Smith, Leslie Hart, Howard Gardner, Vernon and Louise Jones, William Glasser, Larry Lowery, Steven Covey, Linda Metcalf, Lee Cantor, Allen Mendler, and Fred Jones. The strategies selected from these other classroom management programs were chosen and placed in the framework on the basis of their congruence with the values and beliefs of effective leadership, which puts relationship and mutual respect at the heart of the matter. In addition, we have relied on the experience of thousands of professional teachers who have practiced and used these strategies successfully. For the past 15 years, these strategies have been shared with thousands of teachers, new as well as seasoned. As we coached teachers in their classrooms, strategies were adapted and new ones added. We pass on what we learned as we observed teachers applying the strategies from this book in hundreds of unique situations.

■ HOW TO USE THIS BOOK

The following are the structural elements of the presentation of each skill. The accompanying icons are provided as visual clues to remind you of the flow and process of your learning.

 All of the chapters and many of the chapter subsections dealing with specific skills or concepts are introduced with a quote from respected educators to capture and support the outcome of the concepts being presented.

 All of the chapters and many of the chapter subsections begin with a Classroom Connection, which is a classroom story with fictitious names to allow you to immerse yourself in a real-life experience.

 This is followed by a Personal Connection activity to access what you already know. It is the reader's responsibility to create a meaningful avenue of connection from his or her own relevant experience.

Next, the strategy or skill is introduced with research and rationales.

 Benefits for teacher and students are summarized.

 Specific examples for using the skill in the classroom are presented.

 Key criteria are summarized.

Benefits, examples, and key criteria may be presented in varying order.

 Most skills have a practice activity called Checking My Understanding for self-testing.

 The final activity for each technique is a Personal Commitment. This is the crucial action step you will take to bring the skill to life in your classroom.

 Each chapter ends with a summary to use for review or reference.

The following invocation guided our writing of this book and captures our mission and our hopes for you and your leadership of our next-generation citizens:

> May the Great Spirit of Wisdom and Learning
> Provide the inspiration and intuition
> To write this book for the highest good of teachers and students.
> Let our purpose light the way to invite teachers
> Into new ways of thinking about their students and themselves
> And to spark and nourish the creative genius
> That lies within us all.

PERSONAL GOAL FOR READING THE BOOK ■

1. What do you want for yourself out of reading this book? (If you answered, "Less stress, peaceful relationships with students, and strategies for feeling successful in creating a positive learning environment," read on, this book is for you!)

_____

_____

2. What would you like for your students as a result of reading this book? (If you answered, "Less teacher dependence, more respect and responsibility, increased learning, and more community among students," keep reading!)

■ ACKNOWLEDGMENTS

In the spirit of "rethinking" acknowledgments, we reflected on the powerful contributions that others have made to our work. We revisited our gratitude to those heartful people who shared their knowledge, experience, expertise, and spirit with us; without them we couldn't have completed this book.

For inspiration and guidance, we thank the following:

● Dr. Marsha Speck, an educator who applied these skills as a high school principal and assistant superintendent over 12 years ago, an author and expert on staff development, and a friend who guided us from our training manual format to a Corwin publication.

● Diane Roberts, business partner, computer guru, and personal coach, whose steady spirit and good humor saw us through even our roughest times. From beginning to end, she rescued and problem-solved with us through two computer crashes and the 9/11 heartbreaks.

● Schools and districts (over 100) who were courageous enough to create new learning paradigms by offering the Classroom Leadership Training, which teaches the strategies incorporated in this book. They valued the importance of staff development that creates the school climate students need to be successful learners.

● Teachers (over 1,000) who pioneered these ideas in their classrooms, refining them, creating nuances, and sharing their practical applications, which we've incorporated in the stories and examples documented here.

For production, design, and editing, we thank

● Brandy Caroline Lee-Jacob, Pat's daughter, for contributing the artistic design of the icons that introduce each phase of the chapters. Her constructive criticism and thoughtful questions helped give shape and organization to this book. She was a practical and a spiritual resource.

- Parthenia Hicks, a poet and writer, who wrote the first prospectus and encouraged Pat to reconnect with Marcia.

- Cathi Clark, our desktop publisher, for persevering with us through formatting, typing, and reformatting when files got undone between Macs and PC. Her consistent focus and organization helped clarify our inconsistencies with desktop publishing.

- Our reviewers, who supported the need for this work and gave valuable suggestions: Nancy Witherell, Kim Truesdell, Rick Heidt, Jason A. Sanchez, Caroll O. Knipe, Marsha Speck, and Theresa R. Rouse.

- Kristine Dyer, a teacher, Pat's high school buddy's daughter, who took her precious time to read the early drafts online and give thoughtful, specific, practical feedback, which we gratefully used and incorporated.

For putting it all together, we acknowledge each other—for reconnecting, working together long distance, bridging our differences, sharing our strengths, and accommodating for each other's unique styles. And in the end our beliefs saw us through as friends and colleagues!

About the Authors

Patricia Sequeira Belvel is a mother, teacher, educational consultant, and leadership coach for teachers and families. She is also the founder and president of Training & Consulting Institute, Inc., whose mission is to promote leadership skills that will impact and shift management strategies from those that rely on the motivation of reward and punishment to those that invite internal control. She has been leading Classroom Leadership and Family Leadership workshops for the past 20 years, encouraging educators to initiate and support a learning environment, both at home and at school, that invites young people to become responsible, caring, courteous leaders. She is well known for her compassionate, no-blame approach in working with teachers and students. Currently she conducts workshops in school districts, at individual school sites, and for beginning teacher projects in various districts and counties and for both preservice and veteran teachers. Educators from many cultures and districts endorse her work because of the positive impact of the workshop and follow-up coaching sessions for both students and teachers. She holds a BA from College of the Holy Names in Oakland, California, and an MA from the University of Santa Clara, Santa Clara, California. Contact Pat at Pat@trngedu.com.

Maya Jordan is a leadership and learning coach. She is founder of Aiming for Excellence, where she partners with individuals and organizations to coach and design learning programs for realizing human potential. Her background includes 15 years as an educator, with 5 of those as a Mentor Teacher for Santa Cruz City Schools in California, where she trained and coached teachers in Pat Belvel's Classroom Leadership workshops. She conducts workshops for educators on creating success in the classroom. She has developed training for educators on using coaching skills to enhance the quality of relationships and communication in learning environments. She is an international trainer in Effective Communications and Coaching Skills. With 2 years as a Certified Corporate Business Coach, she delivers coach training via teleclasses for Corporate Coach University. She coaches new coaches, educators, and leaders in a wide variety of industries. Contact Maya at: Maya@aimingforexcellence.com.

Dedication

To our first teachers: Pat's mother, Carrie Medeiros Sequeira, and Maya's grandmother, Laura Hartwick, who encouraged and supported our becoming teachers and who modeled positive teaching strategies in our earliest days of life. They were unconsciously competent about the value of personal relationships being the No. 1 prevention.

To Pat's first coach, Jeanne Horan Herrick, who was in Pat's classroom weekly, teaching and coaching her on learning all of these strategies. She wrote the first version of this work and is the source of the heartful aspect to the strategies we want all teachers to use with their students.

To Maya's first coach, Patricia Sequeira Belvel, who brought inspiration and guidance to these practical techniques and made successful teaching a reality. She was honest and objective in pointing out the ways to grow and encouraged demonstrating the same honesty and objectivity while leading the classroom with heart.

Part I

Rethinking Our Role in the Classroom

ॐ

As a man thinketh, so is he.

—Proverbs 23:7

ॐ

Part I creates the setting for all of the strategies that are taught in this book by distinguishing between being a classroom leader and being a classroom manager. Chapter 1 clarifies how our thinking affects our teaching and invites you to reflect on how to make the shift from the stress of being the manager to the freedom of being a classroom leader. Chapter 2 provides an opportunity to look at various teaching styles in order to ensure that your teaching style matches your beliefs.

Shifting From Manager to Leader

1

ॐ

We are what we think. All that we are arises with our thoughts.
With our thoughts we make the world.

Buddha

ॐ

RETHINKING OUR ROLE AS TEACHERS ■

Classroom Connection

Jamal Patel was a fairly new teacher who seemed to work magic in getting his students to produce high academic work and appropriate social behavior. His classroom was orderly and ran smoothly. He had strong personal connections with his students and received excellent evaluations and commendations from his principal and his peers after his first year of teaching. He believed in intrinsic motivation and wanted his students to be motivated from within. He rewarded his students for their good behavior with points that were redeemable at the end of the week for such things as a free homework pass or a new design pencil or a sticker or whatever else was in the "goody box." However, when Mr. Patel was absent, he received numerous phone calls from his principal or his fellow teachers that his students were impolite, unruly, and unproductive with the substitute teacher. On one occasion when Mr. Patel was out for over a week the sub left negative notes about the class's behavior and how they had tried to reverse the point system and see how many points they could lose. Mr. Patel was puzzled. This did not match his experience of these students or his thinking. During a class meeting about this upset over the class behavior with subs, the students revealed that they behaved and performed well when he was there *because they really liked him and they didn't like the substitutes. They said that the incentive system was fun and they liked it but that they really didn't care about the "goody box items." Jamal Patel shared this with his mentor and began to rethink and research the issue of intrinsic motivation. Clearly, the students were motivated by their relationship with him but their motivation had not transferred to the higher level of "doing the right thing" because it was the right thing (intrinsic motivation). They were still pleasing their teacher and getting "goodies" or losing points (extrinsic motivation). Mr. Patel began to rethink his role as the "keeper of the norms" and the manager of the classroom. He began to strategize about how to become more of a leader who could guide the students to take more internal ownership of their behavior. He did this first by sharing his beliefs and thinking about intrinsic motivation with them at a class meeting and asking for their input. He recorded their ideas about how they thought that they could "manage themselves" when a substitute was in the classroom. They created two charts: "What We Need From a Sub" and "What Our Substitute Should Know" (Figure 1.1).*

Many thinkers and teachers, both ancient and modern, have asserted that our thoughts create our reality. We know that how we think about a problem strongly influences our ability to solve the problem. Mr. Patel is a teacher who thinks of himself as someone capable who can turn any upset "upside down" and as a creative force in the classroom who "works magic" with challenging students. He thinks of himself as having influence in his classroom, even though he realizes he may have little influence over what happens outside his classroom, in students' homes and private lives. Thus he had no fears about calling a meeting to involve his students in creating a solution rather than creating one by himself. His thinking was influenced strongly by his beliefs in intrinsic motivation, and when he experienced a conflict in his students' behavior he reevaluated his current practices. On the other hand, if that same teacher, with that same group of students started questioning his ability to "dance out of power struggles" and began to think of himself as unable to "manage these kinds of kids" because, for example, they came to him with too many home problems outside of his influence, he would lose his effectiveness. He would begin to notice all of the times when he was "out of control" and his students were uncooperative, and then he would see the cup as being half empty instead of half full. Our thinking does indeed affect our actions. According to Stephen Covey (1989), when we focus on things outside of our sphere of influence (e.g., changing our students' parents), we will be frustrated and have more worries and less influence, but when we put our attention on the things over which we have influence, our influence and sense of power will increase. We will be empowered to turn any upset "upside down," just like Mr. Patel. This principle is paramount in the story of "the little engine that could," who, while saying, "I think I can, I think I can, I think I can," gradually climbed the impossible hill. *Rethinking Classroom Management* invites you to shift from the narrow focus of the teacher as manager in the classroom to the bigger picture of the teacher as leader in the classroom. Take a few moments to respond to the question below and make your own personal connection to Mr. Patel's story and this idea of how our thinking affects our actions.

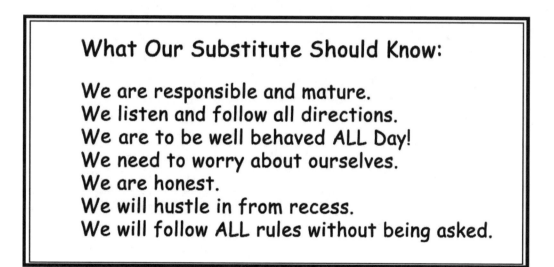

What We Need From A Sub

Understanding we miss our teacher
Trust and caring
Keep our routines
Follow our procedures
Have a sense of humor

What Our Substitute Should Know:

We are responsible and mature.
We listen and follow all directions.
We are to be well behaved ALL Day!
We need to worry about ourselves.
We are honest.
We will hustle in from recess.
We will follow ALL rules without being asked.

Figure 1.1.   Charts Created by Mr. Patel's Class

Personal Connection

How do the ways that you think about yourself and your students empower you to lead?

_____

_____

_____

_____

By the end of this chapter, you will be able to rethink, clarify, and write down your beliefs about your role as a leader in the classroom. This will help you rethink your role in your classroom and discover creative, proactive solutions to problems and issues that concern you. You already know how negative thinking affects your students who come into your classrooms with the "I can't" attitude. This background will help you take a look at your own thinking about your role in the classroom. Let's first look at the many roles teachers play in the classroom, then connect to Mr. Patel's classroom and identify the behaviors that distinguish a classroom leader from a classroom manager.

As teachers we are asked to play many different roles: curriculum designer, instructional guru, parent, counselor, nurse, advisor, custodian, child development expert, organizational planner, classroom manager, spiritual advisor, friend. We come into teaching with great inspiration and aspirations, yet after a few weeks many of us feel that we are perspiring more than inspiring. We are exhausted because we feel like we have been trying to hold 20 or 30 ping-pong balls under water all day long in a struggle for control. Our enthusiasm for teaching becomes diminished when we have to think about our students as objects to be managed and ourselves as "classroom managers."

This is the dilemma and challenge in classrooms today. How do we regain our sense of power and invite our students to be cooperative, responsible members of our classroom without turning into "Robo-Cops" or drill instructors? How do we inspire and lead students to appreciate these social values intrinsically? We all are faced with more challenges in a complex world that require and demand new ways of thinking and being. Students are coming to us with poorly developed social skills. The social and technological changes of this century allow for fewer natural opportunities for children to learn the basic prerequisite social skills of caring, sharing, deciding, acting, and following through. For many students, school is the one stable environment left for learning traditional and basic values of relationship, respect, resourcefulness, and responsibility.

Meeting current challenges in the classroom requires more than traditional classroom management; it calls for teachers to be leaders. Stephen Covey, in his book *The Seven Habits of Highly Effective People* (1989), makes a very clear distinction about how management is focused on "doing things right" whereas leadership is focused on "doing the right things." Management is about efficiency in climbing the ladder (getting our work done), whereas leadership guides students to put the ladder against the right wall (p. 101). Classroom management has traditionally been about methods; classroom leadership is focused on the direction the course of study will take and the vision of how the semester or year will look and feel. Classroom management often is about incentive-based motivation; classroom leadership is about motivation through relationship, inspiration, mutual respect, and common goals.

Teacher leaders like Jamal Patel get students to set sail with them on a voyage of learning. Teacher leaders invite students to be citizens in their classroom rather than "tourists" who "simply pass through without involvement, commitment or belonging" (Freiburg, 1996, p. 32). Teacher leaders invite students to become citizens in the classroom by asking them questions about what they are looking forward to learning this year, how they want to be treated by their teacher and their classmates, and how they are going to work with subs. They create a vision of an exciting year and motivate excitement and interest in their group through personal stories and connections as well as by asking the students to participate in creating the classroom environment. It becomes "our" classroom rather than "my" classroom. Once under sail, with everyone on board the ship, teacher leaders can use some management strategies to teach students the life skills of self-discipline, self-management, and self-reliance, as Mr. Patel did.

On the other hand, if students are not involved in and committed to the journey of the class, many will jump ship and hang onto the harbor, and the teachers will feel impelled to throw them life vests and jump in to save them. Teachers will then spend their time coaxing, bribing, or threatening them to stay on board. As they patrol the waters and the deck to keep the recalcitrant "tourists" on the ship, the teachers will become exhausted and frustrated, and no amount of management strategies will keep them from drowning in a sea of despair and discouragement.

But if the classroom leader creates the vision of the classroom voyage with the class, then he or she can concentrate on ensuring that the ship is sailing in the right direction. The leader keeps learning on track with the compass aligned to the goal.

Examples of Classroom Leadership

- Create a vision of an exciting year by involving the students in planning what they want to learn. Students go through the text or course outline and identify what they are most interested in learning and what is of least interest. Next, they create a list with three other students.

- Help students see connections to what they already know by asking them what they already know about the subject, whether it is eighth-grade math or third-grade social studies. List their responses so that everyone in the class can see them.

- Facilitate class meetings as a forum for students to plan learning activities, plan projects, field trips, and so on and to resolve classroom issues with a solution-focused, "no-blame" format.

- Ask questions out of a genuine interest in helping students resolve their own problems.

This book offers a contemporary alternative to traditional incentive-based classroom management strategies and an answer to a problem that has arisen with their use. From school site to school site, the words vary but the problem is the same: instead of self-directed, internally motivated youngsters, we are seeing more and more students dependent on external motivation to control their behavior. We seem to be educating a nation of students who continually ask us what they should do and what we will give them if they conform—and conversely, they ask us what we will do to them if they don't obey. If we keep treating our students as incapable of having intrinsic values, bribing them with carrots or punishing them with sticks we will create a society of citizens who will be always watching to see what they can get away with or who are dependent on someone to monitor their every move.

Traditional classroom management strategies aimed at controlling behavior are becoming less and less effective. Stickers, stars, awards, and rewards often become frustrating attempts to hold our classrooms together in some sort of orderly fashion. Alfie Kohn (1998) has been leading the way for educators to get off this treadmill by documenting and publishing research to substantiate that "the carrot and stick" systems (rewards and punishments) that rely on quick-fix techniques to get kids "shaped up" actually undermine the prosocial values that we are trying to teach. (See also Deci, Koestner, & Ryan, 2001.)

The role of the teacher in today's society is changing. Over the past 20 years, important social skills that used to be taught at home have become more and more the responsibility of the classroom teacher. Teaching is a powerful leadership position that has the potential to shape our society in a variety of ways. Many children spend more of their waking hours with their teachers than with their parents.

In educating young people today, we are preparing them to enter a complex, rapidly changing world. This demands that we have the vision and heart to assume our role as classroom leader and invite our students to appreciate and acquire the following leadership skills for themselves:

- An abiding respect for themselves and others

- The ability to choose responses on the basis of values rather than immediate feelings

- A clear sense of their capacity for influence and responsible behavior

- The ability to initiate appropriate action and follow through academically and socially

Key Criteria for a Classroom Leader

- Demonstrates an abiding respect for self and others

- Chooses responses based on values and beliefs rather than feelings

- Creates a vision for the students to connect to the academic and social curriculum

- Commits to ask more questions and give fewer answers to students

- Facilitates the learning process through student self-reflection and assessment

- When confronted with problems, shifts thinking to focus on solutions instead of blaming

- Believes that "efficient management without effective leadership is like straightening deck chairs on the Titanic" (Covey, 1989, p. 102)

- Uses strategies to support intrinsic motivation

✔ Checking My Understanding of Leadership

Answer true or false for the following:

_____ 1. Leadership is about doing things right.
_____ 2. Management is about methods.
_____ 3. Leadership is about efficiency.
_____ 4. Leadership is more about direction and goals.
_____ 5. Creating a vision for students is the role of the leader.

Answers: 1F, 2T, 3F, 4T, 5T

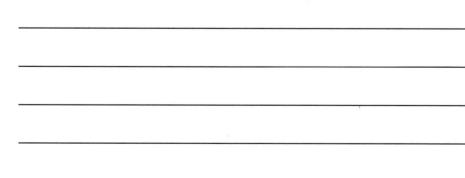 Personal Commitment

What are some issues about your role as the leader in your classroom that you want to rethink? (Think about your experiences with powerful teachers/leaders.)

_____

_____

_____

_____

■ OUR BELIEFS AND VALUES

ᔣ

Proactive leaders make decisions based on their values and beliefs, rather than their feelings.

Stephen Covey, *The Seven Habits of Highly Effective People*

ᔒ

Classroom Connection

Mrs. Esparza's kindergarten class had just come in from a rainy-day recess. The children had played in the rain, and some had explored in the mud. As Manuel and Rhea walked into the classroom, they made mud prints on the rug and were fascinated with their imprints. Mrs. Esparza saw the mud and exclaimed, "What are you doing, deliberately making mud tracks on our new carpet? You are going to miss recess at lunch for making this mess."

The children sat down bewildered. A few minutes later, as her anger was subsiding, Mrs. Esparza realized that they weren't doing it deliberately, it was just young children's curious way of experimenting. In her heart, she knew and believed that children this age often acted before they thought and that she had just done the same thing. She felt bad, so she went over to the table where Manuel and Rhea were sitting and said, "I'm sorry, children, I know that you didn't mean to make a mess. You were just fascinated with the mud. How can we clean the mud off of our new rug and remember to make mud prints outside?"

The children brightened and said, "We can get sponges and buckets and wash it up."

"Good idea. Let's get Mrs. Jenks to help you."

Though we can enjoy the humor of this story and feel for Mrs. Esparza's plight, we can also recognize that Mrs. Esparza's first response to the situation was an example of making a decision on feelings, not on values and beliefs. Many times, even as adult role models, we are unable to control our feelings of frustration, anger, outrage, and disbelief when students' behavior does not match our expectations. Teachers are human too. Much like our students, we can stop thinking when we are seriously upset. The first step to making certain that our actions match our beliefs and that what happened to Mrs. Esparza doesn't happen to us is to articulate our beliefs and values clearly.

Personal Connection

From your own experience as a student, what do you recall teachers doing that you would not choose to have in your teaching repertoire?

_____

_____

_____

_____

From your own experience as a student, what do you recall teachers doing that you want to do in your own classroom?

_____

_____

_____

_____

WHY SHOULD WE EXPLORE OUR BELIEFS AND VALUES? THE CONNECTION TO VIOLENCE PREVENTION AND ANGER MANAGEMENT

As teachers, we are intimately involved in the change process and need to become experts at how we can change behavior, both our own and our students'. So let's begin to challenge our thinking by looking at how our beliefs and values influence how we think about ourselves as a classroom leader and the connection this has to violence prevention and anger management for our students. By the end of this section, you will be able to write your beliefs and values about teaching and use them as a guide for decisions in your own classroom. This will help to cut down on your stress and provide a guide for your decision making. You already know how the leaders you admire most are those who match their actions to their values and beliefs and how dissonant it feels to work for or with people who say one thing and do another.

We are more than role models for our students; we are leaders and teachers of both an academic curriculum and a social curriculum. As part of our classroom curriculum, we are trying to teach our students how to channel aggression and violence in constructive ways—in other words, to think before they act. We teach this both by our modeling and by our talking to them about our own actions. For example, Mrs. Esparza could have said, "I am really angry, too angry to think. Sit down here in these chairs while I cool down." Then after her cerebral cortex had resumed functioning and she was thinking clearly, she could return and speak to the children about how they were going to make amends for their behavior. This is really the key to violence prevention: clarifying our values and beliefs and acting on our thinking rather than our emotions. We model for our students that we can and do make our decisions from our values and beliefs, not our feelings.

As teachers we have been to many workshops. Yet educational researchers have documented that less than 10% of us go back to our classrooms and implement what we learned without coaching (Olson, 1989). We know firsthand that changing a behavior is difficult work. In fact, according to a book by Leslie Hart entitled *Human Brain and Human Learning* (1983), our behavior is organically stored in our brain as a program. Once a program is built, we don't lose it. Our brain fires to the program that is stored, whether it is helpful or unhelpful. If it is unhelpful, the only way we can keep it from being enacted is to build a longer and stronger program of the new, more appropriate behavior so that the brain will fire to the new, longer and stronger program instead. In behavioral terms we used to refer to stored programs of behavior as "habits," not knowing that they are really organically stored in our brain much like on a computer chip and that the brain automatically goes there. How many times have you experienced the automatic response of habit? Have you ever moved into a new place and found yourself continuing to reach for the light switch where it was in your old place? Or remodeled your home and continued to try to put food in the oven where it used to be?

Over 10 years ago, some human resource researchers from IBM, Sears, and PG&E joined forces to determine why employees who went to workshops rarely applied their new learning in the workplace. What they found was that when the teaching or workshop focused only on actions (such as skills and behaviors) there was little hope that employees would integrate the skill into real life or commit to maintaining it. But when the teaching focused on connecting what was learned to personal and cultural values and beliefs, and on aligning one's thinking to support those values and beliefs, employees became committed to the change and were more able to change their actions and behaviors (Hord & Huling-Austin, 1989).

Figure 1.2 shows how changes in behavior happen and why our values and beliefs are so critical to rethinking our classroom management strategies. When we are adults, our beliefs and values shape our thinking, which

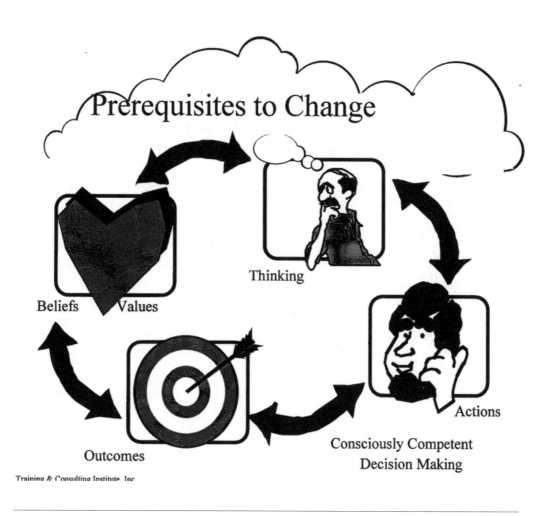

Figure 1.2. Prerequisites to Change

SOURCE: Training & Consulting Institute, Inc.

in turn shapes our decision making and consequently our actions and their outcomes. Notice that the arrows in the figure point in both directions, so that the process is cyclical.

Examples of How Beliefs and Values Shape Our Thinking

- Positive Example: Suppose that I, as a teacher, have a value about respect and beliefs about what respect should look like and sound like. The thinking that follows might be: "I think of myself as a respectful person; I treat students with respect." Then my actions flow from this thinking about myself. The outcome is respectful treatment of students.

- Negative Example: Suppose that I think of myself as someone who has no self-control and who just can't drive by a McDonald's without stopping for French fries. Then even though I know cognitively that I am trying to reduce the number of fat grams that I'm consuming, my behavior will follow from my thinking, and I will find that indeed I can't resist the French fries.

So our thinking really does influence our behavior and our students' behavior. How many students have you heard say, "Well, I just can't do it" or "I've always been chatty." "As a man thinketh, so is he." The exciting part is that we as teachers can help our students think anew—we can help them see themselves differently now that we understand how the change process works.

Personal Commitment

Write down your values and beliefs about students and learning. If it suits your learning style, use the "mind maps" (Figures 1.3 and 1.4) to visually brainstorm and record, on the rays flowing out from the center, your own beliefs about students' needs in the classroom learning environment. Other options are to craft your beliefs from your favorite quotes or poems or to make a list or outline of your beliefs.

Many teachers have found this exercise so helpful that they have posted what they have written in their classroom. Others say that they keep a written copy of them near their desk. Having written values and beliefs serves as a guide for decision making during times of upset in the classroom.

Once you have clarified your values and beliefs, you may want to write a pledge to your students that is based on them and post that in your classroom. (See the pledge that one teacher made to her students in Figure 1.5.)

_____

_____

_____

_____

_____

_____

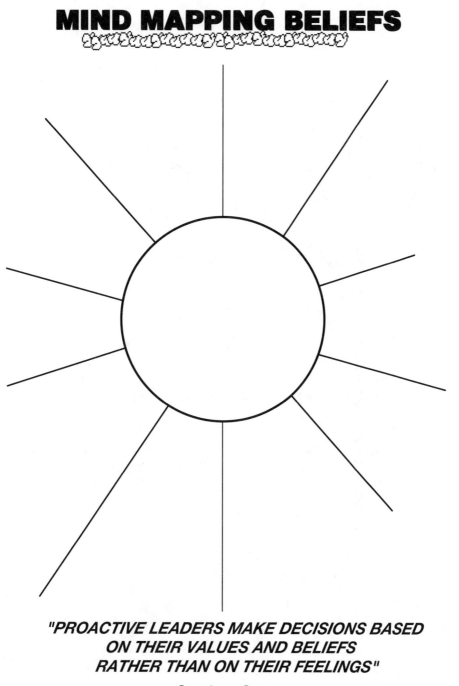

MIND MAPPING BELIEFS

"PROACTIVE LEADERS MAKE DECISIONS BASED ON THEIR VALUES AND BELIEFS RATHER THAN ON THEIR FEELINGS"

Stephen Covey

Figure 1.3.   Mind-Mapping Beliefs

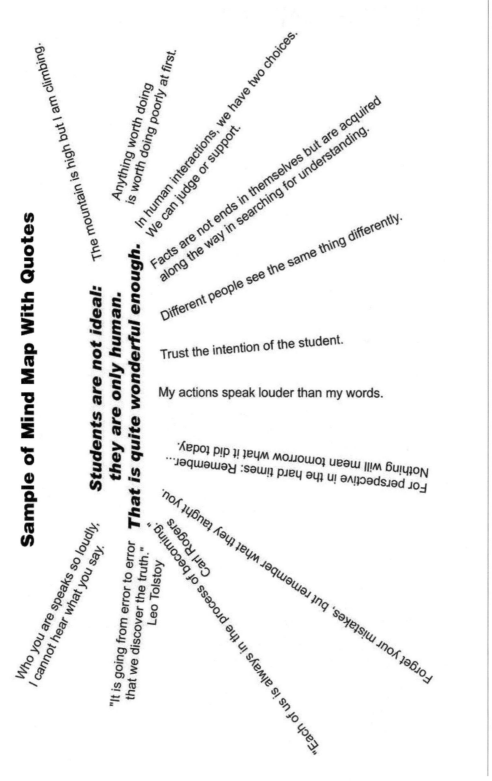

Sample of Mind Map With Quotes

The mountain is high but I am climbing.

Anything worth doing is worth doing poorly at first.

In human interactions, we have two choices. We can judge or support.

Facts are not ends in themselves but are acquired along the way in searching for understanding.

Different people see the same thing differently.

Trust the intention of the student.

My actions speak louder than my words.

For perspective in the hard times: Remember... Nothing will mean tomorrow what it did today.

Students are not ideal: they are only human. That is quite wonderful enough.

Who you are speaks so loudly, I cannot hear what you say.

"It is going from error to error that we discover the truth."
Leo Tolstoy

"Each of us is always in the process of becoming."
Carl Rogers

Forget your mistakes, but remember what they taught you.

Figure 1.4.   Sample of Mind Map With Quotes

16

JENNIFER'S PLEDGE

I promise to:

- *Focus on your strengths & share those*
- *Be aware that my mood & tone affect your mood*
- *Discuss matters/problems privately, whenever possible*
- *See you as the teacher who can enlighten me, especially when we disagree*

Figure 1.5.   A Teacher's Pledge to Her Students
SOURCE: Jennifer Jenkins, Washington Open, Santa Clara Unified School District

Summary of Rethinking Our Roles in the Classroom

As a man thinketh, so is he.
We are what we think.

- How I think about myself as a teacher affects how I lead in the classroom.

- Leaders put relationships with students first and get them to set sail on an exciting voyage of learning.

- Leaders are proactive rather than reactive: their actions are based on beliefs and values rather than on feelings.

- Leaders have their beliefs clearly written as a guide for their classrooms. They let students know how they support and celebrate differences in culture, style, and learning.

Changing Our Style to Match Our Beliefs 2

In any system of humans, the individual within that system who has the widest range of variability will be the controlling element.

Law of Requisite Variety (Cybernetics)

 ## Classroom Connection

Mr. Guzman taught a fifth-grade ESL class where a majority of students came from abusive home settings. Though several other teachers had failed with these students, Edward Guzman was able to engage them in learning because he had the biggest "bag of tricks"—the most strategies—and because he could shift strategies midstream. His prevention strategy was to stop every 6 to 8 minutes and ask a process question about what he had just been teaching, both to check for understanding and to give students a legitimate time to talk and use English in class. He would say, for example, "Think for a minute about any other words you know that mean the same as "caring," in your own language or in English. . . . Now share your ideas with a neighbor." However, even with that prevention in the middle of a lesson, he noticed that the class was restless after 15 minutes, so he asked them to stand up and turn their desks toward the back of the room. He led a quick "brain gym" exercise from Dennison and Dennison's book *Brain Gym Activities* (1992) and then began teaching from the back of the room. Within 3 minutes, the students were back on track (see the subsection "Altering the Setting" in Chapter 7, "Rethinking Classroom Interventions").

Mr. Guzman was the person in the system with the widest range of variability and therefore was the "controlling factor," which means the driver of the bus, the leader in the classroom, rather than the rescuer and enabler or the Gestapo/drill instructor (these classroom management styles will be discussed below). Often students, especially preadolescent and adolescent students, have more variability and options than the adults and thus become the controlling element, the classroom teacher, leader, and guide.

♥ Personal Connection

Think of a time in your classroom where you had an experience like Mr. Guzman's and were able to prevent an upset by guiding your students in a different direction with prevention strategies.

You have the potential to be the person in the classroom system with the widest range of options, the most strategies, and the ability to pick and choose from these on the basis of the needs of your students and your own intuition and style. Prescriptive approaches that tell you, "When students do X, you need to do Y" may prevent you from being a flexible or creative teacher. If you are considering adopting any new classroom management system, it is important that you see the purpose of the strategies and techniques that are presented, understand their brain-based rationales, and assess how strategies mesh with your own beliefs and thinking. Table 2.1, showing a variety of classroom management systems, can assist you in determining if the management system you are using is connected with your values and beliefs.

Reading a book that addresses only skills or outcomes produces very little change. For lasting change, you will need time to reevaluate your beliefs about students and education, then opportunities to apply your new thinking to your situation and practice it until it is integrated. This chapter will develop your role as a leader and guide rather than as a drill instructor or rescuer. It will empower you to create an environment that supports self-control and self-discipline.

■ CLASSROOM MANAGEMENT STYLES

Now that you have clarified some of your beliefs and values about teaching, look at the following classroom scenarios that illustrate various coping styles that teachers use in their classrooms. These styles were adapted for classrooms from a parenting model developed by Dinkmeyer and McKay (1982). Sometimes these styles are consciously adopted, but most often they are the result of our own patterning and experiences. We all have times when we are coping in a style that does not match our values and beliefs, so be compassionate with yourself if you recognize yourself in one of the negative scenarios. All of us have been the teacher in one of the

Table 2.1   Summary of Classroom Management Systems

	Goal	*Central Assumption*	*Key Feature*
Assertive Discipline	Allowing teacher to spend as much time teaching as possible	Teacher attitudes govern teacher behavior	Rules and consequences External controls
Dreikurs' *Children: The Challenge* (1990); Systematic Training for Effective Parenting (STEP; Dinkmeyer & McKay, 1982); Project Accept	Encouraging responsible behavior	Student behavior is goal oriented	Logical consequences
Glasser's (1968, 1986) Control Theory	Increasing opportunities for students to feel good about themselves	Student behavior problems often derive from low self-esteem	Self-awareness
Social Literacy Training	No-lose conflict resolution	Classrooms provide few opportunities for open, honest communication	Open communication
Systematic Management Plan for School Discipline	Addressing student behavior on a schoolwide basis by establishing organizational mechanisms for reducing problems	Problems are endemic to school Organizational factors determine behavior	Organizational change
Behavior Modification	Decreasing negative behavior and increasing positive behavior	Students misbehave because the consequences of misbehavior are reinforcing	Reinforcement
Responsible Classroom Discipline	Preventing disruptive behavior	To effectively manage classroom behavior, it is critical that teachers understand the issues involved in classroom management and not just implement techniques	Multidimensional strategies for managing classroom behavior Problem solving by teacher and students
Classroom Leadership: This Book	Inviting internal control	Our thinking influences our actions, and our personal relationships with children form the foundation for effective leadership	Self-esteem based framework approach supported by coaching and feedback

SOURCE: Class handout created by Jeanne Herrick and Marsha Weil, Stanford University, Summer 1982.

drill instructor scenarios; upon later reflection, we are certainly not proud of our lack of self-control, but it can happen in spite of our best intentions.

Those of us who believe in intrinsic motivation, who want our students to do the right thing because it is the right thing rather than because of extrinsic factors like rewards and punishment, will want to begin to adopt the style of leader and guide. The rescuer style is, in contemporary terms, the codependent or enabler style; it leads students to be very adult dependent and to have a very low sense of competence or resiliency. At times it might be important to rescue a student from himself or herself or from another person, but this should not be the primary style of leading in the classroom. The drill instructor/authoritarian style of coping often sounds like "Do it my way or the highway, sit down and keep still or get out of my class." This style demands that students conform to the teacher's wishes rather than participating in creating a classroom together. It undermines intrinsic motivation and stifles creativity and critical thinking.

Review Table 2.2 on teaching styles and use them to process the teaching style scenarios that follow.

✔ Checking My Understanding of Teaching Styles

Directions: To stimulate further thinking about your beliefs, read the following scenarios that interest you or the ones closest to your grade level and reflect on these questions:

a) How did the teacher/adult cope: as a leader/guide, as a rescuer, or as a drill instructor?

b) How did the student feel? (How would you have felt if you were the student?)

c) Did the student learn a new behavior to replace the old one? (This is the definition of discipline, from the Latin word *disciplina*, teaching of the correct behavior.)

d) What could have prevented the upset from happening in the first place?

You can check your answers with the common responses from most teachers, which are after each of the scenarios.

1. Jennifer Boyd, a kindergartner in Mrs. Hall's class, was working at the Art Center and spilled her paints on the linoleum floor. As Mrs. Hall's aide walked by, she stopped and frowned and said, "Come on, you spilled the paint and you have to clean it up, Jennifer!" Jennifer dropped her lower lip, pouted and did not move but instead sat down near the center. The aide waited. Jennifer pouted. The aide finally cleaned up the spilled paints.

(Continued on page 24)

Table 2.2   Teachers' Coping Styles

Leader/Guide	Rescuer/Enabler	Drill Instructor/Authoritarian
"I keep my ideals, because in spite of everything I still believe that people are really good at heart." Anne Frank	*"He that is kind is free, though he is a slave; he that is evil is a slave, though he be a king."* St. Augustine	*"I was there to follow orders, not to think."* *Defendant in Watergate Trials, 1990*
Provides guidance, asks questions to facilitate students' problem solving for themselves. Thinks students learn more from processing their own mistakes. Focus is on students' needs rather than teacher's needs. Supports rather than judges or interprets motivation to others' behavior. Underlying belief is to trust the intention of the students.	Hovers over students like a helicopter. Thinks teacher needs to protect and rescue students from cruel world and life's lessons. Focus is on the teacher being the savior.	Directs and demands students' behavior. Thinks, "I know best because I'm the teacher." Focus is on conformity and obedience.
Gives message of personal worth with strong teacher-student relationship and positive feedback on emerging social skills (target talk).	Makes rules to protect students "for their own good."	Makes lots of rules to control students and show teacher's personal power.
Asks questions about responsibilities instead of preaching about them.	Makes excuses for students while complaining about their lack of responsibility.	Makes lots of demands: "Do it my way or the highway." Preaches a lot about responsibility.
Role-models how to take care of self and be responsible.	Does *for* students rather than *with* students.	Tells students how to do things.
Shares personal experiences about own struggles with beliefs and actions.	Thinks students need protecting from negative feelings.	Tells students how to feel: "Stop moping and get busy."
Uses questions to facilitate student decision making. Invites processing behavior.	Decides for students what is best.	Provides absolutes, black-and-white thinking that often invites resistance.
Models time frames and structure for student to organize tasks.	Avoids structuring time frames for students to be self-monitoring.	Demands that things be done *now.*
Models and consciously supports doing one's best work.	Uses guilt to shame students: "When will you ever learn?"	Issues threats: "Get that work done now or . . ."
Often asks, "Who owns the problem?" Helps students explore their own solutions to problems.	Preaches and talks about how students aren't capable and need teacher.	Takes ownership of students' problems. Orders students around.
Lets actions speak more than words.	Protects students from natural consequences. Thinks students are victims.	Uses harsh words; takes little action unless angry.
Supports students while allowing natural consequences as life's teacher.	Thinks and says that too many extras "have to be done" for "these students."	Believes that punishment and pain are the best teachers.

Common responses from most teachers: The adult was a drill instructor, then a rescuer. The child felt incompetent. No new behavior was learned. A prevention strategy that would have helped would have been to have some written procedures for painting that both the aide and child would have been familiar with and could have used—for example:

Spills?

Get a Buddy

Get a Sponge

Clean Spill

Then the aide could have asked, "Jennifer, who do you want to get to help you clean the spill?" (see the subsection "Activity Procedures" in Chapter 5).

2. Mrs. Brink's fourth-grade class was working in groups at various centers. Adam had been sent back to his desk to spend 3 minutes because he was continually touching other students' materials and interrupting boisterously. After 2 minutes he returned to the reading group and began working quietly within the group. Mrs. Brinks went to him and said in a whisper, "Adam, you're being very respectful of your group by keeping your voice low and your hands on your own materials, what's your secret?"

   Common responses from most teachers: Mrs. Brink was being a leader/guide by first taking action without a lot of words (sending Adam to his seat for 3 minutes—see the section in Chapter 7, "Removal Procedures"—and then giving him immediate feedback on the new social skill he was practicing when he returned. This was a message of personal worth, using "target talk" (see the subsection "Target Talk" in Chapter 3). Mrs. Brink was able to ignore that Adam had come back 1 minute early because he was now practicing appropriate social behavior. She modeled acting on her values and beliefs and avoided a power struggle by thinking about the bigger picture as a leader rather than focusing on the remaining minute that Adam was supposed to spend at his desk. The goal was accomplished. A prevention strategy would be to have Adam track with beads or cards with tally marks the number of times he wanted to "pester others" and didn't. This would put him in charge of observing himself and lead him to see how much self-control he really had. It could have been set up that he shared with the teacher every 10 minutes or whatever they agreed on (see the section "The Concept of Pure Reinforcement" in Chapter 8, "Problem Solving").

3. Mr. Thomik runs a very orderly classroom and insists that rules be rigidly enforced. When a student talks out of turn, he immediately

reprimands him or her verbally and then puts the student's name on the board. It remains there for the entire week.

Common responses from most teachers: Mr. Thomik is following the drill instructor style of using punishment and humiliation. This style, while often getting conformity, does not invite intrinsic motivation to flourish.

4. Before recess, the principal makes an announcement on the intercom reminding students not to sit or hang from the tetherballs. While a teacher is on yard duty, she notices a student sitting on the tetherballs. The yard duty teacher goes over to the student and tells her that she will sit on the bench at recess for the rest of the week.

   Common responses from most teachers: This is drill instructor style. Sitting on the bench for 1 week will not ensure that the student will think differently the next time; it just reinforces her negative thinking about her behavior. Also, when students feel punished they often focus their energy on anger and resentment toward the punisher rather than seeing their relationship to the problem. A prevention strategy would be to have the tetherball rules written and illustrated by students who enjoy playing with them and then laminated and taken out to the tetherball area by the students who need to be reminded of the rules. Student leaders could be appointed to help other students to remember why sitting on the tetherballs breaks them. Maybe the offenders could help with these projects.

5. Mrs. Commons is delivering a lecture to her 10th-grade students. She has interrupted her lecture twice to quiet Jennifer and Ann's whispered conversation, saying, "Girls, if you can't stop chatting, I'll have to separate you." Both times, the girls apologize politely. A third time, the whispering distracts Mrs. Commons. "Okay, Jennifer, you'll have to move to this vacant seat in the first row," she announces, indicating the empty seat. "Please, Mrs. Commons, we'll stop." "No, Jennifer, I've asked you girls several times now." "We'll be quiet, we promise." The argument continues: "Girls, you told me that before, and you are wasting this entire class's time with all this arguing." "We just had to finish talking about something really important. Now we'll be quiet. Please just give us one more chance." Mrs. Commons sighs and continues teaching.

   Common responses from most teachers: Mrs. Commons has fallen victim to the drill instructor style of teaching—threatening the students—with a little rescuer thrown in—trying to get the students to conform by making them feel guilty. A prevention strategy would be to create group agreements for teacher-directed lessons, with the teacher agreeing to not teach more than 10 to 12 minutes without giving the students "brain talk" time to process the information before she continues the lesson (see the section

"Activity Procedures" in Chapter 5 and the section "Participation: Questioning Strategies" in Chapter 6).

6. Mr. Campos has his eighth-grade remedial class divided into two groups. One group is doing an independent assignment. He is leading a review of a literature assignment with the other group. Each student in the group is formulating a question and challenging one of the other students. Eduardo, who is usually absent or tardy, is participating boisterously and really enjoying finding answers to the questions his classmates pose. Sometimes, however, he interjects out of turn and in his excitement comments on others' questions and answers. Mr. Campos looks at him and says, "Eduardo, it's not your turn, shh, shh, you need to wait your turn, shh, shh. Can't you remember our rules? Now if you call out again, you'll have to leave." The next round of questions begin, and within a couple of minutes Eduardo asks one of the girls a question about her answer without raising his hand. Mr. Campos says, "All right, Eduardo, you are choosing to disobey our rules; you need to go to your seat." Eduardo says, "I was just asking Elena a question." Mr. Campos says, "No, you were interrupting as usual, and you remember our rule—so now you're out of the game." Eduardo leaves the group and kicks his chair over in route to his desk as he mumbles about how unfair Mr. Campos is. Mr. Campos says, "For that, Eduardo, you can just go to the office and see Ms. Willis, the principal."

Common responses from most teachers: Drill instructor takes over. Eduardo loses his sense of connection to the group and the teacher as well as feeling like a failure. Eduardo clearly wanted to participate and needed to be involved. The research on learning and memory says that students should be verbally responding every few minutes in order to retain and make sense of the information (Sprenger, 1999). A prevention strategy would be that instead of using the questioning strategy of sampling, where only one student gets to respond and all of the others are passively listening, Mr. Campos could choose a strategy that would allow all the students to answer, like "group response" or "pair share" (see section "Questioning Strategies" in Chapter 6).

7. The bell rings. All of the students in Mr. Stern's class (you may assume it is middle school or high school level) are busy writing in their journals in response to the instructions on the board. Jeff enters the classroom late but quietly and heads directly for his desk. He pulls out his journal and begins to work on the assignment. After a couple of minutes, Mr. Stern moves to Jeff's table. He says quietly, just to Jeff, "Coming in so quietly and getting right to work was very thoughtful of your classmates." He then leaves Jeff a note asking him, "When can you stay after school to create a plan to get to class on time? Today at noon or tomorrow after school?" Continuing to take the roll, Mr. Stern moves to the table where Sharon has stopped writing and is talking to Cindy. Putting his

hand on Sharon's table, he waits 5 to 10 seconds and moves away. Sharon goes back to writing in her journal.

Common responses from most teachers: The teacher is the guide here and lets his actions speak more than his words. He models respect for his students by talking privately, yet the class observes that the tardiness is not ignored (see Chapter 7, "Rethinking Classroom Interventions"). He uses proximity with Sharon rather than giving her positive attention for a negative behavior by calling her name. With Jeff he uses target talk to acknowledge his quiet entry and welcome him to class but models a firm, assertive, neutral, leadership tone about school rules and involves the student in the problem solving. If students are kept after school, then the time should be spent on problem solving. This is an example of discipline as opposed to punishment. A prevention strategy could have been to have students write in their journals about how they were going to get themselves to class on time.

STRATEGIES AND RATIONALES FOR SHIFTING STYLES

How will we be able to shift from being drill instructors or enablers to a more proactive style of being guides and leaders in the classroom? One of the key areas to rethink is how we frame the upsets that happen in the classroom. There are basically two ways of thinking about behavior problems in the classroom. One is to frame all misbehaviors as delinquent and deviant—as instances of students' choosing to deliberately stray from the classroom expectations. When thinking about behavior from this perspective, the teacher feels a need to control the setting, and the result of effective control is always conformity. Many classroom management systems operate from this point of view and teach control-oriented techniques and punitive consequences, which are guaranteed to produce a high degree of student conformity. Unfortunately, the price we pay for conformity is suppression and the necessity for more and more external controls rather than any internal motivation toward appropriate behavior or internalization of new behaviors.

The other way to think about classroom upsets is from a "social learning problem" paradigm. This view is based on the belief that the inappropriate behavior is not deviant or deliberate but rather that the student has a social learning problem. There are three possibilities:

- The student has learned too much of the wrong behavior.

- The student has not learned enough of the appropriate behavior.

- The student has never been taught the appropriate behavior.

Do children choose to misbehave and violate norms? Do adults choose to "forget items" that they need for work? Let's look at this whole issue of "deviancy" versus "mistakes" or social learning problems. According to the educator Larry Lowery (1989), teachers often assume that children are capable of inference, or the ability to think through the likely effects of a behavior or action, before they actually are. An adult driving alone on the freeway is using his inference skills when he weighs the likely effect of using the carpool lane and assesses whether the benefit to him is worth breaking the law and running the risk of paying a fine. But children cannot infer consequences in this way because they are not developmentally ready. Inference happens in the prefrontal lobe of the brain, which is not fully formed until sometime between the ages of 10 and 12 and in boys often not untill later. Thus, children do not pick up an object to throw and then think, "Wait, this is heavy. If I throw it into the window, the window will break, then the principal will call my parents, and then I will get in trouble." They pick up the object and without thinking hurl it at the window—even though afterwards, when asked, they may be able to tell us that they shouldn't have thrown it. Their impulsive actions are not deviant because deviancy requires the prefrontal lobe of the brain to be fully formed. Further, even adults with fully formed prefrontal lobes can momentarily "forget" to weigh consequences of an action. Programs and habits can be so strongly imprinted in us that our brains automatically fire there, like the "go to" menu on a computer.

To adopt the leader/guide style of classroom management, we must be able to think of discipline problems as social learning problems rather than problems of deviancy (Table 2.3). Alfie Kohn (1993) states that "rewards and punishment work very well to get one thing and that one thing is temporary compliance" (p. 161). Such compliance is at the heart of deviancy control models.

Examples of Strategies for Shifting Styles

- Think about upsets as social learning problems.

- Remember that the prefrontal lobe of the brain forms from ages 10 to 12.

- Put up a visual reminder in your classroom, such as a picture or phrase.

- Post your beliefs about kids near your desk or file cabinet.

- Get a buddy teacher to "coach" you on seeing it differently.

- Move your watch or ring to a different hand or finger as a reminder of your new way of thinking.

- Look at a student's hands and remember that he or she is someone's "darling child."

Table 2.3   Comparison of Deviancy Control Versus Social Learning Approach

Deviancy Control	*Social Learning Approach*
Conformity	Self-direction
Suppression	Decision making
Dependence on external control	Fostering of internal control
Teacher not viewed as connected to classroom system	Teacher viewed as part of system
Teacher exerts more control over target students through use of consequences. This produces a need to exert still more control through consequences.	Target students invited to self-assess and create plan with teacher.
Examples:	
∞ Demerit systems	∞ This book
∞ Assertive discipline	∞ The California Development Project
∞ Token economy systems	∞ Glasser's (1990) quality model

 Personal Commitment

When children have an academic learning problem, what do you do? How do you support them? How can you apply those same theories and practices when children have a social learning problem?

_____

_____

_____

Summary of Shifting Our Style to Match Our Beliefs

- In the leader/guide style of classroom management, the teacher moves beyond control by including the student and inviting him or her to develop internal control over his or her own behavior.

- The teacher is seen as a creator rather than as a victim.

- The teacher views misbehavior as a social learning problem.

- The teacher provides a climate for self-direction and decision making by asking questions.

- The teacher honors individual differences for self and student.

PREVENTION FRAMEWORK

I. Personal Relationships for Trust

- Student Teacher Relationship
- Gifts Without Strings (NCR)
- Target Talk (Knowledge of Results)
- Room Design for Proximity
- Class Meetings

II. Prerequisites for Success

- Leader Creates Climate for:
  - Brain Compatible Environment
  - Teacher and Student Self-Esteem
- Social Skills
- Academic Curriculum

III. Parameters for Cooperation

- Class Agreements
- Procedures
- Directions
- Room Design for Organization
- Transition Tasks

IV. Participation for Involvement

- Opportunities for:
  - Simultaneous Involvement During Instruction
  - Active Listening During Input
  - Active Engagement During Learning Activities

Part II

The Four "P's" of Prevention: Personal, Prerequisites, Parameters, and Participation

∽

An ounce of prevention is worth a pound of cure.

Aesop's *Fables*

∾

art II, on prevention strategies, is the foundation for creating a powerful learning environment in your classroom. It contains the prevention leadership skills to be effective in 85% to 90% of the situations that cause stress in the classroom. Our purpose in this section is to give you a framework of skills to build relationships that will create a positive community of learners who are practicing respect, cooperation, and personally motivated participation. As you become aware of how you already use these skills and then increase their use, you will reduce classroom tension and gain a feeling of confidence. Notice how your work on beliefs in Chapter 1 builds a foundation for positive relationships to grow and be nurtured. Begin to integrate your beliefs with the leadership techniques in this section and create a plan for action based on your rethinking.

The Prevention Framework (see page 30) outlines the strategies that will be introduced in this part of the book. It sets the stage for maximum classroom success. Each chapter will present one of the four "P's" of prevention. It will also act as a quick and easy self-assessment for you to refer back to if you are using interventions in more than 2% to 3% of your situations. By spending time with the "Personal Commitment," "Checking My Understanding," and "Personal Connection" exercises, you will have the self-knowledge, practice, and relevant application to use each strategy in your unique classroom environment.

Leadership Principles of Prevention

Successful Classroom Leaders:

- Nurture self-esteem
- Build supportive relationships
- Focus more on preventing than intervening
- Rely more on the positive than the negative
- Encourage intrinsic motivation
- Make decisions on the basis of their values and beliefs rather than their feelings

---

PREVENTION FRAMEWORK

I. Personal Relationships for Trust

- Student-Teacher Relationship
- Gifts Without Strings (NCR)
- Target Talk (Knowledge of Results)
- Room Design for Proximity
- Class Meetings

II. Prerequisites for Success

- Leader Creates Climate for:
  - Brain Compatible Environment
  - Teacher and Student Self-Esteem
- Social Skills
- Academic Curriculum

III. Parameters for Cooperation

- Classroom Agreements
- Procedures
- Directions
- Room Design for Organization
- Transition Tasks

IV. Participation for Involvement

- Opportunities for:
  - Simultaneous Involvement During Instruction
  - Active Listening During Input
  - Active Engagement During Learning Activities

Personal Relationships for Trust

3

The First "P" of Prevention

જી

We become teachers for reasons of the heart. But many of us lose heart.
How can we take heart, alone and together,
so we can give heart to our students?

Parker Palmer, *The Courage to Teach*

જી

Classroom Connection

Dave was a fourth-grade student in a typical school who was known for the challenges he brought to his new teacher each year. After he had been in his fourth-grade class a few months, other teachers began asking, "Why is Dave doing so well in your room, Lynn?" They explained to Lynn that when they had had Dave in their classes, he had run around the room, crawled on the bookcases, and generally caused havoc for most of the year. They wanted to know Lynn's secret.

At the time, Lynn was unaware of what she did that allowed Dave to be successful. She commented, "He must think I'm the Wicked Witch of the West! My reputation must precede me, or he thinks I've got a broom or whip hidden in the closet." In truth, Lynn had no idea.

Coincidentally, however, Lynn was invited to Classroom Management Training, which was her opportunity to shift from unconscious competence to conscious competence in her teaching. As she examined her relationship with her students, she discovered that she instinctively knew that the only way she could spend positive time with Dave was to let him in early every day to get the class pencils ready. They had time to chat as they prepared the room. From these daily doses of positive time together, their relationship gained trust and gave him a feeling of importance. With that as the foundation for the day, Lynn was able to help Dave be more on target in class. He still had his problems on the playground and at home, *but in her classroom he was learning and having a relatively successful year. Lynn found that she used similar relationship-building techniques with other students: she would smile, comment on their new shoes, or touch their shoulder as she passed. She made it a habit to ask them about their weekend, invite them to help with the overhead, or assist with after-school projects. She realized how much these interactions, based on her caring and respect for these learners, had created her ability to keep the classroom moving forward.*

 ## Personal Connection

What are you already doing with the majority of your students that builds a trusting relationship?

■ THE FOUNDATION: TEACHER-STUDENT RELATIONSHIP

The quality of the teacher-student relationship is the single most important factor to consider when rethinking classroom management. Over a span of many years, the research consistently indicates a high correlation between a caring teacher-student relationship, academic achievement, and cooperative student behavior (Brophy & Good, 1970, 1974; Poplin & Weeres, 1992; Rosenshine, 1971). Emmy Werner (1996), a psychologist at the University of California at Davis, studied resiliency for over 40 years in children of disadvantaged homes. She discovered that resilient children consistently had a caring adult in their lives. Outside of family members, the "caring adult" most frequently cited by these children was a favorite teacher.

The teacher-student relationship is the heart of classroom leadership today. It is the foundation for all that we do. When a positive relationship is weak or absent, attempts to use *any* managerial strategies will be ineffective. But it is equally important to note that creating positive teacher-student relationships will not solve all classroom problems.

Teachers want to make a difference. With the fast-paced classroom settings and high demands of the curriculum, urgency is created that often puts our relationships on the back burner. The unintended result is a boiling pot of hopelessness and violence in our education system and it threatens to blow at any time. When students feel disconnected from the human side of their learning, they lose their confidence and vitality. Parents and students are relying on teachers to heal this fear and pain. Through trust and respect, teachers can model the needed relationships to turn students in a positive direction. By taking daily steps toward rebuilding their commitment to making a difference, teachers can take back the role of proactive participant rather than victim and develop students who are citizens in a community of learners.

One study that elicited comments from teachers, students, and parents about their schools (Poplin & Weeres, 1992) reported that participants felt the crisis inside schools was directly linked to human relationships. Most often mentioned were relationships between teachers and students. Where positive things about the schools were noted, they usually involved reports of individuals who cared, listened, understood, respected others, and were honest, open, and sensitive. Teachers reported that their best experiences in school were those where they connected with students and were able to help them in some way. They also reported, however, that there was precious little time during the day to seek out individual students. Students also noticed teachers' lack of time to speak to them individually. Parents said they wanted an honest dialogue between themselves and their children's teachers. Even more important, many parents feared that poor relationships between teachers and their children damaged their children's sense of confidence and vitality. Students of color, especially older students, often reported that their teachers, school staff, and other students neither liked nor understood them. Many teachers also reported that they did not always understand students ethnically different from themselves. When relationships in schools were poor, fear, name calling, threats of or incidents of violence, and a sense of depression and hopelessness were present. This theme was prominently stated by participants and so deeply connected to all other themes in the data that the authors concluded this might be one of the two most central issues to address in solving the crisis in schools.

Table 3.1 outlines the basic prerequisites for building positive classroom relationships. When these are in place, teachers and students operate from a positive, respectful position that fosters self-esteem and creates a learning environment conducive to academic achievement and positive connection to school.

Table 3.1   Foundations for the Positive Student-Teacher Relationship

- *Valuing differences* in cultures, learning styles, gender, race, religion, and thinking by using language, activities, words, deeds, and visuals that support student diversity

- *Calling forth the best in students* by inviting them to be participants in the learning process and encouraging strengths

- *Focusing on the positive* by finding the good and helping students see their strengths

- *Being caring, nurturing, and respectful*; treating the students like younger equals and friends of the family

- *Exhibiting genuine concern and curiosity* by inquiring about the students' concerns, being curious rather than judgmental, and listening more than talking

- *Maintaining a firm, neutral, assertive presence* by understanding that body language gives 80% of the message, basing actions on values, not feelings, and holding the limits

■ GIFTS WITHOUT STRINGS

ৎ

If you would win a man to your cause,
first convince him that you are his sincere friend.

Abraham Lincoln

ৎ

When you have developed a belief system that honors the foundations of the positive teacher-student relationship, you are ready to implement the relationship skills that are the backbone of preventing upsets in your classroom. The first of these is "gifts without strings," or noncontingent reinforcement (NCR): positive reinforcement given to students independent of their behavior. There are no strings and no conditions attached to this personal gift. It is free and totally independent of any student behavior to earn it. Carl Rogers (1961) refers to this concept of gifts without strings as *unconditional regard,* and Stephen Covey (1989) refers to it as *deposits* in the emotional bank account of another. It might also be described by the title of Ann Herbert's book *Random Acts of Kindness* (1992), which started a positive kindness movement.

In the story of Dave, his teacher Lynn would invite him into the classroom early to sharpen pencils and spend positive time together. She did this frequently because he was a student likely to bring challenges to the classroom. Lynn knew it was important to provide gifts without strings frequently to students with strong emotional needs. Many kids come to us with emotional bank accounts that are close to empty. We often call these kinds of students *target students.* In an attempt to get their needs met, they often display inappropriate behavior.

Noncontingent reinforcement is the key to every successful relationship and is essential in the teacher-student relationship. It forms the foundation for trust and security and provides the bonding and connection that every teacher and student needs to have a caring community of learners. It is a tool for being inclusive of even the most extreme diversity and calls forth the best side of students. By itself a bonded relationship will not solve every problem, but without it effective leadership and a cooperative environment are often dependent on external control.

Teacher effectiveness research (Kohn, 1996) has found that a characteristic shared by successful teachers is the bonding, caring, and genuine concern that they exhibit toward their students. This characteristic is key to prevention of violence in schools. There is more cooperation in those classrooms where noncontingent reinforcement is more predominant than contingent reinforcement. As we are shifting the climate in the classroom to support intrinsic motivation, gifts without strings need to outweigh all the adverse conditions in the educational system that are outside of our circle of influence (an example is grades).

Examples of Noncontingent and Contingent Reinforcement

- Noncontingent Reinforcement:

  1. Letting a student write the key words on the board during a teacher-led discussion is noncontingent reinforcement because there is no reason for the selection of that student: no conditions were attached to her being chosen.

  2. Greeting students at the door and smiling at them and talking about topics that interest them are examples of noncontingent reinforcement when done for no reason other than to show genuine caring and concern.

- Contingent Reinforcement:

  1. On the other hand, if a student gives the correct response to a question and the teacher smiles in response, that is contingent rather than noncontingent reinforcement because the smile was contingent on the correct response.

  2. A student scored the winning point in a basketball game and is congratulated on her skill. (Although this may be a nice thing to do, it is an example of contingent rather than noncontingent reinforcement—why?)

Examples of Gifts Without Strings to an Individual

- Engaging a disconnected student in conversation about a shared sports experience

- Initiating a discussion with a student about clothing fads, colors, or style

- Chatting with a student about brothers, sisters, pets, interests, or personal life

- Asking a student to help collect papers, record points, or put up overheads

- Smiling or winking at a student at the beginning, middle, or end of class

Examples of Gifts Without Strings to a Whole Class

- Greeting students at the door when they enter

- Telling students a story from the teacher's experience relative to the topic

- Using humor: joke of the week contest, funniest cartoon, etc.

- Playing a musical instrument or sharing a poem, story, or hobby

- Setting aside time to discuss past or future weekend stories

- Asking students for their ideas about curriculum, procedures, homework, etc.

- Circulating through the classroom and teaching from various areas, smiling at various students

- Sitting among the students and reading your book during free reading time or doing your work while they do theirs

- Letting students determine what activity they will do next

"I'm concerned I've been doing this wrong. I often tie rewards to positive behavior……"

You haven't been wrong! Now you can use your new awareness to use fewer strings until you find you won't need them at all.

The important point here is: Gifts Without Strings should be increased and used whenever possible to foster internal motivation. For now, build as much of this "just because" strategy into your daily interaction. Become very conscious of how to foster intrinsic reinforcement and use extreme care when using extrinsic reinforcement.

You may be thinking……

Benefits of Gifts Without Strings

- Sets the stage for intrinsic motivation
- Forms foundation for trust
- Fosters sense of security
- Creates a comfortable climate
- Creates a positive association with teacher
- Increases probability of cooperation
- Models tone for students to emulate
- Increases motivation to perform

Key Criteria for Gifts Without Strings

- Positive reinforcement
- Unconditional, given for free, independent of any behavior
- Suitable to student's age, stage, and style
- Provided frequently in large doses for target students

Checking My Understanding of Gifts Without Strings

Determine which of the following meet the criteria for gifts without strings (G). Mark G for those and S for strings (contingent).

_____ 1. Teacher invites anyone who wants to join her for lunch in the park to meet at 11:30.

_____ 2. Teacher states that if the class works quietly for 20 minutes she will show a special PBS video on endangered species.

_____ 3. Teacher tells a student who often delays completing work on time that if she'll finish early she can have some free time.

_____ 4. Teacher has a popcorn party for students while reading one of their favorite novels.

_____ 5. Teacher announces that all who pass a test with 90% or more correct will have an opportunity to create questions for the next day's quiz.

Answers: 1. G, 2. S, 3. S, 4. G, 5. S

❤️ *Personal Commitment*

How will you develop a personal relationship with the whole class?

_____

_____

_____

_____

■ TIPS FOR HANDLING STUDENTS' UPSETS

ᔐ

Man's inability to communicate is a result of his failure to listen effectively, skillfully, and with understanding to another person.

Carl Rogers, *On Becoming a Person*

ᔐ

Communicating during upsets requires skill and attention if we want to protect our teacher-student relationship and preserve a student's self-esteem. One of the greatest gifts the teacher can give is time to listen. Remember the story of Dave? When Dave had upsetting mornings at school, it would affect the ability of the entire class to learn. When his teacher Lynn handled these upsets in a positive manner, Dave felt understood, and the rest of the class could carry on with their learning without disruption. This is where we really are tempted to act as rescuers or drill instructors and either tell the target student how to solve the problem or fix the world for him or her. It is absolutely critical to maintain our leader/guide role when handling students' upsets and mistaken perceptions. If it is not possible to maintain some semblance of neutrality and sanity, it is best to postpone the conversation until at least one person has a cool and objective attitude. There is a direct correlation between how people feel and how they behave.

▧ Examples of Ways to Check in With Students to Assess Emotional States

- Students choose a feeling word from a classroom chart.

- Students write in a journal about how they are feeling.

- Students draw a picture of how they are feeling.

- Students indicate how they are feeling when attendance is called by signaling a number between 1 and 5 by holding up fingers or by saying the number out loud, with "1" being "not so good" and "5" being "great."

- Students signal with "thumbs up" or "thumbs down" to indicate how they feel today.

- Students fill out a personal feelings worksheet (available from Borba, 1994, or the Child's Work, Child's Play Catalog, available from www.childswork.com, (800) 962-1141. The teacher can use this information to get a snapshot of the current feeling of the class.

The recent brain research of Robert Sylwester (1995) shows that when we are confronted with perceived threat, danger, or stress, two response systems may engage in the brain: the reflexive (reactive) and the reflective. The reactive mode constricts our behavior, triggering a survival alert. But the same sensory information often travels simultaneously to the cortex, producing more thoughtful reflection. From there, the brain may send out a message to counteract the reflexive message. Most students are not familiar with strategies to reduce stress and engage their reflective mode. A variety of skills can be taught for students to learn to manage their upsets (see Chapter 8, "Problem Solving"). Learning anger management and seeing teachers model it can help to reduce violent behavior in the classroom.

▧ Examples of Skills to Help During the Initial Conversation With an Upset Student and to Model a Reflective Approach

1. *Listen with your heart* by hearing the words and also what isn't being said. Give your undivided attention by facing the student and maintaining eye contact. Keep your body language neutral. This creates a safe place for students to share and lets them know their feelings are valuable.

2. *Acknowledge what you hear* without blame or judgment. Nod your head or say, "I see." This shows you care about their feelings and you are willing to take the time to listen.

3. *Repeat back* to the student what feeling and perspective you hear. Ask if your description is correct.

✓ Checking My Understanding on Acknowledging Feelings of an Upset Student

Below, choose the response that best acknowledges the student's feelings.

1. "The coach yelled at me when I dropped the ball and the whole team laughed."

   a) "It couldn't have been that bad."

   b) "Sounds as if that really hurt your feelings."

   c) "Don't let it get you down, you'll have plenty of other chances to get the ball."

2. "I hate it when I don't get picked till last!"

   a) "Sounds like you would like to get picked sooner."

   b) "I can't believe that at your age you are still worried about that."

   c) "I'm sure you get picked sooner sometimes."

Answers: 1. b, 2. a.

■ TARGET TALK: CREATING REINFORCEMENT FOR POSITIVE CHANGE

∽

Treat people as if they were what they ought to be, and help them to become what they are capable of being.

Goethe

∾

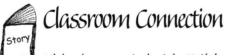 Classroom Connection

Michael was a student in Katie's classroom who struggled with aggression. During group work, Michael would often grab all of the colored pens from the basket on the middle of the table, take the best ones, then throw the others to *his peers at the table, causing upset and bedlam for the other students. Katie and her coach had prearranged for the coach to catch Michael before he threw the pens and use the power of specific language to shape him into being more thoughtful of others.*

Just as Michael was reaching his hand into the basket, the coach, who was standing near the table, said, "Oh Michael, look how thoughtful you are of others, taking one pen for yourself and then passing the rest in the basket to your table friends. What helps you share so kindly?" Michael looked at her, passed the basket, smiled, and shrugged his shoulders. The coach moved on to another table. One month later, when the coach returned to Katie's classroom, Michael came up to her and said, "Lady, lady, remember me? I'm the thoughtful one." The coach probed for some consciousness: "How is it that you are being so thoughtful, Michael?" He said, "I've just grown up, that's all!"

This real-life classroom story illustrates the power of our words to shape a student's thinking about himself. The teacher and the coach structured a setting for success and then used "target talk" rather than praise to give Michael and the other students around him some feedback about social behavior.

❤️ Personal Connection

As you explore this new section on "target talk," think about the Michaels in your classroom who struggle with problems and have not yet developed the "brain program" for appropriate behavior. How could you use the power of immediate feedback, combined with powerful language, to begin to help students to think about themselves differently and thus act differently? Generally teachers have three types of goals for students: academic, social, and cognitive. Identify four to six life skills that you want to encourage in your students in the next few months.

Students and teachers can select one or two that they want to develop and write them on a card, decorate it, and keep it on their desk. Figure 3.1 shows a card that lists several traits for students to select from; students can then write down on their card what the trait they have chosen looks and sounds like.

Create a clear picture of how these skills will look in your students. What behaviors, language, and effects on classroom climate will you expect?

_____

_____

_____

_____

I'm a person who is _____ .

It looks like_____ .

It sounds like _____ .

thoughtful	independent	loyal	peaceful
self-directed	trustworthy	altruistic	affectionate
considerate	loving	careful	compassionate
cooperative	curious	dedicated	diligent
trustworthy	motivated	enthusiastic	empathetic
responsible	someone with a sense of humor	friendly	caring
honorable	inspiring	patient	merciful
confident	conscientious	noble	supportive
organized	mature	sympathetic	patient
prepared	courteous	tolerant	self-controlled
a decision maker	persevering	peace-making	dependable
honest/truthful	resourceful	positive	flexible
a good sport	a team player	friendly	a problem solver
a critical thinker		kind	hard working
sensible			

Figure 3.1.   Card for Students to Select Traits They Want to Develop and Work On

Believing in the art of communicating competence is a prerequisite to being a builder of the positive classroom possibilities. A teacher must operate from the belief that putting emphasis on the effective elements of being a responsible person in the classroom will increase those desired characteristics and behaviors.

Mastering the objectives requires some students to shift their thinking and their behavior. Remember the research reported in Chapter 1 about how connecting learning to values and beliefs paved the way for thinking that made application of new skills much easier? Words do trigger pictures in our minds. If I say, "Don't step in the mud puddle," what image do you picture? The mud puddle and your foot in it, right? Try it with a child. This is why it is so important to phrase our directions and feedback with words that will trigger the pictures that we want our students to see (Figure 3.2).

The use of feedback that reflects the appropriate outcomes produces valuable pictures and information about how feedback works well in the learning environment. You already know the value of giving students immediate feedback on academic skills. Feedback on social skills is equally

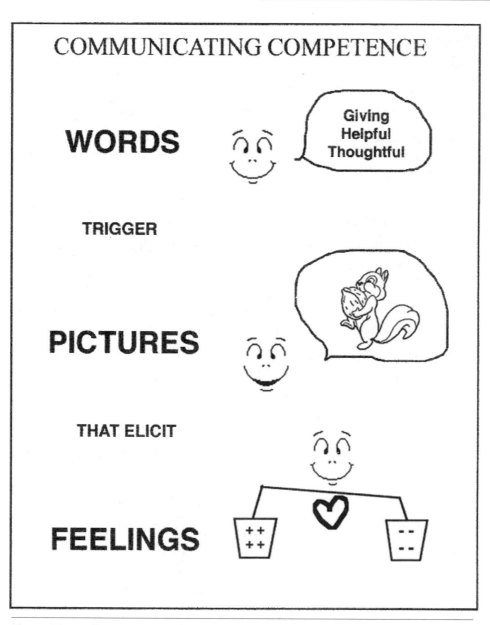

Figure 3.2. Communicating Competence

important. A helpful question for educators is: How can we teach our students these important skills while supporting their learning with meaningful practice?

Target talk is a powerful way to give immediate feedback on social skills. It is the strategy of helping students develop our cultural values and beliefs. It provides immediate feedback during the formative stage of learning and practicing a new life skill (social skill). This feedback describes specific target behaviors that are being taught and helps students know how they are contributing to the classroom community when using them. For example, you might connect an observable behavior of the student (like helping another student find a lost item, waiting one's turn to speak, or remembering to bring materials to class) to a life skill or value (caring, responsibility, or patience).

Examples of Target Talk

- Carmen, how responsible of you to bring a notebook, pencil, and book to the group. How did you remember all three things today?

- Fernando, that was very resourceful, making your own colors when you noticed we were running low on paints. How did you think of that?

- Your teamwork helped your group be successful today. Staying focused on the topic was the key. How did you make that happen?

- You really modeled a peaceful response during group discussion today by asking questions and listening before responding. What helped you do that?

- You showed caring when you included your classmate in the game today. What's your secret?

- You have shown improvement in following our procedures about staying with your group during activities. That requires a lot of self-control—what's making the difference for you?

Target talk can be delivered in several ways:

- *Verbally*: Either publicly or privately, depending on the student's needs

- *In writing*: In a private note or on a bulletin board of celebrations

- *Indirectly*: Spoken to another so as to be overheard by the student

- *"You" messages:* Using the student's name or the word *you* at the beginning of the sentence and connecting it to the specific outcome the student has created give ownership of the behavior to the student.

Examples of Student Focus Versus Teacher Focus

- Correct, Focus on Student: "You were so responsible in your team when you helped everyone get back on track."

- Incorrect, Focus on Teacher: "I liked it when you got your team back on track."

Teachers are often in the habit of using "I like," "I noticed," or "thank you," all of which tie the behavior to the teacher's external motivation and take away student ownership. Save your "I" messages for your feelings or your opinions, and thank students when they are truly doing you a favor.

The goal of target talk is to help students shift their thinking about themselves and their relationship to each other and the community at large. It is given only when the behavior is new and emerging and is not used to manipulate other students into conforming or becoming "teacher pleasers."

Target talk helps a student begin to think about him- or herself as a person of value. Though it is contingent on behavior, it is the highest form of contingent reinforcement and one that we all need to receive in order to feel competent and affirmed. It is the second most powerful leadership skill after gifts without strings in creating a positive relationship. Target talk is to the social curriculum what positive feedback is to the academic curriculum.

✚ Benefits of Target Talk

- Creates a positive self-image
- Maintains and increases prosocial behavior
- Develops awareness of social impact on the group
- Creates responsibility for their success, experts at their own behavior
- Strengthens relationship to self and others
- Fosters awareness of competence
- Teacher curiosity is motivating

Table 3.2 compares "Conformity thinking behavior modification" with "Competence thinking target talk" and is adapted from Linda Metcalf's *Counseling Toward Solutions* (1995). The behavior modification approach provides less connection with the desired outcome and is usually said to manipulate other students to follow suit and get in line. Usually the student who receives it is not in need of the feedback. Competence thinking target talk helps the student build awareness of the social value of the new skill being learned. It gives immediate feedback to support this learning.

Using target talk may be a new behavior/skill for you. If so, you can expect to feel somewhat awkward, phony, and mechanical in your first attempts at it. Be easy on yourself and practice in a safe environment. Start with using it privately with one or two "target students," then expand when you feel comfortable. Some people find it helpful to write out their statements and tell their students or their family that they are practicing noticing positive contributions. They might want to try it too!

Table 3.2   Teacher Statements Exemplifying "Conformity Thinking Behavior Modification" Versus "Competence Thinking Target Talk"

	Conformity Thinking Behavior Modification	Competence Thinking Target Talk
Elementary School	"Students, thank you for working well today."	"You have included others in your group and have completed your entire graph. How have you managed to be so cooperative with each other?"
High School	"Class, the science lab looks great today. Because of your help, you can use the CD player during your lab today."	"This room was a mess earlier. You seem to have really teamed together to fix it up. How have you transformed it in such a short time?"
Athletics	"Fellows, you did great basketball drills today. You did much better than yesterday."	"Guys, your performance today was a perfect example of teamwork. Everyone led one of the drills, and you all helped each other run the zone. How did you turn this team around?"
Special Education	"Jamal, you stayed focused nicely this morning. Good for you! You are earning your points for a computer reward for this afternoon."	"Jamal, you were responsible to yourself and others this morning. You kept focused on athletics and resisted others' attempts to distract you. What helped you have so much self-control?"

☞ Key Criteria for Target Behaviors

- State specific target behaviors in precise observable language.

- Place focus on student's competence with "You" rather than "I."

- Include outcome or result word to connect to values and beliefs.

- When appropriate, include a self-reflecting question to promote internalization.

- Provide immediate feedback: time target talk as close to social behavior as possible.

- Use a neutral tone of voice.

✔ Checking My Understanding of Target Talk

Some of the following statements meet the criteria for target talk and some do not. Label those that have the criteria "TT" (target talk). Refer back to the first four key criteria.

_____ 1. Everyone was cooperative during silent reading today. You came in quietly, picked one book, and sat down to read silently. How were you able to do that?

_____ 2. Michelle, you are practicing patience, reading your library book while waiting your turn to paint. What helped you?

_____ 3. You came in from the fire drill nicely.

_____ 4. Jason, you're being respectful of others by raising your hand and waiting your turn to speak. What helped you remember?

_____ 5. Everyone remembered what to do after the bell rang. How did you do that?

_____ 6. The table groups were very thoughtful of others this morning by remembering to use working voices during work time. How did you remember?

_____ 7. Everyone is ready for the test.

_____ 8. Good organization, everyone has their desk cleared and pencil out, ready for the test. How is it that we were better organized than yesterday?

Answers: Nos. 1, 2, 4, 6, and 8 are target talk.

Personal Commitment

When you finish the practice task, write your own target talk statements based on your goals for your whole class and particular students. How will you shift the students' thinking about their behavior and build competence? Strategize ways you can remember to provide "target talk" daily to help students see themselves as socially appropriate members of the classroom community.

_____

_____

_____

_____

_____

_____

_____

_____

■ ROOM DESIGN FOR TEACHER PROXIMITY

꙰

*Students say they like classrooms where they feel they know the teacher
and the other students. While students appreciate a well-organized
and orderly environment, they do not like one in which the teacher
is detached and treats the classroom as a whole
rather than as a roomful of individuals.*

P. Phelan, A. Davidson, and H. Cao, "Speaking Up: Students'
Perspectives on School"

꙰

Classroom Connection

Reynaldo is a new student in Rozalinda Kounin's classroom. He told her he is worried about coming into the class so late in the year. He likes how Ms. Kounin has her desk at the back of the room and how all the desks are in groups. He asks her if he can sit back near her desk to be near her. She tells Reynaldo that she moves around the room a lot and is rarely at her desk unless it is before or after school. Roz knows that Reynaldo needs her proximity as a way to feel secure and connected. She makes a point of teaching from an area near his desk, as well as Dave's and Michael's. Roz knows that students need to feel that they have access to their teacher. She walks among them during class as a way of connecting and preventing problems and also to let them know that she is present for them. Sometimes she walks to their desk and places her hand on their shoulder or their chair as she is teaching and while they are working as a way of connecting and giving them support.

♥ Personal Connection

Consider your current room design and assess the ability of students to get to you. Can you travel easily around the classroom?

_____

_____

_____

_____

Teachers who have a good relationship with the class can use their presence and position to leverage appropriate behavior without saying a word. Body language is 80% of the message we give people. By moving through the classroom, teaching from various areas and perspectives, we give the message that we care. We are part of the group, confident, relaxed, and available. Proximity can also be a subtle, nonverbal, first-level intervention strategy. When we stand near students, our body gives the message that they need to tune in and keep to our agreements. It is also an easy way to provide equal access for all students (never being more than five steps away from anyone). Rather than stand at the flip chart, the board, or the overhead, use students to help. Let them be your hands to record ideas or answers while you direct them. Then you are free to move about the classroom.

Key Criteria for Teacher Proximity

- Teacher has a firm neutral presence.
- Relationship with students is trusting.
- Room design fosters easy teacher movement.
- Proximity can be used as a prevention or intervention.

Benefits of Teacher Proximity

- Builds a sense of connection to students
- Minimizes distractions
- Maintains more time on task
- Provides equal access to teacher for *all* students

Figures 3.3 and 3.4 show various room arrangement options and their advantages and disadvantages.

For more information on placement of students and groups within the room arrangement, see Chapter 4 on room design and placement of target students.

Room Arrangement Options

	Advantages	Disadvantages
1. Closed circle or rectangle 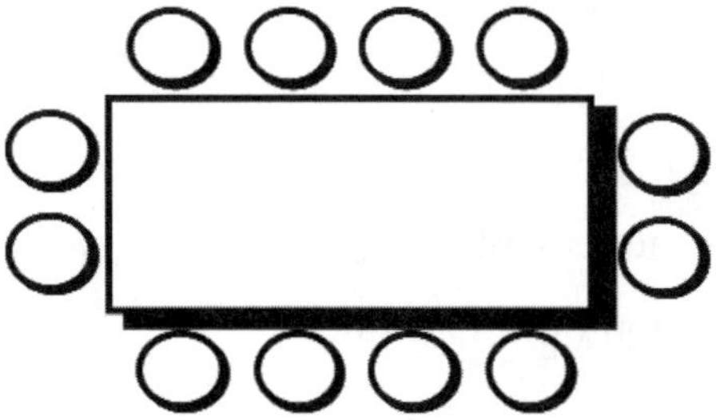	• Encourages eye contact, personal with others. • Especially appropriate when group is working on interpersonal issues.	• Can encourage interpersonal conflict and confrontation. • No single focal point • Not conducive to using group memory.
2. Semi-circle or rectangle with tables 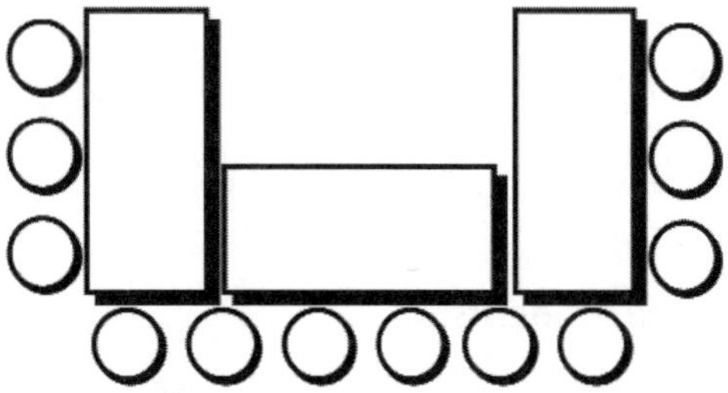	• Allows group to focus on group memory. • Status differential minimized while roles are clear. • Reduces interpersonal conflict.	• Tables can be barrier.
3. Semi-circle without tables 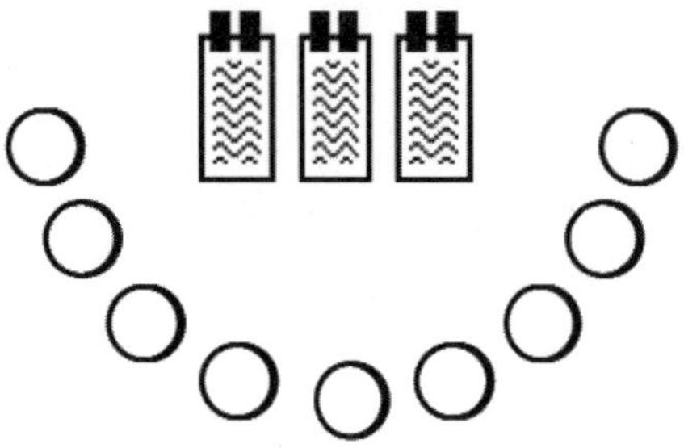	• No barrier between students. • Can accommodate larger groups. • Single focus on task.	• Initial discomfort for students who are used to having tables. • Writing materials have to be placed on floor.

Figure 3.3.   Room Arrangement Options

Room Arrangements

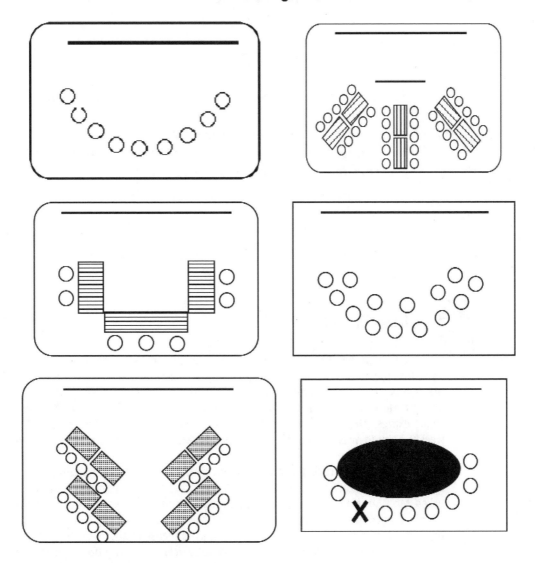

Figure 3.4.   Room Arrangements

♥ Personal Commitment

Consider how you can increase the use of proximity in your classroom. How can you design your classroom to ensure free flow and easy access for you and the students?

_____

_____

_____

■ CLASS MEETINGS AS A PREVENTION STRATEGY

ᔒ

How can we possibly prepare our students for full participation in a democracy if we structure our classrooms autocratically? It is an amazing feature of our democratic educational system that we have settled so universally on an autocratic social organization of our classrooms. Thus arises the need for democratic class meetings.

Spencer Kagan, *Cooperative Learning*

᠋ᦉ

 ## Classroom Connection

The first week of school, Mr. Wun's sixth-grade social studies class had their first class meeting. Mr. Wun's goal for the first meeting was to successfully create a procedure for coming to the meeting and to involve the students in the process. He wanted them to look forward to the meeting as a time that they could express themselves and feel like they were a part of a community. The weekly agenda was posted all week, and the students knew that Friday there would be a meeting.

Mr. Wun asked students to bring ideas that could open the meeting with a spirit of celebration. After class that day, Timothy, one of the quieter students, asked Mr. Wun if he could bring a CD that was popular right then to start the meeting. Mr. Wun discussed the content of the CD and asked if Timothy would bring it on Thursday for him to take home and to please choose a track that had appropriate language and content for school. Luckily, Timothy had a great rap tune that had the perfect lyrics to open the first meeting. When meeting time came, Mr. Wun challenged the class to safely bring their chairs to make a circle by the end of the track on the CD. Most of the class loved the music, and they arrived safely in a circle by the end of track, which gave Mr. Wun the opportunity to acknowledge the spirit of respect and success in taking on the circle challenge as a group. He then asked for other ideas on how to start future meetings and chose a student to record them on the whiteboard. Several students mentioned during that time that they liked the track that Timothy had brought, which made Timothy feel appreciated.

On another whiteboard was the question: How will we make class meetings fun, fair, and successful? It was the first topic on the agenda for the next meeting.

♥ Personal Connection

What are the classroom issues that might go on the class agenda for group discussion and decision making?

_____

_____

_____

_____

CLASS MEETINGS AS A PREVENTIVE STRATEGY ■

Class meetings provide the perfect environment for teaching social skills and building relationship and community. They offer an ongoing opportunity for students to get to know each other and for the teacher to model a commitment to relationship building. At the beginning of the year, the skill may be as simple as having everyone bring his or her chair to a circle without hurting anyone. The next time, you may add that it be in a reasonable amount of time. Skills can then build in future class meetings with listening, respectful feedback, acknowledging, sharing similarities and uniquenesses, practicing discussion etiquette, creating procedures, and crafting rules and agreements. Later in the year, when relationships are stronger and the students are familiar with the meeting format and required behavior, problem solving may become a part of the meetings. This is where the big payoff shows up. To have a safe, open forum for students to solve problems as a community is the crossover to real life and being a responsible citizen with solid skills.

 ## Benefits of Class Meetings

- Prevents problems by getting group agreement
- Supports a brain-compatible environment
- Offers a place for group participation in creating classroom standards, rules, and procedures
- Builds a sense of community and connectedness

- Creates a structure for practicing life skills

- Provides opportunities for autonomy and influence

Guidelines for Class Meetings

Class meetings can be of several types:

- Problem solving

- Planning activities, parties, field trips, etc.

- Learning and practicing social skills

A specific time for meetings should be set aside on a regular basis: for example, every Wednesday before lunch, before PE, before recess, the first Thursday of the month, the last 15 minutes of the period.

The length of the meeting should vary with the developmental age of students:

- Kindergarten: 10 to 15 minutes

- Primary grades: 15 to 20 minutes (maximum)

- Middle grades: 20 to 30 minutes

- Secondary grades: 15 to 45 minutes

Examples of Ideas for Class Meeting Structure and Activities

1. Have a clipboard available between meetings to write down agenda items.

2. Compliments Activity:

   - Before the meeting, students prepare the compliment card shown in Figure 3.5.

   - With the same compliment card, a word can be chosen the week before. Then each student is asked to notice someone that week who displays an example of the word and to bring it to the meeting.

   - Names can be drawn the week before and then students have to find a compliment for each person whose name is drawn.

3. Inside Outside Circle: The students sit in two circles facing each other and practice social skills such as getting to know someone new, introducing yourself to someone, giving a compliment, active listening, sharing, or working out a problem together.

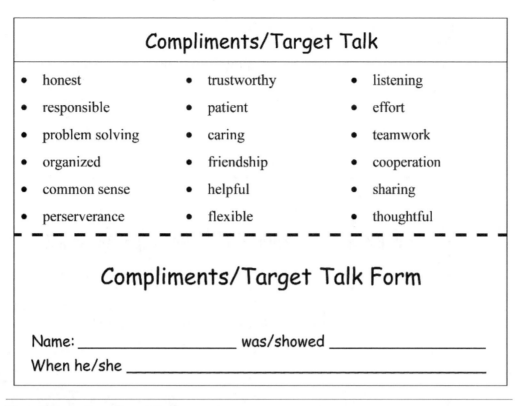

Compliments/Target Talk		
• honest	• trustworthy	• listening
• responsible	• patient	• effort
• problem solving	• caring	• teamwork
• organized	• friendship	• cooperation
• common sense	• helpful	• sharing
• perserverance	• flexible	• thoughtful

Compliments/Target Talk Form

Name: _____ was/showed _____

When he/she _____

Figure 3.5   Compliment Card

4. Circle Game: To begin the meeting, go around the circle with each person using a sentence starter:

   - My favorite color is . . .

   - My favorite treat is . . .

   - My favorite movie is . . .

   - My favorite after-school activity is . . .

   - My favorite thing to do on the weekend is . . .

   - My favorite sport/playground equipment/PE game is . . .

5. Opening fingerplay, song, rhythmic chant, favorite cut from a CD, short game

Key Criteria for Class Meetings

- Everyone is seated in a tight circle.

- Meeting lasts 10 to 45 minutes.

- Agenda is created together (after meeting procedures and positive meeting behavior are in place).

- Meeting is a forum for compliments and acknowledgment.

Personal Commitment

How can you see the class meeting fitting into your weekly plan?

_____

_____

_____

Summary of Personal Relationships for Trust

● When a positive relationship is weak or absent, attempts to use *any* managerial strategies will be ineffective. A strong relationship between teacher and students is the most important building block for success (Figure 3.6).

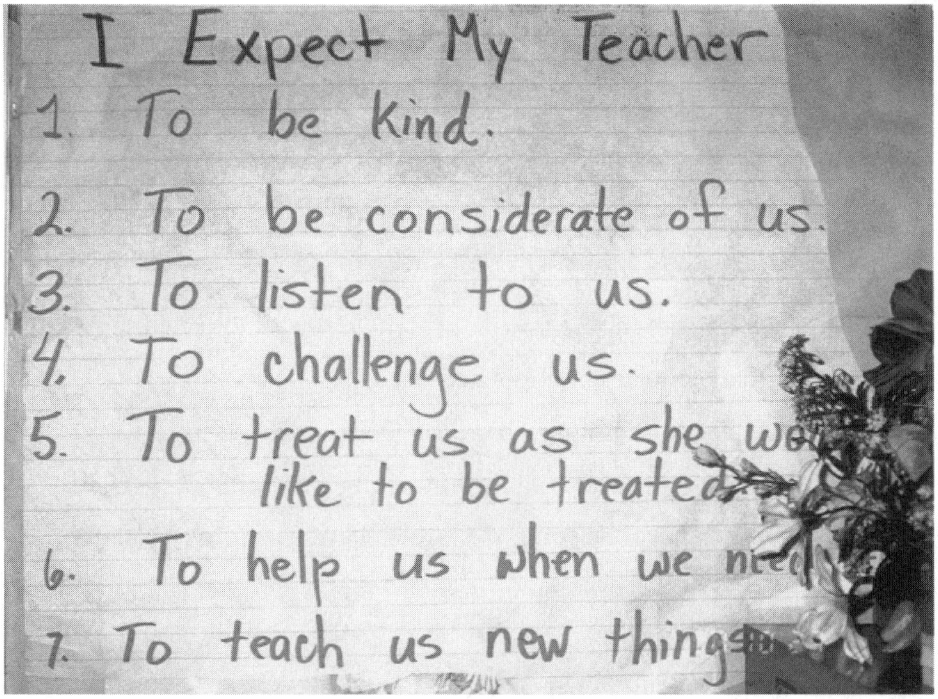

I Expect My Teacher
1. To be kind.
2. To be considerate of us.
3. To listen to us.
4. To challenge us.
5. To treat us as she wo
   like to be treated
6. To help us when we ne
7. To teach us new thing

Figure 3.6.   One Class's Expectations of Their Teacher

- It is essential that teachers maintain neutrality and a nonjudgmental attitude during student upsets to protect their relationship with the student and to preserve the student's self-esteem.

- Gifts without strings, given freely and independent of student behavior, are the key to fostering a trusting and secure teacher-student relationship.

- Target talk is the strategy of providing specific information (feedback) to the learner during the formation of learning a new social skill or behavior. It allows the learner to know what and how progress is being made so it can be increased and maintained.

- A teacher who has a bonded relationship with the class can use his or her presence and physical position to encourage and support appropriate behavior and academic success. Proximity of the teacher fosters more time on task, fewer distractions, and equal access to the teacher.

- Class meetings provide an ideal environment for practicing social skills and building relationships.

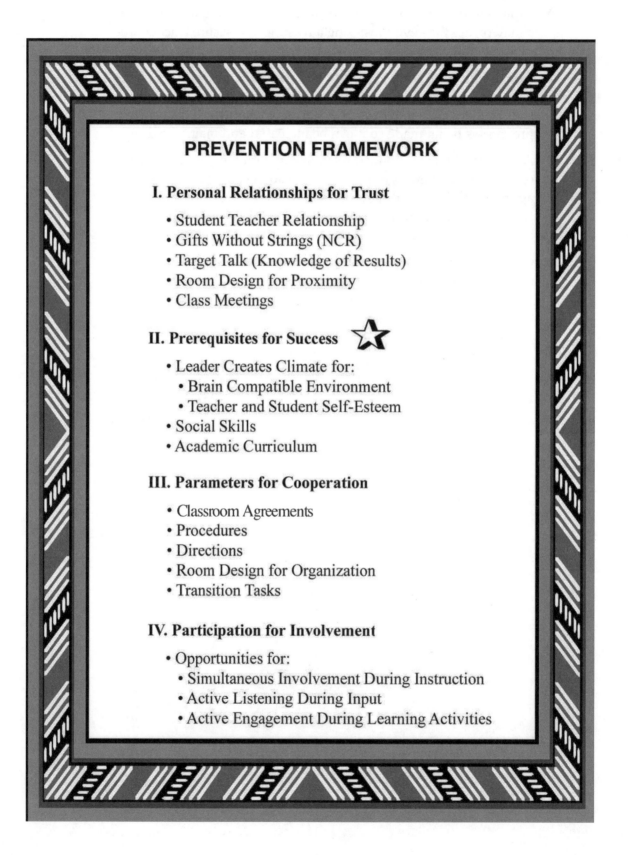

PREVENTION FRAMEWORK

I. Personal Relationships for Trust

- Student Teacher Relationship
- Gifts Without Strings (NCR)
- Target Talk (Knowledge of Results)
- Room Design for Proximity
- Class Meetings

II. Prerequisites for Success ☆

- Leader Creates Climate for:
  - Brain Compatible Environment
  - Teacher and Student Self-Esteem
- Social Skills
- Academic Curriculum

III. Parameters for Cooperation

- Classroom Agreements
- Procedures
- Directions
- Room Design for Organization
- Transition Tasks

IV. Participation for Involvement

- Opportunities for:
  - Simultaneous Involvement During Instruction
  - Active Listening During Input
  - Active Engagement During Learning Activities

Prerequisites for Success

4

The Second "P" of Prevention

∽

By focusing on fulfilling fundamental emotional needs, teachers can enhance students' motivation to learn.

Spence Rogers and Lisa Renard, "Relationship-Driven Teaching"

∾

Prerequisites are the second prevention strategy to consider in rethinking how you as the classroom leader can create a climate for success in your classroom while preventing a majority of classroom management upsets. We know that many students come into our classrooms without their basic emotional needs met. Rethinking prerequisites will help you to meet some of those needs within the context of teaching your curriculum, rather than as a separate add-on curriculum. Although we all want our students to share the responsibility for their success, they can do so only if we do our part in ensuring that their fundamental emotional needs are met, at least in our sphere of influence, our classroom. As you read the following story, begin to think of what prerequisites might be missing for the student.

 ## Classroom Connection

Lupe Acosta was a 6-year-old student in the K-2 classroom of first-year teacher Sharon Chen in a high-poverty district. Lupe barely spoke and was quite primitive in her behavior at school. Sharon struggled with how to meet the needs of the other, equally needy children and Lupe at the same time. The entire school community knew that Lupe was coming to school without the basic prerequisites to achieve, yet here she was in a classroom with 23 other children, 5 of whom also came from homes where there was abuse, little supervision, and a lack of stable parenting.

Early in September, after Lupe's erratic antisocial behavior had escalated, the principal asked a district mentor/coach to come in on a daily basis and support Sharon in providing a "brain-compatible" environment for herself as well as the students. The coach observed Lupe running around the perimeter of the room, throwing books onto the floor from every shelf she passed, laughing and making noises, while the teacher and three aides (special ed and speech) were monitoring children at the centers. Lupe grabbed the coach's pen and called her the "f___ lady." The coach waited for Lupe to circle the room again and then tried to engage the child in tracing her hand with the pen that she had taken. The distraction worked, and a bond was forming. The coach was trying to assess what Lupe's needs were. She knew that Sharon already had a bonded teacher-student relationship with Lupe. The next task was to build an environment in which Lupe as well as the other students could feel comfortable and secure because Lupe's behavior was violating everyone else's safety.

❤ Personal Connection

Can you picture yourself in Sharon's situation? How would you help a student like Lupe be successful?

_____

_____

_____

_____

_____

This chapter will help you fulfill your responsibility for students' success by assessing whether the fundamental emotional, social, and academic conditions are in place for your students to be 85% successful in your classroom. You already know how intimidating it can be for you to take a class when you lack the prerequisites for it. Your own experiences will help you as you plan how to prevent this from happening to your students. The three main sections of this chapter will cover three areas for you to explore and will enable you to rethink ways to help students be successful in your classroom.

1. "Environmental Prerequisites" describes how to create a "brain-compatible" classroom and shows how to incorporate the dimensions of self-esteem into planning of the classroom learning environment.

2. "Social Skills Prerequisites" provides guidelines that students need to work successfully in groups.

3. "Academic Curriculum Prerequisites" shows how to plan your instructional activities for students' success.

These three sets of prerequisites must *all* be in place for students to be successful learners in the classroom. Students must master these skills and concepts or the teacher must accommodate the lesson to their stage of mastery before new learning can occur.

In the story about Lupe, many of the environmental prerequisites were not in place for her to be a successful learner. For leaders in the classroom, the kind of situation described in this story can seem overwhelming—just one more thing to think about and, if we don't take the responsibility, a source of frustration and upset all year long so that neither teacher nor student will feel successful. When we take the time to assess each of the three areas of prerequisites—environmental, social, and academic—before teaching any lesson or designing any learning activity, our students will be more successful; when they are successful, we will feel successful. Our assessment can be conducted formally through pretests or one-on-one diagnostic inventories or informally through observation or teacher inventories where students self-assess what they know, don't know, and might want to know. When the prerequisites are still in the formative stage, not at a mastery level, the leader needs to accommodate for the missing elements.

Examples of Accommodation

- Adapting the task itself—that is, altering or omitting parts of the task for certain students

- Changing the instructional strategy—for example, from direct instruction to peer teaching

- Modifying the activity, using the research on different intelligences—for example, from an intrapersonal task, in which each student works alone, to an interpersonal task, in which some students who are missing prerequisites work in groups or with partners who have the necessary prerequisites to support them

- Providing for the use of visual aids or supports (calculators, word banks, computers, etc.)

Such strategies accommodate both the teacher and the students and often allow the teacher to go on in the curriculum to a new concept, principle, or theory while the prerequisite skills are still being practiced but are not yet mastered. For example, in teaching a lesson on writing business letters, if the objective is to teach the format and some students have not yet mastered punctuation, the teacher might provide a frame on a chart for them to use as a reference. Students who have not mastered punctuation can check their business letters when needed, rather than waiting for the entire class to reach mastery. We hear a lot about "differentiating instruction"; rethinking prerequisites is another way do it. Incorporating the ideas that follow about environmental prerequisites—creating a brain-compatible classroom learning environment and incorporating the dimensions of self-esteem—will give both students and teachers the opportunity to succeed at learning.

■ ENVIRONMENTAL PREREQUISITES

The Leader's Creation of a Brain-Compatible Environment

♋

I am the decisive element in the classroom. It is my personal approach that creates the climate. . . . As a teacher, I possess a tremendous power to make a child's life miserable or joyous. . . . I can humiliate or humor, hurt or heal. In all situations, it is my response that decides whether a crisis will be escalated and my children's self-esteem supported or violated.

Haim Ginott, *Teacher and Child*

♋

Classroom Connection

Lupe frequently complained of a tummy ache and headaches. Sharon and her coach knew that these physical symptoms were often a sign of fear and insecurity in new situations. They brainstormed after school on what types of gifts without strings might help Lupe feel more secure and connected to teacher and classmates and might also decrease the aggression that was running her. The coach reviewed with Sharon how aggression was decreased with structure and teacher proximity. Sharon used that rule of thumb along with what she knew about Lupe's needs to be helpful.

Lupe was used to helping out at home with the cooking and younger children. Sharon decided that she would invite Lupe to come in every morning and count and staple together five pieces of newsprint or scrap paper that the children could use at the math center. This would provide a connection to Sharon for Lupe, help for Sharon, a structured outlet for Lupe to pound out some pent-up anger, practice in counting for Lupe, and a product that the class would need and use.

Sharon noticed that when she assigned centers, no matter where Lupe was assigned she always went to the playhouse. The coach suggested that they continue to use the information that the child's behavior was giving them: For the next few weeks, Sharon would just assign her there because that seemed to be a place that Lupe associated with comfort and success. Sharon knew that until Lupe could get comfortable and safe in her environment, learning was not going to happen.

By October, Sharon wanted to have times in the day when the playhouse was closed. But she didn't want to simply close the playhouse, because that would have gotten her into a power struggle with Lupe. So instead, paradoxi-

cally, she made Lupe feel comfortable and safe by enlisting her help in closing the playhouse and thereby allowing her to feel in control of the situation. She assigned Lupe the task of standing in front of the playhouse with a signal (swinging her arms like a railroad signal) and holding a sign that said, "Playhouse Closed." Once all of the other children were settled at their desired centers, Sharon was free to invite Lupe to one of the teacher-guided centers for a learning activity. While Lupe was there, the special ed teacher or aide was able to give her immediate feedback on both her social skills and her academic skills: for example, "Lupe, you are so thoughtful of Eric, sharing the unifix cubes. Let's check and see if you are remembering the pattern. Check here against the model Ms. Sharon made." At the end of centers activities, Sharon gathered the students to share what they had learned about themselves or about the lesson at the center they had chosen.

❤ Personal Connection:

Finish the following sentence: "Reading this story reinforced my own ability to. . . "

_____

_____

_____

_____ ○

A brain-compatible classroom like Sharon's is one in which educators recognize the brain as the primary organ for learning and create an environment that prevents the brain from shutting down or "downshifting" (MacLean, 1990). A brain-compatible classroom learning environment is generally defined as one in which the leader supports learning and thinking by ensuring that the learner has access to that large part of the brain, the cerebral cortex, where thinking and learning are processed. The research on education and the brain that has been conducted over the past 15 years, whether by the early leaders in the movement, like Leslie Hart (1983), Paul MacLean (1990), and Susan Kovalik (1993), or, more recently, by Caine and Caine (1991), Robert Sylwester (1998), Eric Jensen (1998), Marilee Sprenger (1999), and Martha Kaufeldt (1999), has all documented the importance of having a classroom environment that is brain compatible. Researchers often identify between five and nine elements necessary for such an environment. In our prevention framework, we will use the six most connected to classroom management:

1. Absence of threat

2. Immediate feedback

3. Meaningful content

4. Collaboration with peers

5. Opportunity to make choices

6. Learning paced for relaxed alertness

By the end of this section, you will be able to compare and connect these six elements to the four dimensions of self-esteem and plan which ones you want to focus on and foster in your classroom. This will enhance students' motivation to learn and your motivation to teach. We read how Sharon Chen's success with Lupe was due to her incorporating these elements into her classroom. Now we too can be more consciously competent about what the brain needs for learning by using more practices that support the thinking brain for our students and ourselves and eliminating practices that make the brain downshift and inhibit the ability to learn.

The Six Elements of a Brain-Compatible Classroom

Trust or Absence of Threat

ॐ

Excess stress and threat in the school environment may be the single greatest contributor to impaired academic learning.

Eric Jensen, *Teaching With the Brain in Mind*

ॐ

In our opening story, what was Lupe trying to do when she threw the books around the room? Some recent brain research may help us to answer this question.

When a person perceives a threat, whether that threat is real or only imagined, the brain has a strong physiological response. MacLean (1990) documents how the blood supply is actually cut off to the cerebral cortex, the thinking area of the brain, and the brain "downshifts" to the more primitive limbic or brain stem area of the brain. This brain stem area, which is part of what is often called the "reptile brain" because it is primitive and, unlike the cerebral cortex, shared by lower orders of vertebrates, is concerned with survival functions and emotions and motivations connected with them, such as fear and anger, and its stimulation can lead to impulsive action, as illustrated in Figure 4.1.

Sylwester (1998) uses terms like *reflexive* and *reflective* to define the separate response systems in the brain that get triggered during environmental stress. Martha Kaufeldt (1999) uses the analogy of a computer that is overloaded with too many programs opened and not enough RAM. When

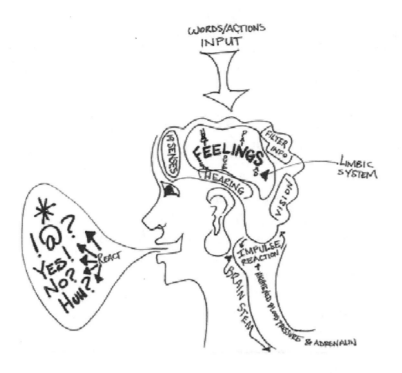

Figure 4.1.   Diagram of the Brain and Its Responses to Input

SOURCE: Adapted by Brandy Caroline Lee-Jacob from MacLean (1990).

the learning environment evokes fear, the fear has an effect like that of insufficient RAM: other programs get shut down so that the available RAM can be focused on surviving the situation. When the brain is in this mode, the learner is putting energy into defensive behavior to protect him- or herself rather than creative or learning behavior. The adrenal system sends out messages to the nervous system, sometimes producing such symptoms as an upset stomach, a headache, clammy hands, or pains in the chest (anxiety). These are all clues that some sort of physiological response is happening. Under this kind of duress, most learners are unable to do the following:

1. Access critical or creative thinking skills

2. Pick up visual or auditory clues from the teacher

3. Perform complex intellectual tasks

4. Solve problems or communicate clearly

5. Recall or access prior knowledge

The brain is literally paralyzed with fear and shuts down to defend the organism from the perceived attack. This organic, physiological response is outside of the person's control.

The aggression that dominated Lupe's behavior when she grabbed the books and threw them around the room was most likely her way of protecting herself in an environment where she felt she had no connection and no control. Because the teacher, Sharon Chen understood that, she was able to think about it differently, and because she thought differently, she was able to respond differently. The outcome was more facilitative, and this positive approach brought Lupe into the community of learners.

Examples of Classroom Strategies to Prevent Real or Perceived Threats

- *Nurture a strong bonded student-teacher relationship.* As Rogers and Renard (1999) have documented, and as we noted in Chapter 3, personal relationships between teachers and students have a strong impact on achievement. This is because "the brain does not naturally separate emotions from cognition, either anatomically or perceptually" (Caine & Caine, 1991, p. 82). When students believe that their teacher cares about them personally and makes deposits in their emotional bank account, motivation to learn increases (Rogers & Renard, 1999). Sharon Chen applied this research with Lupe and had success within a couple of weeks, as soon as Lupe felt safe and secure and trusted Sharon. Over the year, the aggression that had dominated Lupe's behavior diminished significantly and she was able to participate in the classroom as a learner.

- *Ensure that students have adequate time* to complete tasks and that there are warnings and visual signals for students to prepare to shift subjects or tasks: for example, visual overhead "teach timers" that show how many minutes students have to complete a task and count down or up so that students can watch and monitor themselves (available from several teacher supply companies, including Stokes Publishing, phone 800-550-5254 or e-mail customerservice@stokespublishing.com). We all know the frustration of starting a task and getting interrupted so that we lose our train of thought and the pattern-seeking brain loses its pattern. Leslie Hart (1983) refers to learning as "the acquisition of useful programs" (p. 86), and when information does not become part of a program, it is usually not retained. Kovalik (1993) supports the same concept. She stresses that a student needs time to identify the patterns and assign meaning to them and then to develop a program to use the new learning. If this time is not given, the original time given was wasted and now both teacher and student are frustrated. Madeline Hunter, a UCLA-affiliated pioneer in the early 1980s on planning effective lesson design, used to say that if we wanted to "cover information" we should come to class with a shovel. In other words, we need to teach less and with more time for depth and meaning. Learning requires uninterrupted blocks of time to acquire mastery with meaning and without fears about having to race the clock.

- *Use perception surveys* to assess if your students feel safe and secure in your classroom and how they perceive the relationship.

- *Create parameters for classroom interaction,* such as class agreements, that focus on preventing put-downs, embarrassment, or any type of teasing or harassment. Develop with the class a "caring menu" (see Chapter 7) , and teach them how to make amends when they make a social mistake. All of Chapter 5 addresses structures such as daily agendas that provide students with a sense of security and safety in the classroom.

- *Encourage risk taking and intrinsic motivation* by eliminating punishment, loss of privileges, and all extrinsic competition and rewards.

- *Use questioning strategies that give students an opportunity to feel safe* by either volunteering a response or having their answer or response shared first in a small group with a partner. The age-old strategy of calling a student's name and then asking a question or vice versa often violates the "relaxed alertness" we are trying to promote in our classrooms (see Chapter 6).

- *Play calming music and allow students a vehicle for expressing feelings,* such as journal writing

Collaboration With Peers.

The basic nature of the student is to want to question, discuss, argue and share. . . . Cooperative learning channels this natural intelligence toward positive academic and social outcomes.

Spencer Kagan, *Cooperative Learning*

Collaboration is a crucial skill for adult life. In a survey done by the American Society for Training and Development and the U.S. Department of Labor (Carnevale, Gainer, & Meltzer, 1989), the qualities that employers valued most in employees, in order of priority, were dependability, proper attitudes, and getting along well with others. The ability to read and other academic skills such as math were ranked below these social behaviors. Yet most employers found employees unable to work collaboratively.

As teachers, we can encourage and invite our students to be a supportive community of learners, or we can inhibit and prevent this important social and emotional skill from developing. In Sharon Chen's classroom, it would have been easy to take the more cautious approach of using only teacher-directed and small group instruction, given the number of high-risk students. But because Sharon believed in children's need to work together, she orchestrated settings to teach them this important life skill during center time. She had students collaborate with each other at centers, under the monitoring of adult aides who could support appropriate social interaction with feedback.

One of the most intrinsically motivating activities for human beings is talking. Notice how in teachers' workshops the need and urge to talk is primary. As teachers, we can channel this basic internal need to talk by planning and structuring situations so that the talking will be about the learning. This also begins to teach students how to work together.

Children naturally want to help each other. Students should be given multiple opportunities to work with each other for common goals—academic, social, or cognitive. This is how they will learn to collaborate at work in their adult lives. They can be assigned to a partner or a group or they can choose one depending on the objective of the exercise. The section on social skills prerequisites later in this chapter will give you some specific, detailed, practical guidelines for when to have students work in pairs versus larger groups as well as when to allow choice and when to provide structure.

Classroom Strategies to Support Collaboration With Peers

- Students writing and reading together ("buddy-reading")
- Class projects and homework that require other students' input
- Class meetings where students solve problems and plan together
- Cooperative learning activities

Immediate Feedback

∽

The single most dynamic influence on the brain's chemistry may be positive feedback, which is essential for the development of a good self-concept and healthy self-esteem.

Robert Sylwester, "The Downshifting Dilemma"

∾

During the formative stage of learning a new skill, learners need to get immediate feedback to prevent them from practicing or applying a skill or concept incorrectly. Hart (1983) refers to this as "program building." It fixes the new learning's key points in students' stored memory. Recall how Lupe got feedback from her teachers when she came to the learning centers and how this helped her begin to think differently about herself and see herself as a cooperative learner. Students can get this feedback from

- *The materials,* as in programmed learning or self-paced learning

- *The teacher* as she monitors the classroom and stops to comment on the correctness of the task and prompts them to fix an error

- *Themselves* and their own perception of when they feel that they have mastered a particular skill or concept

- *The task itself,* such as an inquiry or experiment and the results

 ## Examples of Classroom Strategies to Support Immediate Feedback

- Teacher's intervention, during practice tasks, of walking around and spending less than 5 seconds with each student while giving one positive comment and one to grow on if needed

- Literacy rubric charts, or charts that districts and schools create so that students can measure their own competency by comparing their work to work that would be an "A" paper or a 4.0 paper, or a "B" paper or a 3.0 paper, using the standards outlined by the state

- Peer editing of written work, as taught in many literacy programs

- Target talk (see Chapter 3) to give students feedback on their social skills

- Multiage grouping where students teach each other

- Reciprocal teaching strategies

- Class meetings where students share their observations about each other's success

- Self-assessment tools, such as asking students to look at a page of problems, then to circle all of the ones that they could do easily with green and to cross out the ones that would stump them in red

Opportunity to Make Choices

♋

We cannot expect children to accept ready-made values and truths all the way through school, and then suddenly make choices in adulthood.

Constance Cami, "Toward Autonomy: The Importance of Critical Thinking and Choice Making"

♋

The power of choosing is the ultimate determiner of success. Students and people in general can be invited to be cooperative when they have choice. On the other hand, resistance can be invited when choice is not offered.

Choice opportunities give a great opportunity to teach consensus, in which everybody wins, versus voting, which promotes winners and losers. Consensus can help establish the win-win atmosphere that is necessary for the classroom to be a good learning environment. For example, suppose that Sharon Chen's class has a class meeting in which the majority of children choose an activity that Lupe, the child who struggles with aggression, does not like. An opportunity opens here for children to begin to learn give and take. They can learn about and use consensus to reach an agreement rather than voting. The teacher leader can help the group work out how Lupe might cope or how she might agree to their choice today and have her choice the next day. There are so many times when children don't have choices due to circumstances outside of our sphere of influence that it is critical for us to create as many opportunities as possible for choice in our own classrooms. Children learn to make "good choices" by getting to make a few bad ones.

Examples of Classroom Strategies to Support Multiple Opportunities for Choice

- Use the multiple intelligences research to design learning activities for students to choose from. Thomas Armstrong offers useful examples in his book *Multiple Intelligences in the Classroom* (1994).

- Give students a choice on their homework based on an objective: for example, "You need to demonstrate and practice retention of the following skills. . . . Choose how to do that for your homework tonight."

- Give them a choice on what type of test they will take.

- Give them a choice on what to study next from a list of possibilities.

Meaningful Content

❧

To minimize extrinsic rewards, educators need a curriculum that is worth learning and a pedagogy that helps students see why it is worth learning.

Catherine Lewis, Eric Schaps, and Marilyn Watson, "The Caring Classroom's Academic Edge"

❧

Meaningful content is content that connects to the students' real world and is age appropriate. Whether the curriculum is powerful and meaningful depends on your students' ability to see a use for it in their real lives. It also depends on students' ability to connect what they learn to their prior knowledge. As Kovalik (1993) reports, "Learning takes place when the brain sorts out patterns using past experiences to make sense out of the input the brain receives" (p. 51). Connections that the learner makes between new information and prior knowledge are often referred to as "brain hooks."

When we perceive learning as meaningful, we attend with intrinsic motivation and do not need to be coerced into learning. As Frank Smith wrote in a "Learners' Manifesto" in his book *Insult to Intelligence* (1986), "Learning does not require coercion or irrelevant reward. We fail to learn only if we are bored, or confused. . . . If we understand, then we learn" (p. 62). Lupe learned more skills in "playhouse" than she could learn at the more structured academic centers because that was meaningful to her. She learned, for example, to measure and sort and to read directions for how to diaper the baby.

Examples of Classroom Strategies to Help Students Find the Curriculum Meaningful

- Ask students what they already know about the subject, topic, theme, concept, etc., and list visually on board or easel.

- Ask students what they want to know about the lesson.

- Teach from firsthand, "being there" experiences such as going on a field trip.

- Have students explore through hands-on experiments and teach from their learnings or mistakes.

- Learn and use three to five different models of teaching other than direct instruction for introductory lessons: for example, concept attainment, role play, the jurisprudential model, the Socratic model, scientific inquiry, or synectics (Joyce & Weil, 1992). Incorporate thematic instruction into your curriculum (Kovalik, 1993).

Pacing of Learning for Relaxed Alertness

∽

Students' behavior and performance are affected by their teacher's tempo.
Vernon F. Jones and Louise S. Jones, *Comprehensive Classroom Management*

∾

This element encompasses not just the pacing of a particular lesson but the pacing of learning and the tempo of the entire school day. Martha Kaufeldt, in her book *Begin With the Brain* (1999), devotes an entire chapter to creating a classroom atmosphere of relaxed alertness. Drawing on Caine and Caine (1991), she shows, with examples from her own personal teaching experiences, that relaxed alertness is not the same as being calm and mellow: "The goal is to create a climate that balances low threat with evidences of challenge, that does not leave learning to chance" (Kaufeldt, 1999, p. 15).

As classroom leaders, we need to learn how to generate interest and enthusiasm while still creating a calming effect on our students by adjusting our own personal pace in the classroom to accommodate theirs. For example, Sharon had a very even-tempered disposition, and she took time to listen and observe her students to meet their needs. Sometimes she needed to pick up the pace to hold their interest, even though this wasn't her favorite or natural style.

Examples of Classroom Strategies to Support Pacing for Relaxed Alertness

- Include quick 1- to 3-minute physical activities such as "Simon says" or Brain Gym activities (Dennison & Dennison, 1992).

- Observe students' nonverbal cues for boredom, confusion, or restlessness.

- Ask students to signal you by crossing their arms over their chest or putting their hands on their head or chin to let you know if you are going too fast or too slow.

- Break activities up into short segments using strategies like "think, pair, share," a questioning strategy that structures students to share with a partner (see Chapter 6).

- Provide students "brain talk" time for 30 seconds to 2 minutes to let them process your teaching and connect it to their prior knowledge (see the section "Questioning Strategies" in Chapter 6).

- When showing a video or film, stop after 10 to 12 minutes and have partners or groups discuss content or write down the favorite or least favorite thing they have learned.

- Remember that we can attend for the number of minutes of our developmental age plus 2 and that most research suggests that even adults tune out after 10 to 12 minutes (Sprenger, 1999).

- Vary the instructional strategies used. Direct instruction should not occupy more than 15% of your day.

- Assign paperwork (seatwork) judiciously; students who feel buried in paperwork are not in states of "relaxed alertness," and a lot of classroom management problems happen with very little learning during these isolated seatwork periods. Have students work together on seatwork activities.

Benefits of a Brain–Compatible Learning Environment

- Promotes student motivation
- Ensures student success
- Provides "brain hooks"
- Creates an environment where inquiry and experimentation is valued
- Develops self-direction and autonomy
- Creates climate of fairness and respect

Self-Esteem

❧

Only a child who feels safe dares to grow forward healthily. His needs for self-actualization, esteem, belonging, love and safety must be gratified.

Abraham Maslow, *Toward a Psychology of Being*

☙

Classroom Connection

Reflect back on the story of Lupe and how she came to school without having her basic human needs of belonging, love, and safety fulfilled. Her teacher, Sharon Chen, could have spun her wheels trying to get Lupe's family to change, a socio-logical challenge beyond the role or influence of classroom teachers, or she could do what she did, focus her energy on her circle of influence her classroom. Once Lupe felt secure and connected to Sharon, she could begin to build some connec-tions to the class. Stapling and sorting the stacks of "drawing paper" that the class used at centers gave Lupe a sense of self-esteem and competence in the eyes of the other students. Allowing her and others to choose when they went to cer-tain centers began to give them a feeling of influence and power over their own lives. All of the literacy-based centers had varying degrees of activities to accom-modate a range of learners, from those at a very low level who were still learning about print to those at a high level who were ready to write their own stories. Students could choose among sticker boards, computers, and traditional journal entries, and they were taught to help each other. During the first few weeks of school, Sharon set up the centers with the same tasks at each center. She taught the children the social skills of moving from place to place, using the materials, staying at their center until the music stopped, and all of the other routines that they needed to know before there could be challenging academic learning. Sharon knew that for now the emotional objectives took precedence over the academic objectives, and she used materials matched to a level at which the students could work independently (independent level) rather than a level at which they would require her guidance and support (instructional level; see the section "Academic Prerequisites" later in this chapter).

Personal Connection

How did the teacher, Sharon Chen, support self-esteem in this story?

_____

_____

_____

Whereas the brain research describes how learning happens in the cerebral cortex, the self-esteem research described in this section describes the emotional connection to learning. As you explore self-esteem, look for how the findings of the self-esteem research from the past are closely aligned with those of present-day brain research. This section will help you develop the skills to create a learning environment that supports the dimensions of self-esteem. Such an environment will also be brain com-patible. Your role in the classroom will be simplified, and you and your students will share a caring and powerful learning environment. When you see the connection of the effective to the affective—of the thinking cerebral brain to the emotional, feeling aspects of our students' self-esteem—you will be comfortable and confident about creating an environment that supports both, at the same time, with the same strategies.

As we begin, it will be helpful to make a distinction between self-image, self-concept, and self-esteem. Self-image is the picture that I have of myself—how I look and how I project myself in the world. This is usually a right-brained, nonverbal view of myself. Self-concept is the idea I have about myself, a more left-brained, logical notion. Self-esteem is more of a feeling or perception I have about myself that is based on my self-image and my self-concept. It evolves from three sources: heredity, environment, and our perception of both. Self-esteem gives us a sense of security, connectedness, competence, and power over our own lives—feelings that are, in fact, basic needs for all human beings (Maslow, 1999). Others often recognize it as a "sense of self-respect, confidence and positive pro-social purpose" (Reasoner, 1982, p. 3). Ultimately it is "appreciating my own worth and importance and having the character to be accountable for myself and to act responsibly toward others" (California Task Force on Self Esteem, 1990, p. 18). As will be discussed below, many characteristics of what is now called "resiliency" mirror the dimensions of self-esteem.

Because self-esteem is a perception, it can change with the tide of popular opinion. It is not necessarily the truth. How many times have you heard a youngster say, "I don't have any friends"? And yet you see just the opposite. So we might say that self-esteem is our "experience" of ourselves. And that experience affects our actions because it is how we think about ourselves.

We said that self-esteem originates partly in our heredity, our genetic disposition for thinking positively or negatively. Because this is not an area that we can alter, at least not at this time, let's look at the other two sources, environment and perception. Five environmental factors can have a profound influence on how a child feels about him- or herself (Figure 4.2):

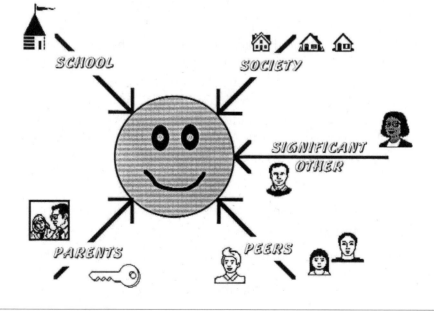

Figure 4.2.   Influences on a Child's Self-Esteem

1. Parents are the first and primary teacher for their children and therefore hold the key to their child's self-esteem. What parents do stays with you always, and what they fail to do can never be done by others. Parents fulfill the child's physical and emotional safety needs from the moment of birth and continue to do so as a child matures. They also make choices about the kind of school and day care environments that their children attend, and this too influences how children see themselves. We get our feelings about ourselves from how we are treated by the significant people in our environment.

2. Significant others are people that the child looks up to and trusts. They can include teachers, counselors, custodians, family members, coaches, religious leaders, and scout leaders. We often say that teachers hold the spare key to a child's self-esteem due to the number of hours students spend with their teachers and the powerful influence teachers have on students' lives.

3. School environment plays a pivotal role in how students feel about themselves. This begins with the secretary in the office and includes the parents and aides in the classroom, the yard duty personnel, the cafeteria workers, the custodians, the school nurse, and everyone else who interacts with the students.

4. Society contributes to children's self-esteem because it forms a context and a culture for reflecting on how one fits into the bigger picture. Society can be the neighborhood, schoolmates, television, church groups, political groups, and other social groups that students join.

5. Peers too contribute to students' feelings about themselves, but not nearly as much as parents and teachers. When students are interviewed anonymously, they report that their parents are their most significant people in their lives. Yes, even adolescents!

For over 40 years, researchers have been studying "target students," students who are potential or actual problems to themselves or others. In the 1960s, the focus was juvenile delinquency; in the 1970s, youth at risk; in the 1980s, the effects of drugs and alcohol; in the 1990s, why kids joined gangs; and today it is resiliency factors.[1] These studies consistently point to two variables that are missing in the lives of young people at risk. Though different terms are used, the common thread is the outcome. Students at risk consistently lack

- Feelings of connectedness or belonging

- A sense of autonomy or power over their own lives; a sense of having choices

People who do not feel included in a prosocial group, and who feel that they have no influence over their own lives and are victims of their situation, do not do well academically, socially, cognitively, or spiritually. Researchers from Piaget (1969) to Alfie Kohn, from Montessori (Standing,

1962) to Caine and Caine (1991), from Hawkins et al. (1998) and Kounin (1970) to Benard (1993) and Krovetz (1999) have substantiated that feelings of connectedness and feelings of autonomy and power are the greatest determiners of students' success in school and in life and that educators consequently need to create a climate that fosters these two factors.

Connectedness and autonomy happen to be two of the four dimensions of self-esteem; the other two are security and competence. All four are crucial to consider when creating the classroom learning environment. You might recognize them as corresponding to the basic human needs defined by Abraham Maslow (1999) in Psychology 1A: safety and security, belongingness and affection, respect and self-respect, and self-actualization. Notice how they also are naturally related to the elements of a brain-compatible classroom.

Table 4.1 frames the dimensions of self-esteem and strategies taught in this book that support each dimension. These dimensions of self-esteem develop in the following order:

1. *Security* is first and is the foundation for all of the others. It is created when the environment is consistent but not rigid. It is related to the factors of absence of threat and learning paced for relaxed alertness in a brain-compatible classroom.

2. *Connection and bonding* cannot happen if a child does not feel safe and secure. It is related to students' need to collaborate and work together in a brain-compatible classroom.

Table 4.1 Effective Teaching Strategies for Building Self-Esteem in Students

1. Sense of Security Need for consistency in the environment	3. Sense of Competence Need for knowing what you do well
• Bonded teacher-student relationship • Gifts without strings • Handling of personal upsets • Parameters for class interaction • Principles of intervention • Limit setting • Absence of threat • Adequate time for tasks	• Immediate feedback • Target talk • Meaningful content • Charting of progress and growth • Self-assessment
2. Sense of Connectedness Need for belonging to group	4. Sense of Power Need for feeling included in the decision-making process
• Bonded teacher-student relationship • Getting cooperation • Alterations to physical setting • Listening • Class meetings • Collaboration with peers	• Opportunities for input • Cooperative activities • Reinforcement that recognizes gradual and intermittent progress and focuses only on successes • Problem solving • Class meetings • Choices about tasks

3. *Competence* is built by success and knowing what one does well. It is related to the factor of immediate feedback necessary in a brain-compatible classroom.

4. *A sense of autonomy and influence or power* cannot be developed until the other dimensions are developing. It is related to the factors of opportunity to make choices and meaningful content in a brain-compatible classroom. It involves giving students options and input into the decision-making and problem-solving process.

Benefits of Self-Esteem

- Feelings of self-confidence
- Inner motivation
- Security in social settings
- Critical thinking
- Pride in work
- Enthusiasm
- Curiosity
- Willingness to risk

Key Criteria for Brain-Compatible Classrooms and Dimensions of Self-Esteem

- Students need to feel safe physically and psychologically in order to learn.
- Students need to connect and collaborate with each other to develop cooperation.
- Students need immediate feedback during the formative stages of learning.
- Students need choice and participation in classroom practices.

Checking My Understanding of Elements of Self-Esteem and a Brain-Compatible Classroom

1. Compare the elements of a brain-compatible learning environment and the elements of self-esteem, and match the elements of one to the elements of the other by drawing lines to connect them.

Brain-Compatible Classroom	*Self-Esteem*
• Absence of Threat	• Sense of Security
• Immediate Feedback	• Sense of Connection
• Meaningful Content	• Sense of Competence
• Collaboration With Peers	• Sense of Power
• Opportunity to Make Choices	
• Pacing of Learning for Relaxed Alertness	

Answers:

- Absence of Threat connected to Sense of Security
- Collaboration connected to Sense of Connection
- Meaningful Content connected to Sense of Power
- Immediate Feedback connected to Sense of Competence
- Opportunity to Make Choices connected to Sense of Power
- Pacing connected to Sense of Security and Power

2. Read the following scenarios. Label which elements of a brain-compatible classroom or dimensions of self-esteem are being supported and which are being violated.

a) Mr. Campos has his eighth-grade remedial class divided into two groups. One group is doing an independent assignment. He is leading a review of a literature assignment with the other group. Each student in the group is formulating a question and challenging one of the other students. Eduardo, who is usually absent or tardy, is participating boisterously and really enjoying finding answers to the questions his classmates pose. Sometimes, however, he interjects out of turn and in his excitement comments on others' questions and answers. Mr. Campos looks at him and says, "Eduardo, it's not your turn, shh, shh, you need to wait your turn, shh, shh. Can't you remember our rules? Now if you call out again, you'll have to leave." The next round of questions begins, and within a couple of minutes Eduardo asks one of the girls a question about her answer without raising his hand. Mr. Campos says, "All right, Eduardo, you are choosing to disobey our rules; you need to go to your seat." Eduardo says, "I was just asking Elena a question." Mr. Campos, "No, you were interrupting as usual, and you remember our rule—so now you're out of the game." Eduardo leaves the group and kicks his chair over in route to his desk as he mumbles about how unfair Mr. Campos is. Mr. Campos says, "For that Eduardo, you can just go to the office and see Ms. Willis, the principal."

_____

_____

_____

_____

Answers:

- Sense of connection is supported when teacher sits with group.

- Sense of security and absence of threat are violated when teacher reprimands student in front of class, blames student, and sends student away from group.

- Sense of power is violated when teacher threatens student and orders him to go to principal's office.

b) Mrs. Brink's fourth-grade class was working in groups at various centers of their own choosing. The theme for this unit was pioneering. Some groups were making dioramas, some were planning a camping trip where they would be pioneers, and some were creating and practicing for a play about the early pioneers in California during the Gold Rush days. Adam had been sent back to his desk by his peers to spend 3 minutes because he was continually touching other students' materials and interrupting boisterously. After 2 minutes he returned to the reading group and began working quietly within the group. Mrs. Brinks went to him and said in a whisper, "Adam, you're being very respectful of your group by keeping your voice low and your hands on your own materials. What's your secret?"

_____

_____

_____

_____

Answers:

- Sense of power and opportunities for choice are supported when teacher lets students choose centers to work at.

Answers continued:

- Meaningful content is supported when teacher gives students themes and options for learning.
- Security and absence of threat are supported when teacher makes sure other students' materials are protected.

Personal Commitment

Which element of a brain-compatible classroom or dimension of self-esteem can you implement in your classroom learning environment?

_____

_____

_____

SOCIAL SKILLS PREREQUISITES ■

∽

The profession of teaching calls on us
not merely to produce good learners but good people.

Alfie Kohn, *What to Look for in Classroom*

∾

Classroom Connection

Heidi Ruecker was an itinerant science teacher in her district. She visited several schools and team-taught science lessons with K-12 teachers. In many classrooms, Heidi and the classroom teacher struggled with students who could not work in groups of four at their lab tables. Disruptions, upsets, grabbing materials, wandering around, and general bedlam resulted. Yet in other classrooms, things went smoothly and students worked together cooperatively. While debriefing with one of the classroom teachers, Isaac Farfan, after class, Heidi asked him how he got his students to work together. He shared that at the beginning of the year he assessed them as to their social skills and then taught them the social skills they needed before the academic learning activity. He discussed with her how the first few lessons that they did in September were all review lessons where the academic curriculum was the secondary objective. During those lessons, he made the social skills his primary objective.

♥ Personal Connection

What did you learn from the story that you might want to know more about?

_____

_____

_____

_____

Many of us wonder how we can teach one more thing. Now do we have to teach the students social skills too? If our goal is for them to be successful learners and caring members of a democracy, then the answer is yes. On the other hand, it does not have to be "one more thing"; it can be done in the context of your review lessons at the beginning of the year. By the end of this section, you will have the skills to help your students to work cooperatively with each other in partners or groups. You will find that your students are more enjoyable and less teacher dependent as well as better able to make a contribution to our culture and our society. You now know how important it is for peers to collaborate with each other and feel a sense of connection and community as learners.

Levels of Social Skill Development

To be successful members of the class and to do many learning activities, students must have some basic social skills. Let's look at the skills people need to work together in order to complete a task or a project (Table 4.2). For classroom settings, they can be categorized as follows:

Level 1: connecting/bonding skills

Level 2: interactive skills

Level 3: communication skills

Level 4: decision-making and problem-solving skills

These are also key elements identified by employers in the study done by the U.S. Department of Labor (Carnevale et al., 1989) as the skills that employers want in the workplace.

These skills are learned most naturally in the order of the levels, which is based on students' developmental stages. As children develop, they move from parallel play and a self-centered world to playing and working with others. Lupe, the little girl in the story that opened this chapter, was still at the stage of parallel play even though she was 6 years old, so many classroom activities were beyond her level of social development.

Table 4.2   Social Skills for Working in a Group

Level 1: Connecting/Bonding Skills	
• Uses others' names	• Cleans up area
• Looks at others	• Moves quietly to/from group
• Stays with a group	• Gathers and shares materials

Level 2: Interactive Skills	
• Gives ideas	• Says "thank you"
• Talks about work	• Includes others
• Asks questions	• Listens to others

Level 3: Communication Skills	
• Repeats what has been said	• Paraphrases
• Encourages	• Acknowledges
• Shares feelings	• Expresses appreciation
• Disagrees in agreeable way	• Contributes ideas

Level 4: Decision-Making and Problem-Solving Skills	
• Listens to different points of view	• Implements solutions
• Generates solutions	• Gets a group back to work
• Defines the problem	• Uses a process for decision making
• Summarizes	

As Figure 4.3 shows, to do partner work students need to have mastery of Level 1, connecting/bonding skills, and an emerging sense of Level 2, interactive skills. Students do not have the social prerequisites for working in groups of three or four students unless they have mastery of Level 1, connecting/bonding, Level 2, interactive skills, and at least half of Level 3, communication skills. Groups of more than four students require mastery of Levels 1, 2, 3, and half of Level 4. Conflict resolution that is real and not mimed requires mastery of Levels 1, 2, and 3, with an emerging sense of Level 4. These are general guidelines for deciding how to structure group work in the classroom; naturally, some students will be stronger or weaker than others. Often it will be necessary to have certain students work only

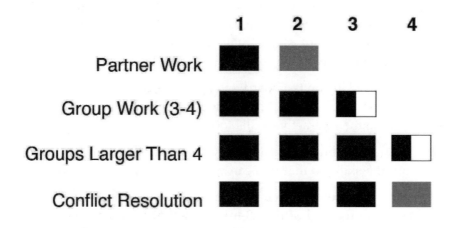

Figure 4.3.   Relation of Social Tasks to Mastery of Social Skill Levels 1 Through 4

with partners while other students who have the prerequisite social skills are working in groups. This is the challenge when designing learning activities. Students need to be aware of these levels and be actively involved in assessing themselves in order to have a goal to acquire the missing skills.

Assessing Your Students' Level of Social Skill Development

Many students have been raised in very structured day care environments with very little opportunity for choice, where adults have supervised and decided their every move. They have been deprived of the natural opportunities and natural consequences needed to learn social skills for working with others in their homes and in their neighborhoods. They come to school as isolationists with very few social skills. Before we teach them the required social skills for our classroom and ultimately the workplace, it is critical to assess their stage of social development.

Examples of Strategies for Assessing Social Skill Development

1. It is important when assessing to know the common developmental stages for students in your age group. The numerous Gesell Institute books on child behavior with titles such as *Your Eight-Year-Old* and *Your-Nine-Year-Old* (see, e.g., Ames & Haber, 1989, 1990; Ames, Ilg, & Baker, 1988) summarize these stages for different age levels.

2. Create an enjoyable learning review activity for students such as putting a puzzle together or identifying or matching some geometric shapes—some task that is at their independent level so that you will be free to observe them rather than monitor and teach them.

   ● Begin by observing them for a short 6- to 10-minute activity with a partner. Let them know that you will be coming around looking for these skills; that will make them aware of this pretest you are giving them and set the stage for more success.

   ● Post the skills on the board, overhead, or chart, and begin with the first level, connecting/bonding skills; for older students, include the interactive skills too.

   ● Create a clipboard or computer printout of the students' names and the skills so that you can walk about and observe.

   ● Put the list up on a chart or board and ask students to self-assess at the end of the 10-minute activity. Students can share with a partner, write in their journal, or share verbally with the class. You could also ask the class about how competent they feel about a particular skill and have them signal you with arms crossed over chest or with one to five fingers up (e.g., "Signal me with one to five fingers: one if you felt you didn't include others at all and five if you felt that you worked hard to include others"). This gives you immediate feedback not just about the skill but about students' awareness of their ability. It also gives the students ownership of the process and some understanding of the importance of the skill.

Teaching Specific Social Skills and Helping Students to Practice, Process, and Self-Assess Them

Social skills can be taught in a variety of ways other than direct instruction. Direct instruction (telling, preaching, and moralizing) is actually the least effective model of teaching to use for attitudes, values, and beliefs.

 Examples of Strategies for Teaching Social Skills

- *Skits*: In small groups, students create 3-minute skits of correct and incorrect social skills.

- *Dramatization*: Teacher and selected students model correct and incorrect social skills.

- *Observation of successful students*: Take a field trip to another classroom.

- *Video*: Make a video of students in your school who are demonstrating the skills correctly, or have the student who is weak on social skills make a video of correct examples.

- *Acting out scripted role plays*

Examples of Strategies for Practicing Social Skills

1. You can get students involved in choosing which social skills they want and need to work on. They can self-assess which social skills are easiest and which are hardest to practice and select and write down one to practice from the list in Table 4.2.

2. Teachers can create academic review activities in which the primary objective is to practice a particular social skill. While students are practicing the skill, the teacher monitors and records and gives written and/or verbal target talk feedback: for example, "Julio and Kareem, how did you know to include Erin in your project?"

"Danielle and Kishama, you were really encouraging each other when you got stuck, how could you remember to do that?"

Examples of Strategies for Helping Students Self-Assess and Process Social Skills

1. After the activity, students can be given time in a structured way to reflect on the social skill they selected and to analyze and evaluate how they did. Figure 4.4 shows a form that might be used for facilitating that process.

2. To get feedback on a social skills activity, you can use the following forced-choice response options dependent on grade level: "Yes/No," "Always/Never/Sometimes," or "A little/Some/A lot." Sample statements to respond to might be:

    - Others in the group helped when I had a question.

    - We disagreed in an agreeable way.

    - We used names in our group.

    You can also ask students to rate their skill performance on a scale: for example, "On a scale of 1 to 5, with 5 being high and 1 being low, rate yourself and reflect on how today was better than yesterday and why. What did you do differently?"

Such processing and self-reflection are crucial for students' development of any skill we want them to understand, practice, and internalize. An increasing body of research is disproving the assumption of the "teach and hope" method that the use of social skills in one setting will transfer to a different setting automatically (Gajewski, Hirn, & Mayo, 1998). The implication for us as educators is never to assume that because the students were doing it last year they can do it this year!

Benefits of Students' Social Skills Development

- Students develop an intrinsic motivation for using social skills that comes from internalizing the value of those skills.

- Students treat each other with respect.

- Students learn self-evaluation.

Fill in the blanks:

A social skill we enjoyed **PRACTICING** today

was _____ because_____

The **SOCIAL SKILL** we used the **best** was

_____ because _____

One Thing **I** learned about GROUP WORK was

It is **HELPFUL** to _____ when _____

Figure 4.4.   Form for Student Evaluation of Social Skill Learning and Performance

🔑 Key Criteria for Social Skills

- Social skills must be assessed and taught before students work together.

- Students need to be involved in assessing themselves.

- There are four levels of social skills, and they are developed sequentially.

- Assuming that students know these skills from past school experience is a grave mistake.

- Students need to learn and practice these skills as citizens in the classroom.

✔ Checking My Understanding of Social Skill Learning

Mark the following statements about social skills true (T) or false (F).

_____ 1. To work with a partner, students need to have Level 2 social skills.

_____ 2. Group work requires only connecting/bonding skills.

_____ 3. Working in a group of more than four people requires communication skills.

_____ 4. Expecting students to resolve conflicts requires them to have only connecting/bonding, interactive, and communication skills.

Answers:

4. False: they need decision-making and problem-solving skills too.

3. True.

2. False: they also need some communication skills.

1. False: they need all of Level 1 and some of Level 2.

🏃 Personal Commitment

Which social skills will you focus on with your students? Which skills do they need to learn and practice as citizens in the classroom?

_____

_____

_____

_____

_____

_____

_____

ACADEMIC CURRICULUM PREREQUISITES ■

⸙

We have all grown up with the platitude
"Practice makes Perfect." Don't you believe it!
Again, knowledge of principles of learning makes the difference
between efficient practice and practice which is a waste of time,
yours and the learner's.

Madeline Hunter, *Teach More—Faster!*

⸎

 ## Classroom Connection

Tanya Garza was a student in Mr. Tsai's fifth-grade class who continually came to him for help, every few minutes, after he had given her group their assignment. The other students in the group seemed to work semi-independently, helping each other and moving through the practice tasks that he had gone over during their instruction time with him. Tanya had done just fine during Mr. Tsai's instruction, and he assumed that she was being either lazy or dependent and needy of his attention. Thinking like this created a lot of upset and stress for Mr. Tsai. Upon consultation with his peer coach, he learned about how some students could work at their instructional level with guidance from a teacher but when sent to work independently were totally lost and did not have the prerequisites to proceed on their own. He was puzzled that the other students in the group breezed through the tasks until he realized that for them the work was probably too easy.

♡ Personal Connection

_____

_____

_____

_____

_____

How did you relate to Mr. Tsai's frustration?

We all know how much easier it is to teach a lesson when the students have the prerequisite skills for the new learning. What challenges the best of us is what to do when all students don't have those skills. As a teacher, Mr. Tsai was often puzzled when students could seemingly do the practice task with the group but struggled when asked to do a few on their own. In this section, we will review some key points of learning theory that will help reduce your frustration when students "can't do" the assignments, relieve your worry about whether they can't or won't do the task, decrease students' dependence on the teacher, and help students and teachers alike to feel successful.

Stages of Learning

Learning theory identifies two stages of learning: the formative stage and the summative stage. During the formative stage, we are forming the information in our brains, but it has not been stored as a program. During the summative stage, we have stored the information, can recall it, and have mastery of it. As we consider prerequisites for our students, we are most concerned about the formative stage, when the learning is still in process.

There are three stages or levels of mastering knowledge, information, skills, and concepts:

1. *The frustration level*: The learner knows just a little but cannot operate above 55% success level on the tasks.

2. *The instructional level*: The learner is able to be successful when a teacher is supporting and guiding the new learning. Students initially practice all together as a group, and then as the teacher assesses more success they practice alone with minimum feedback from the teacher.

3. *The independent level*: The learner can perform at 75% to 85% success level and has mastery of the material. The student is able to work without support or guidance and is practicing to retain the skill or concept.

Clearly, the level at which our students are operating will determine whether we design an academic task as independent homework or seatwork or as a practice task with teacher support.

Standardized test scores such as the Iowa Test of Basic Skills (ITBS), the SAT 9, and California Achievement Tests are norm-referenced scores that indicate where a student "ceilings out." Often these scores are interpreted as students' independent level when in fact they represent the frustration level for the skill, not the instructional or independent level. A simplified rule of thumb to determine mastery levels is to drop the student's standardized test score one grade level to obtain his or her instructional level (where he or she can be successful with the help of a teacher, aide, or fellow student) and drop that score two grade levels to obtain his or her independent level (where students work without help). For example, if a student's frustration level (or level on standardized tests) on reading is at Grade 4, his or her instructional and independent levels are likely to be at Grades 3 and 2 respectively:

Academic Reading Level

Frustration	4.0
Instructional	3.0
Independent	2.0

Designing Practice Tasks With Practice Theory

❧

Within 24 hours of a one-hour learning period, at least 80% of detailed information is lost without practice.

Tony Buzan, *Use Both Sides of Your Brain*

❧

Many teachers experience Mr. Tsai's frustration with homework and independent seatwork assignments. Both tasks require independent practice, with the prerequisite that the learner is at 85% to 90% mastery. When designing homework or classroom practice tasks, we need to keep in mind four principles from research on practice theory to ensure mastery of the new learning.

Practice Levels Need to Be Shaped Toward Independent Practice

Just as we teach a child to ride a bike, in the classroom we use shaping to structure the initial practice, holding on so that students don't fall or fail. We structure or lockstep them through the first few practice tasks as a whole group so that everyone is successful, then let them try a few on their own. Eventually they are doing them on their own. This is like riding the bike around the block all alone. It may take several days for some students and only one day for others. We also need the practice sessions to be short (10-12 minutes) and intense (i.e., quickly paced and frequent during the early stages). This may mean we do a quick practice before the end of the period, another at the start of the next day, and so on.

Examples of Shaping Practice

- Several students are at the board; some are at their desks with paper; the teacher verbally leads the practice.

- The teacher and a student are at the overhead with same practice tasks as students at seats. The teacher leads the class verbally, someone records on the overhead, and students record on their papers as recording happens on the overhead.

- Students who have mastery lead the practice in small groups for those who are still in the early stage of learning.

Practice Needs to Be Monitored During the Initial Stages

The teacher and/or a student with mastery monitors the students, roaming the room, observing them, and giving them immediate feedback to prevent practicing mistakes (see the section "Immediate Feedback" earlier in this chapter).

Accuracy Level Required for Each Practice Is 85% to 90%

One of the most critical findings from the effective schools research in the 1990s was the high correlation between success rate on individual tasks and student achievement as measured by standardized tests. According to the research, students must be practicing at a 85% to 90% success rate in order to move on to independent practice (Hunter, 1995a; Weil, 1990).

Practice Needs to Be Distributed Over Time to Ensure Retention

Research on human memory indicates that without practice we forget 80% of all detailed information within 24 hours (Buzan, 1974; see also Hunter, 1995a). Thus, it is important that practice sessions be distributed over time and scheduled on a regular basis to reinforce the new learning as well as to ensure retention. New learning without a regular and distributed review—that is, daily review for the first 7 to 10 days and then less frequent practices distributed over time—actually wastes the original effort put into the lesson and places the student at a serious disadvantage when it comes time to recall the new learning at a later date. Transition activities at the beginning of each period or subject are an ideal means of distributing practice sessions in a sequential and structured way to ensure retention. Teachers can actually go through their lesson plan book and plan which skills are "must-knows" and need to have practice sessions on them distributed throughout the year so that students will retain the skills when they are tested in April or May.

Benefits of Using Practice Theory to Design Practice

- Increases retention of curriculum
- Decreases stress of frustration
- Increases student success
- Decreases adult dependence

Key Criteria

- Shape students toward independent practice to ensure mastery.
- Monitor during initial stages of practice to provide feedback and prevent error.
- An 85% to 90% accuracy level is required for each shaping practice session.
- Practice needs to be planned and distributed over time to ensure retention.

Checking My Understanding

What level of success indicates that students can move to independent practice? Answer: %06-58

Personal Commitment

How can you use the information about distribution of practice to plan homework?

_____

_____

_____

_____

Summary of Prerequisites for Creating a Climate for Success

- The leader creates classrooms to support self-esteem and a brain-compatible environment.

- The brain cannot function well under stress because activity is then diverted from the cerebral cortex to more primitive areas of the brain. Problem solving needs to wait until the feeling of threat has diminished and the brain is once again capable of reflective thought.

- The dimensions of self-esteem and the elements of a brain-compatible environment are identical in the practices that foster them and in their outcome.

- Forty years of research confirms that when students feel disconnected and without influence and power over their own lives, they do not succeed in school or in life as productive members of society.

- Students and teachers need to work and learn in an environment that supports the whole person: the thinking brain for learning and positive feelings of self-esteem for healthy living.

- The teacher assesses and teaches social skills and uses these as a guide for determining whether students will work alone, in pairs, or in small or larger groups.

- The teacher uses practice theory research to plan practice that supports retention of learning.

NOTE

1. For juvenile delinquency research, see Kounin (1970); for research on youth at risk, see Benson (1997); for research on the effects of drugs and alcohol, see Hawkins, Lishner, and Catalano (1998) and Botvin and Griffin (1999); for research on gangs, see Howell and Gleason (1998); and for research on resiliency factors, see Benard (1993) and Krovetz (1999).

PREVENTION FRAMEWORK

I. Personal Relationships for Trust

- Student Teacher Relationship
- Gifts Without Strings (NCR)
- Target Talk (Knowledge of Results)
- Room Design for Proximity
- Class Meetings

II. Prerequisites for Success

- Leader Creates Climate for:
  - Brain Compatible Environment
  - Teacher and Student Self-Esteem
- Social Skills
- Academic Curriculum

III. Parameters for Cooperation

- Classroom Agreements
- Procedures
- Directions
- Room Design for Organization
- Transition Tasks

IV. Participation for Involvement

- Opportunities for:
  - Simultaneous Involvement During Instruction
  - Active Listening During Input
  - Active Engagement During Learning Activities

Parameters for Cooperation 5

The Third "P" of Prevention

∽

Tell me, I'll forget. Show me, I may remember.
But involve me and I'll understand.

Chinese Proverb

∾

Classroom Connection

As the class entered the room on the first day of Sally Jones's eighth-grade math class, a note on the board read: "What will we need to have happen for us to have a great semester in math class?" Ms. Jones invited her students to take out their math notebook and silently write their ideas about this question. After 5 minutes, she had them get into groups of three and put their ideas together. She asked the groups to write their top five group ideas on bright colored Post-it notes. Next, as a group, they came up with categories for the successful math class and made a chart for each. Their categories included "Understanding the Math," "Tests and Quizzes," "Fairness," "Homework," "Group Work," and "Respect." The groups then pasted their Post-it notes under the most appropriate category on the chart. Next, the charts were divided up and given to groups of students to synthesize. The information was to be summarized in a few suggestions for (a) classroom agreements, which would apply all the time, (b) activity procedures, or behavior expectations that would apply only to certain types of activities but would apply every time they happened; and (c) directions, or details on how to carry out specific activities that might vary from day to day. The following day, the teacher had the groups report their suggestions, and the class decided how to use them to make it a great semester in math class.

 *Personal Connection*

What are the classroom settings you will want parameters for?

_____

_____

_____

_____

A critical characteristic of effective classroom leadership is establishing and agreeing on classroom parameters. Parameters create a way for students to take responsibility for a safe environment through their behavior and participation. The key ingredient of true working parameters is student participation. To begin to have students go deeper in creating parameters with the teacher, there has to be trust and a strong relationship. Students have to see the teacher's beliefs in action. If the invitation to participate is only superficial, with the real intent being to manipulate the students or appear to be caring, the students will see through it. They will say what they think the teacher or other students want to hear. Then they will begin tuning out or planning how to get around the parameters. This is counterproductive to intrinsic motivation. Knowing what is socially efficient in the classroom is in itself great knowledge. However, if it is presented without real understanding and commitment, it is useless and in fact more of a problem than a tool.

Teaching is a stressful profession in that the teacher is receiving over 500 stimuli an hour and making well over 1,000 decisions a day (Hunter, 1989). Decisions must be made on the spot. By the end of this chapter, you will understand five techniques that will reduce the number of stimuli that you must deal with and the number of on-the-spot decisions that you must make. With as much student involvement as possible, you will be structuring the following parameters of the classroom environment:

1. Classroom agreements for safety and responsibility

2. Procedures for social behavior and self-direction

3. Directions for clarity and independence

4. Transition activities for retention and focus

5. Room design for learning and cooperation

Parameters are the set characteristics or boundaries that are necessary for the group to feel physically safe and psychologically secure in the school environment. The parameters established for most school settings are usually a combination of school rules, classroom standards, classroom rules, and activity procedures for various settings such as the cafeteria, playground, office, phone area, restrooms, and bike area. Parameters also include activity procedures and directions for in-class tasks and the structure of classroom seating for individual, whole-group, and small group work.

The safety and security that parameters provide lay the foundation for creativity and learning. You already know how a sense of security and an absence of threat are key basic human needs and prerequisites for learning. This chapter will allow you to clearly define the structures necessary for your environment, tasks, and classroom interactions.

In most areas of life, we learn to balance the amount of freedom with the amount of structure we need. As classroom leaders, it is our primary role to assess each group of students for how much structure and how much freedom they will need to be successful. It is best to provide more structure at the beginning of the year and then move toward greater freedom as the year progresses. Parameters require preplanning about where students will work, who they may work with, how much time they will be given, what they should do when they are finished, how they will treat each other, and how they will get help. Thinking through these questions and assessing your group's level of social skills determines the amount of structure or freedom that you as a leader will provide.

Our purpose in this chapter is for you to rethink and develop an effective set of parameters tailored to your beliefs, your students, your curriculum, and your personal teaching style. Planning for the involvement of your students in this process is key to its success.

CLASSROOM AGREEMENTS ■

It is an axiom in some educational circles that young people "have to learn to live by the rules," but it is even more important that they develop into persons who act on the basis of internal values. Preoccupation with rules creates a kind of oppression such that even the most well-meaning adults lose sight of underlying values. It is much easier to write another procedure than to teach a young person to respect the rights of others.

In classrooms where social skills are focused on and practiced, the teacher and students need fewer management strategies. They can easily apply leadership concepts by going beyond rules that legislate morality and instead promote the idea of treating everyone in a caring, respectful manner. These skills are referred to as "megaskills" by Dorothy Rich (1988) and "lifeskills" by Susan Kovalik (1993).

Imagine going to a teacher workshop and entering the room to find these rules:

Workshop Don'ts:
- No Coffee Breaks
- No Bathroom Breaks
- No Talking at Any Time

How would you feel? You might want to get up and leave, or perhaps you would try to negotiate (if you were courageous). The word *rules* holds a negative connotation because it carries the memories of situations where we were not involved in creating the standards. It creates a constricted feeling of powerlessness and conformity.

The idea behind rules is to make the environment safe and consistent, which is important in learning environments. But the piece that is often left out is the dialogue and participation of those who will live by the rules. The important part is not the rule itself but the process of talking about the values and beliefs that we all bring to the classroom and creating a forum for building understanding: opening our minds to the ideas of others, understanding the viewpoints present in a community of learners, and coming to agreement on what we will need as a group to learn together and then making it a reality. This process requires that each individual commit to taking responsibility for his or her part. It involves learning along the way and taking time to see what the stumbling blocks are and what skills need extra processing time.

Classroom agreements are the three to five norms or guidelines for behavior that demonstrate our values and provide a reminder of how we will treat each other. They allow us to feel both physiologically and psychologically safe within the classroom environment. Agreements state behavioral expectations that remain constant even though the instructional activities change during the day or period. They are the specific observable behaviors of our values in action. They form the foundation for guiding desirable behaviors and provide teachers and students with a sense of security within the classroom environment because the expectations are clear, consistent, and out in the open. Once they are agreed on, classroom agreements should be posted and visible as a reminder of our values.

Classroom agreements are genuine class creations rather than lists of rules superimposed by a higher authority. They are made with the students in a process that first involves discussing the values that the students and the teacher hold. The list below was drawn up by Pam Locke's seventh-grade classroom at Regnart School in California.

Our Values

- Respect
- Kindness
- Honesty
- Responsibility
- Fairness
- Compassion

In classrooms that are guided by the teacher (acting as leader/guide) rather than controlled by the teacher (acting as drill instructor), classroom agreements take on the appearance of value-based guiding principles. Such principles can be illustrated by quotes, poems, mottoes, lists, or themes that are decorated and displayed (Figure 5.1).

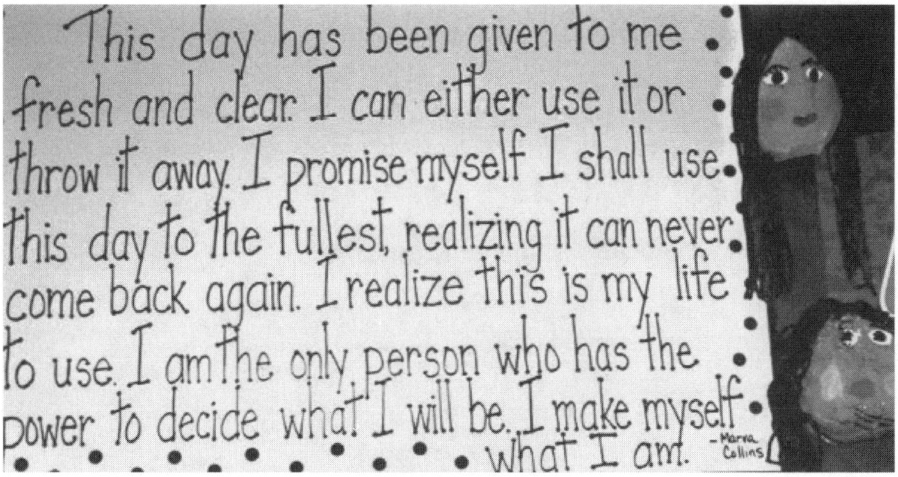

Figure 5.1.   Inspirational Quote to Base Classroom Agreements On

To understand these more general value-based norms or guiding principles on which agreements on behavior will be based, students need to know what the values look like and sound like. This requires processing, brainstorming, role-playing, and practicing the behaviors that go with each value. For example, what would fairness look like in your classroom? How would students show respect? What language, actions, gestures, and postures would be required? Class meetings can be an effective forum for developing this clarity and practice with values. Reading, writing, and art activities can be designed to reinforce the understanding of the specific behaviors of a "lifeskill," "megaskill," or guiding principle. Role-playing the positive and negative behavior or brainstorming all the ways "not" to act can be fun and can shed light on the subtle distinctions. When the value is being exhibited, positive feedback from the teacher is needed to point out the behavior and the impact it has on others. This is not the traditional use of feedback to compliment, reward, or find fault. This is genuine sharing of how the positive behaviors affect the students and the group. The teacher is transformed from the enforcer to the facilitator who holds the vision and guides the students to their agreed-upon goals.

Given the importance of creating positive pictures for the brain (discussed in Chapter 3), agreements should be stated in positive terms, spelling out the behavior we want rather than the behavior we don't want. Sometimes we may have to make exceptions to this rule: some statements are hard to phrase in positive terms. A common example is "no put-downs." But when these exceptions come up, it is important to talk about the positive picture and make sure the students are clear on the behaviors that will be acceptable and what outcome these will have. Why do they want to avoid put-downs? What do they want to encourage or support in each other?

The following norms were taken from teachers' classrooms and contain all the criteria of correctly designed classroom agreements. (See also Figures 5.2 and 5.3 for other elementary classroom agreements.)

Treat each other kindly. No put-downs.

Be respectful. Listen when someone is talking.

Be helpful. Help others when they ask.

Be fair. Always include others.

Be responsible for yourself.

Figure 5.2.   Example of Classroom Agreements

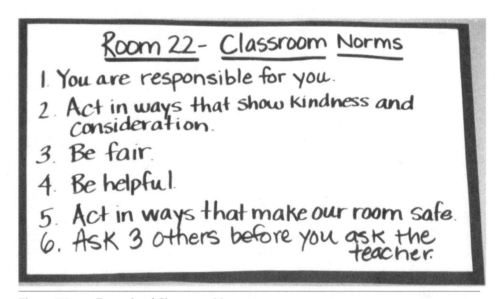

Room 22- Classroom Norms
1. You are responsible for you.
2. Act in ways that show kindness and consideration.
3. Be fair.
4. Be helpful.
5. Act in ways that make our room safe.
6. Ask 3 others before you ask the teacher.

Figure 5.3.   Example of Classroom Norms

🙂 Examples of Elementary Classroom Agreements

- Ask before borrowing or touching.
- Walk in the classroom.
- Use indoor learning voices.
- Keep legs of chair on floor.

🙂 Examples of Secondary Classroom Agreements

- Exert self-control.
- Use appropriate "school" language.
- Ask before borrowing.
- Use your common sense.

🙂 Examples of Elementary Classroom Mottoes and Quotes

- "Walk safely in the classroom" (motto surrounded by student pictures of what "safely" will look like)
- "In the garden of respect, good things grow" (an artful bulletin board with each flower having a description of a respectful behavior)
- "We Care!" (poster with student photos around the border)

🙂 Examples of Secondary Classroom Mottoes and Quotes

- "In our world, in our home, in our school, no one is as smart as all of us!"
- "Be the best you can be!"

Agreements' observable expectations for students' behavior are created in the trust that the students are capable of meeting them. To convey this trust, the teacher does not have a predetermined set of consequences for breaking agreements. Having set consequences would give students the message that the teacher did not trust them and indeed expected them to break the agreements. So although the teacher shows consistency in responding to violations of agreements, he or she retains the flexibility to treat students differently depending on their individual needs and the unique situation and to come up with a fitting logical consequence that will make amends. This is at the heart of intrinsic motivation: it invites the student to internalize and have ownership of the norms. As discussed in Chapter 1, intrinsic motivation reduces the teacher's role as enforcer, unlike a system of rewards and punishments, which makes it necessary for the teacher to be an enforcer at all times and to maintain that role indefinitely. As Alfie Kohn (1993) points out, "Rewards and punishment work very well to get one thing . . . and that one thing is temporary compliance" (p. 161).

Classroom agreements can be referred to in connecting behaviors to social and academic impact when teachers give feedback: "Sheryl, when you asked to borrow Karen's pen, you showed her that you respect her things and that you care about her." The agreements become a reference point that makes it relevant to be responsible. They can also be referred to as reminders of agreed-upon student responsibilities: "Thao, when you use Julian's eraser without permission, he looks upset and unsure if it will be there when he needs it." And students can use them in group work. For instance, one student might tell another, "Sean, remember our Agreement #3, we support and encourage each other. Help us out here." (See the section "How to Maintain Student Cooperation with Agreements and Procedures" later in this chapter.)

Benefits of Classroom Agreements

- Provide students with a sense of security
- Foster a sense of power by involving students
- Give clear expectations for which students can display responsibility
- Create a positive climate
- Increase academic learning time
- Reduce classroom stress
- Enable students to monitor themselves when the agreements are posted
- Enable teacher to be a facilitator rather than a security guard

Key Criteria for Establishing Classroom Agreements

- Agreements are unchanging: They apply to all activities at all times.

- Agreements describe only critical and observable behaviors. If more general value-based guiding principles are used, they must be developed and processed so the specific behaviors that they encompass are known to each student.

- Keep the number of agreements to a minimum (three to five). Phrase agreements in a brief, positive way.

- Post agreements in a conspicuous place and review them regularly.

- Agreements do not include consequences for their violation.

- Agreements are age appropriate, and students are involved in the creation process.

Checking My Understanding

1. For items a) through e), rephrase the statement to reflect a positive picture of the agreement.

   a) No horsing around in line.

   _____

   b) No talking in class.

   _____

   c) Don't push and shove in the classroom.

   _____

   d) Don't use other people's supplies without permission.

   _____

   e) No put-downs.

   _____

2. Which of the following might apply to the classroom at all times? Which agreements might require some class process time to clarify? What activities could you use to build understanding of the positive behaviors?

a) Use equipment properly.

b) Place homework in basket before class begins.

c) One student speaks at a time.

d) Treat each other with respect.

e) Walk in the classroom.

f) Turn in neat assignments.

g) Raise your hand to speak.

h) Stay in your seat.

i) Wait your turn.

Answers:

2. Might apply to classroom all the time: a, b, d, e. Might need time to process: a, c, d, e, f, i

e) "Encouraging comments only" or "We uplift each other" or "Use encouraging comments."

d) "Ask before borrowing others' supplies."

c) "Keep your hands, feet, and stuff to yourself" or "Honor each other's space."

b) "Save social conversation for breaks."

a) "Keep to your own space in line."

1. Possible Options for Rephrasing:

❧ Personal Commitment

Imagine you are a student in your class. What three to five critical expectations would you want to present to your teacher for class for consideration? Phrase them as positively as you can.

_____

_____

_____

_____

How will you support your students in creating meaningful conversation and understanding around classroom agreements?

_____

_____

_____

_____

ACTIVITY PROCEDURES ■

*The classroom as a sacred space means the school as a safe place. . . .
As I read some of the accounts of Santee and Columbine, the common
thread is that before the classroom became physically dangerous,
it became emotionally dangerous.*

Rabbi Harold Kushner, Speech at the 56th Annual Meeting of the
Association for Supervision and Curriculum Development, 2001

Classroom Connection

On the second day of math class, Sally Jones had the student groups from the first day present their suggestions to the class. This was an opportunity for them to categorize which suggestions were about behaviors and which were about logistics, as well as which behaviors were desired all of the time (to be spelled out in classroom agreements) and which were for behaviors specific to certain activities (to be spelled out in activity procedures or directions). For each of the categories, Ms. Jones asked the students to think of ways that arrangements had worked or not worked in the past. They talked about what roadblocks came up and how they could face these hurdles in their year together. At the end of the class, they had a list of behaviors that were specific to the activities of group work, homework, getting help, and tests and quizzes. They also had some of the logistics that went with each of those tasks. They sorted the list to find the more general values and "all the time" behaviors that they wanted to see in their class that year (under the categories of "Fairness," "Respect," and "Understanding Math").

❤ Personal Connection:

Review the list of activities below and mark any that occur within your own classroom. Add any of your own activities that may be missing.

Sharing	Free time
Silent reading	PE
Discussion	teacher-directed lesson
Biology lab/lecture	Paired research
Clean-up	Cooperative learning groups
Oral reports	Rainy day
Chalkboard practice	Computer lab
Test taking	Class meetings
Filmstrips/movie/videos	Vocabulary review
Personal activity time	Substitute
Guest speaker	Readers' workshop
Shared reading	Field trips
Writers' workshop	Getting help
Homework	Independent practice
Journal writing	Sharpening pencils

One of the most important sets of parameters to establish is the activity procedures for the classroom. Activity procedures are the written specific social/behavioral expectations for the various activities that occur within every classroom and that will hold for every time the activity takes place. You are familiar with how much students vary in the level of social skills that they come to school with. It is necessary to teach, describe, and model the appropriate social behaviors that will be needed for various activities. By *social skills,* we mean how students move and interact, what tone of voice they use, and how they get help when they need it. These change from activity to activity and need to be visible in the same way as the academic charts, such as those on place value and parts of speech, that are posted around the room to help students remember academic skills during the formative stages of learning. The social skills that are used in cooperative groups are quite different from those used during oral reports or a teacher-directed lesson. Once agreed upon, classroom procedures clearly define and establish the social parameters for specific activities, distinct from directions, which establish the task-related parameters of a specific activity. For many students, learning to work together in a group is a new experience; creating activity procedures becomes a teaching strategy. Many students need to process the distinction between home/private behavior and school or public behavior.

✚ Benefits of Activity Procedures

- Maintain consistency
- Provide students with a sense of security
- Serve as a reminders to teacher and student

- Provide focus for target talk and limit setting
- Prompt self-direction and less dependence on teacher

Key Criteria for Activity Procedures

- Procedures are phrased in positive terms: for example, "Use whisper voice."

- Procedures include all the social behavior of activities.

- Behaviors described are observable.

- Students are involved in formulating.

- Teacher should post, review, and check understanding of procedures before the activity begins.

- Procedures should be posted only during the formative stage of learning the behaviors of the activity.

- As with classroom agreements, only the teacher should be aware of the possible consequences for violating a procedure.

Table 5.1 shows some questions to address when you are formulating activity procedures.

Table 5.1   Questions to Address When Formulating Activity Procedures

1. How do you want the students to work?
   - Together?
   - Individually?

2. How do you want them to communicate?
   - Silently?
   - Using a "library voice"?
   - Using a "two-finger voice"/"2-inch voice"/"6-inch voice" (all terms to describe how far sound should travel from mouth)?
   - Should they talk one at a time?
   - Should they call out?
   - Do you want them to brainstorm?

3. How do you want them to solicit help?
   - Raise their hand?
   - Write their name on the board?
   - Use a signal card?

4. Where do you want them to sit?
   - At their desk?
   - In a particular area?
   - At a table?
   - Is moving around ok?

5. What should they do when they are finished?
   - Select an activity?
   - Begin the next task?
   - Read silently?

6. How will they be using time?
   - Will they be under time constraints?
   - How many minutes will they have?

7. What materials will they use and how?

Figures 5.4 through 5.10 show a variety of activity procedures for different activities and grade levels.

Examples of Activity Procedures

1. Journal Time, Silent Reading, Transition, Tests
   - Work silently.
   - Stay in your space.
   - If you finish early: draw, dream, read.

At the Beginning of Class

- Get out horn and Warm up
- Read board, get out charts
- Talk to neighbor

Be Ready!

What do you do... When you are not being worked with

- Listen to whoever is being worked with
- The part may apply to you!
- Sit quietly

Be Ready!!

Figure 5.4.   Procedures for Music Class

2. Small Work Group

- Stay with your group.

- Remain in area.

- Use "2-inch voice" (soft, low voice)

- Seek help from:

    a) Neighbor
    b) Close group
    c) Group name on board

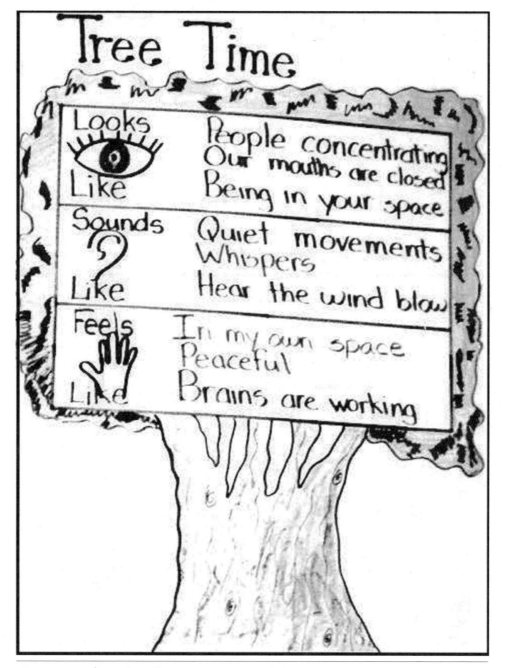

Figure 5.5.   Procedures for Using a Quiet Workspace Loft Called the Treehouse

Intrapersonal
Time

1. Work silently.

2. Stay in your
   seat.

3. If you finish early,
   read, draw, dream.

Figure 5.6.   Procedures for Intrapersonal Time

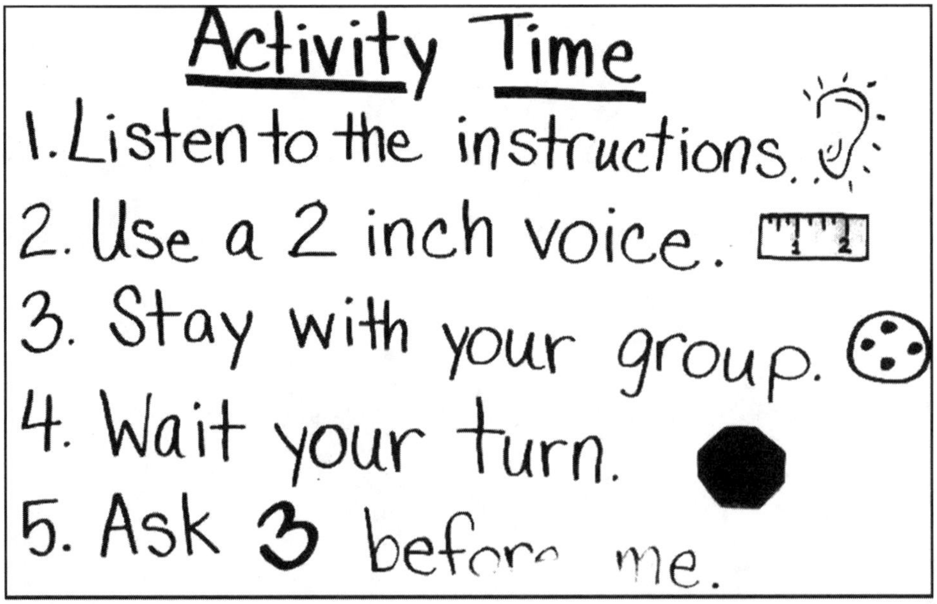

Activity Time
1. Listen to the instructions.
2. Use a 2 inch voice.
3. Stay with your group.
4. Wait your turn.
5. Ask 3 before me.

Figure 5.7.   Procedures for Group Activities

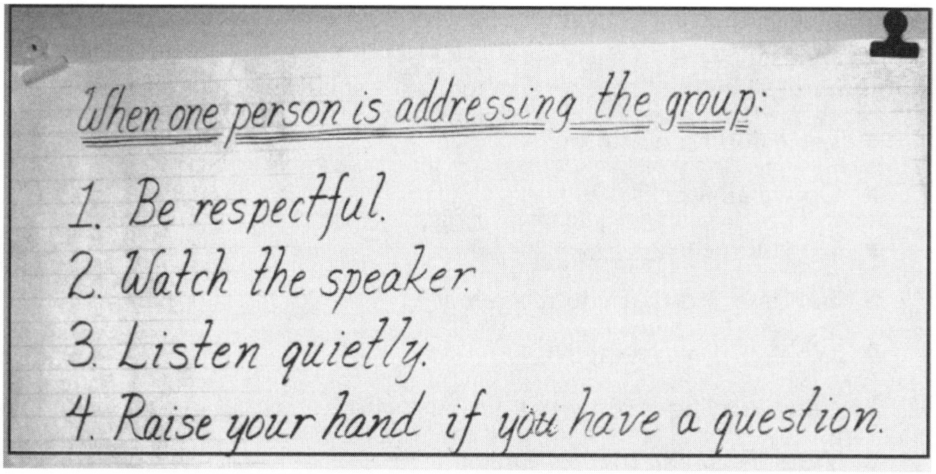

When one person is addressing the group:

1. Be respectful.
2. Watch the speaker.
3. Listen quietly.
4. Raise your hand if you have a question.

Figure 5.8.   Procedures for One Person Addressing the Group

3. Direct Instruction: (11-16 minutes/ key points)

- Use active listening.

- Raise hand to speak.

- Stay put.

4. Cooperative Learning Group (Focusing on a Specific Cooperative Skill)

- Work only with those in your group.

- Stay in area assigned to group.

- Use "thinking voice" (quiet voice).

- One person in group talks at a time.

- Ask 3 Before Me!

Procedures can also have students in a group take on group roles. For example, one group member might be the "encourager/gatekeeper," who makes such remarks as follows:

- Can you add more to this?

- Can you help finish the story/sentence?

- Let's take turns.

- What do you think?

- How do you feel about it?

- Listen, we want to hear from everyone.

- Please cooperate.

- Positive comments only.

- Who haven't we heard from yet?

- Our group works best when everyone helps.

Another might be the "checker," who makes such remarks as follows:

- Let's stop for a minute.

- Do we all agree?

- Do you mean _____?

- I understand that you're saying _____.

- What_____ is saying is _____.

- Can we all agree on what was just said?

- Would you like that repeated?

Other possible roles are recorder, timekeeper, speaker, and supplier.

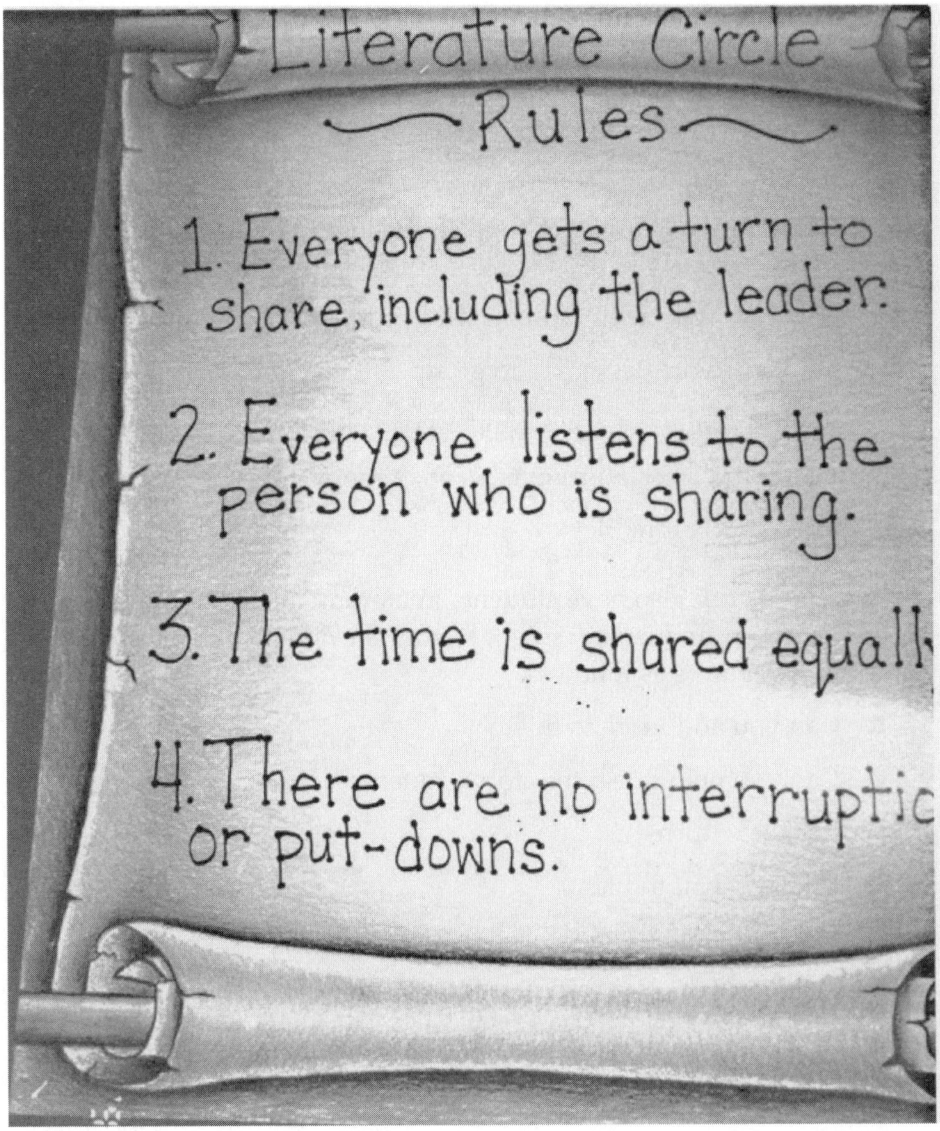

Figure 5.9.   Procedures for Literature Circle

Figure 5.10.   Tone of Voice Procedures (Teacher or Student Can Move Arrow on Left)

MAINTAINING STUDENT COOPERATION ■
WITH CLASSROOM AGREEMENTS
AND ACTIVITY PROCEDURES

Once classroom agreements and activity procedures are created, they will need to be maintained if students are going to continue to be motivated to participate in them.

Examples of Strategies for Maintaining Student Cooperation With Agreements and Procedures

1. Process how following agreements and procedures is going.

   - *Elementary Classroom Example*: "Today everyone seemed to have an easy time remembering their working voice. Can anyone share what made that work for you today?"

   - *Secondary Classroom Example*: "Today everyone put extra effort into including others during the group discussions. What was different about today than yesterday? How did that happen?"

2. Implement agreements and procedures consistently.

   - *Elementary Classroom Example*: In a team contest, Ann calls out her answer without raising her hand. The teacher ignores Ann's answer and gives the question to a member of the opposite team who has a raised hand.

   - *Secondary Classroom Example*: The bell has rung and the teacher is handing out the test questions. Joe sees his girlfriend outside the door. He eases out the door and talks to her until the test begins. Then he slips back in the room and begins working. The teacher walks up to Joe at the end of class and says quietly, "You left the room after class began; see me after this period."

3. Review agreements and procedures periodically.

   - *Elementary Classroom Example*: Mr. Nelson noticed that several students were dawdling on the way to the materials table. The first thing the next morning, he reviewed the procedures and had several students model how to get materials. He also used "target talk" statements more frequently for students who were following the procedures for the next few days.

   - *Secondary Classroom Example*: Ms. Drury observed homework in the basket at the end of the period. The procedure for turning in homework was to place it in the basket at the beginning of the period. A monitor placed the work in a folder on the teacher's desk as soon as everyone was seated. The following day, she reviewed procedures for turning in homework and then pointed out that credit could be given for homework that was turned in at the beginning of the period.

Knowledge of the seven intelligences (Armstrong, 1994) can offer creative ways of remembering and reviewing agreements and procedures.

1. *Musical Intelligence*: Agreements or procedures are made into a song (a familiar tune can be used).

2. *Linguistic Intelligence*: Agreements and procedures are written down and posted.

3. *Spatial Intelligence*: Graphic symbols and pictures are posted next to written words.

4. *Bodily-Kinesthetic Intelligence*: Gestures are created to go with agreements and procedures.

5. *Logical-Mathematical Intelligence*: Agreements and procedures are numbered and sequenced.

6. *Interpersonal Intelligence*: Small groups are involved in responsibility for review of agreements and procedures.

7. *Intrapersonal Intelligence*: Feelings are associated with agreements and procedures for each individual.

DIRECTIONS ■

ꗧ

Communicate unto the other person that which you would want them to communicate unto you if your positions were reversed.

Thomas G. Crane, *The Heart of Coaching*

ꗧ

Classroom Connection

Patrice Guzman prepared her class for an art lesson where they would be using watercolors. They reviewed the procedures for group sharing: each would have a role, and they checked that each group knew who was the "supplier," the "checker," the "encourager," and so on. Patrice then gave them verbal directions about how to clean up watercolors, which they had never used, and explained how important it was to clean up and wash off the spaces around each of the watercolors. As the art period was ending, Patrice noticed Danny Jacob at the sink, running water full blast on the watercolors. "Danny Jacob," she cried, "what are you doing?" He said, "Washing the watercolors like you told us to." Alas, she realized that there were no written guidelines for cleaning up watercolors, nor had she modeled exactly what she wanted. Her picture was very different from his!

Personal Connection

Have you ever had an experience like Patrice's where an upset happened because your picture for an activity was different from that of your students? What could you and Patrice have done to prevent this kind of upset?

_____

_____

_____

Directions describe the details and "how-to's" of the activity. Directions are specific instructions that apply only to the current task. They usually do not include social behaviors. Activity procedures are different because they are social/behavioral expectations that apply every time a specific activity and/or type of lesson occurs. Take the example of a Readers' Circle. The procedures are the same every time the activity takes place: move quietly and safely to the circle, keep your paper, book, and pencil quiet while reading, and so forth. The tasks, however, may vary from one Readers' Circle to the next (and those are the directions that need to be gone over and posted for that day).

One important kind of directions is the daily agenda. This is a structure that allows students to know what will happen and creates a sense of safety and competence. It may be possible to include the students in creating it each day by having some choices and by giving a student the responsibility to post it in the morning.

✔ Checking My Understanding

Label the following examples with (A) for classroom agreements, critical expectations for behavior that remain constant even when the activity or lesson changes; (P) for activity procedures that always apply to a specific activity or type of lesson; and (D) directions for a specific task.

_____ 1. Work without talking to other students.
_____ 2. Walk in the classroom.
_____ 3. One student speaks at a time.
_____ 4. Come to class on time.
_____ 5. Work five problems before checking answers.
_____ 6. Eat only in designated areas.
_____ 7. Choose a selected activity when you finish your work.
_____ 8. Enter classroom silently.
_____ 9. Take care of physical needs during breaks.
_____ 10. Choose a group leader and recorder.
_____ 11. Stay in work locale assigned to your group.

Answers:

A: 2, 4, 6, 8, 9   P: 1, 3, 7, 10, 11   D: 5

Personal Commitment

1. Select an activity that your class currently engages in.

_____

2. List activity procedures for it—both those you would like to establish and those that are already established.

_____

3. List directions that may change over time with this activity.

_____

TRANSITION ACTIVITIES ■

ら

Before you can begin something new, you have to end what used to be.
William Bridges, _Transitions: Making Sense of Life's Changes_

こ

Classroom Connection

Mr. Menendez wanted to make the most of every minute of class time. He always had an activity posted on the whiteboard when the students entered. The students knew that they stopped talking when they entered the room. They knew to look at the board to get started on a short 5-minute task. The tasks varied during the day, but some were at a consistent time each day. Silent reading was one of the consistent daily activities. When morning recess was over, the students knew it was time for silent reading. There was a song that they sang as they came in, and they all had to have two books by the time the song ended. This was a time when students could practice reading and get settled down from recess. It also set the stage for the Readers' Workshop that followed. After 5 minutes of reading, they put their books away and began the Readers' Workshop. At other times of the day when the students returned from lunch, PE, and first thing in the morning, other 5-minute activities were posted on the whiteboard: for example, math drills or puzzlers, journal writing, spelling practice, organizing *materials, or reviewing science or social studies logs. They developed procedures for many of these activities and reviewed them when necessary (every day at the beginning of the year, after holidays, when they had substitute teachers, etc.).*

 ## Personal Connection

What are you currently doing to get your students focused at the beginning of class segments?

_____

_____

_____

A transition activity is a brief (2- to 5-minute) activity that immediately directs the students' attention to learning at the beginning of class. You know how important it is to provide structure for students as well as a quick practice on previously learned concepts and skills. A transition activity can serve as the structure for a quick review and practice of information or can prepare students for the lesson that is coming. It is usually done "intrapersonally" to allow time for students to settle down and get their brains ready to learn after they have come into class or before they begin a new area of study. Recall the principles of practice theory in Chapter 4. When practice is not distributed, the new information is removed from awareness and is unavailable to form new memory connections. Since retention is a process based on linking and associating, the fewer items that are available for recall, the less likely it is that the new learning will be registered and connected. Introducing a transition activity at the beginning of each period or subject is an ideal way to distribute practice in a sequential and structured way to ensure retention.

Benefits of Transition Activities

Allows the teacher to do the following:

● Observe

● Take roll

● Count lunches

● Read notes

● Make personal contact with individual students

● Set up for the lesson

- Do organizational tasks

- Allow the students maximum use of academic learning time

- Give class structure and routine to class

- Foster a sense of security and competence

- Provide opportunity to practice and retain learning

- Build group cohesion and bonding; serves as an inclusion activity

- Support the brain-compatible environment by giving students time to settle down so that their brains are ready to learn

Types of Transition Activities

A transition activity can be as follows:

- A reinforcement and practice for previously learned skills

- A check test or homework on previous day's lesson

- An ongoing activity related to previous instruction

- An activity in which the students organize for a complex task

Examples of Elementary Classroom Transition Activities

1. Practice Activities:

    - Students review previously taught sight words by filling in a puzzle.

    - Students put reading vocabulary words in the "ABC" order.

    - Students copy and solve five or six math problems as a review before math lesson.

2. Ongoing Scheduled Activities:

    - Students write words or draw pictures in picture dictionary booklets.

    - Students copy the daily agenda each morning.

    - Students match science vocabulary with definitions in text.

3. Organizing for a Complex Activity:

    - Students set up manipulatives before math manipulative lesson.

    - Students set up place value boards before lesson on place value.

    - Students set up art materials before lesson on watercolor.

    - Students set up balances before science lesson.

4. Check Tests of Homework on Previous Day's Lesson:

- Students are given a quick check test on last night's homework before getting a new lesson.

- Students are given a quick test on what they learned yesterday before moving on to new material.

- Students are given a timed math test on "5 times" facts before they are taught multiples of 6.

Examples of Secondary Classroom Transition Activities

1. Practice Activities:

- Students practice calisthenics with student leader before PE lesson.

- Students in chemistry class write the symbol for chemical elements learned yesterday.

- Students identify dependent clauses from list on chalkboard as review of yesterday's lesson.

- Students do 10 to 12 problems when they first enter classroom before instruction.

Correcting Transition Activities

Transition is not intended to create more work for the teacher to correct. Because transition is a short practice at the independent level, it should not require teacher correction. Most transition activities, such as student organizational activities or ongoing scheduled activities like journal writing, do not require daily correction.

Examples of Inexpensive Methods for Correcting Transition Activities

- Answers can be shown on a transparency and students can self-correct.

- Students can correct each other's practice.

- Class leader/monitor can read off answers.

- Class monitor can correct practice activity or check test.

- Answers can be put upside down on bottom of sheet.

- Students can self-correct from blackboard; then the best score of the week can be recorded.

If correcting would lengthen the time of the transition, it should be done at another time: at the end of class, before recess, or as another transition activity. Correcting one's own practice or a peer's practice can serve as a reinforcement of the skill or concept.

Key Criteria for Transition Activity

- Begins before lesson.

- Lasts 2 to 5 minutes.

- Provides brief practice on previous learning or allows students to organize for a complex activity or is an academic task that is part of an ongoing classroom routine

- Is related to the subject area about to be covered.

- Teaching is absent/task can be performed independently.

Checking My Understanding

Mark (T) for examples that meet all the criteria for a well-designed transition activity. Mark (NT) for those that do not.

_____ 1. While teacher is taking the roll, and before a math lesson, the students practice their math facts by taking a 3-minute timed test.

_____ 2. As students come into their English class, there is a short (5-minute) assignment on the blackboard based on the previous night's homework assignment.

_____ 3. While teacher takes roll, the students sit and wait for class to begin.

_____ 4. During roll taking, PE students update their fitness record card with data from yesterday's exercises.

Answers: 1T, 2T, 3NT, 4T.

Personal Commitment

Plan a transition activity. If it needs checking, how will you make sure the students do the checking?

_____

_____

_____

■ ROOM DESIGN AS AN EFFECTIVE PARAMETER

༄

Clearly the need for effective management exists in both work settings and learning settings. In both cases, smooth well-running classrooms where time, space, and materials are used efficiently, maximize the opportunities students have to engage material in a meaningful way.

Carolyn Evertson and Catherine Randolph, *Classroom Management in the Learning-Centered Classroom*

༄

Classroom Connection

Serena Holland was a fairly new teacher who had used room design to build relationship and wanted to take her use of room design to the next level. She wanted to provide a design to foster whole-group and small group work as well as the privacy necessary for individual work. She knew she had several challenging students coming to her class and wanted to place them in the best possible seating arrangement for success. One was a student who was very social and had the reputation of disturbing the class. Another was a shy, quiet student who had been falling through the cracks. Last year there had been distractions caused by a backup of students when getting materials. There had also been a problem with movement to activity centers. She had several ideas for placement of materials and centers to create more space and flow.

Personal Connection

What have you done to place challenged students for optimal success?

_____

_____

_____

One of the most critical factors to consider when setting the stage for preventing management problems in a classroom is the physical arrangement of the furniture, supplies, and resources within the classroom. In Chapter 3, we explored how room design can be important to building positive relationship. In this section, we will explore how classroom design can facilitate flow of people, learning, and materials.

In the well-designed classroom, the teacher can see and be seen by all the students and can move about freely. The students can see presentations and displays such as agendas, the class motto, instructional charts, and procedures. High-traffic areas run smoothly without backup or congestion. Materials are easily accessible and kept in an organized system. There is a delicate balance between an interesting classroom and an overstimulating environment. It is best to have space with a minimum of clutter.

The arrangements of the desks and materials can do either of the following:

- Inhibit or facilitate teacher and student movement

- Encumber or encourage successful management and learning

- Reduce or enhance connection between students and teacher and between students

Key Criteria of Room Design

- Design is strategically preplanned for teacher and student movement.

- Room arrangement supports classroom procedures for giving individual feedback and giving group instruction.

- Room design fosters teacher's ability to make contact, "work the crowd."

- Teacher's desk is at back or side of room.

- Arrangement uses the principles of proximity.

- Academically and/or socially challenged students are optimally placed.

- Supplies, centers, and resources are easily accessible.

Benefits of Good Room Design

- Fosters sense of security

- Minimizes distractions

- Allows a flow of people and materials

- Maintains more time on task

- Students feel more equal access to teacher

Optimal Placement

Students who are potentially challenged academically or socially sometimes are overcome by problems of aggression, resistance, distractions, withdrawal, or dependence. They may be gifted students or students at risk. These students need special teacher consideration when desk arrangement within the classroom is being planned. As soon as a student begins to feel his or her own sense of power over the problem, these considerations can be phased out.

Students who are struggling with aggression need some degree of separation from other students in order to have their own sense of space. For example, they need to be seated close to the teacher for support and physical presence. If the teacher uses cooperative learning groups, an aggressive student needs to be in a group where the teacher can be close enough to provide support and to prevent the variables that invite aggression from happening—for example, someone challenging the student's answer. Some teachers have found that inviting the student to sit at their desk or to come to sit near the group they are working with also provides this safety net.

Students who are struggling with resistance to being and participating in the classroom also need some degree of separation and space from the teacher to reduce the need for constant intervention. This allows for selective listening and creates space for the resistance to defuse. They do not need as much teacher proximity. They need to be isolated from social interactions that will pull them off focus, and they need some choice in the separation.

Examples of Optimal Placement Options for Various Behavior Problems

1. Some degree of separation from other students

   - Aggression: angry outbursts, name calling, manipulation, physical, attention getting, etc.

   - Resistance: to help prevent delays

   - Distraction by other students

2. High degree of teacher proximity

   - Aggression

   - Distractions by noise, activity, or thoughts

   - Withdrawal: responding to internal stimuli and physically withdrawing (e.g., yawning, rocking, talking to self, daydreaming, leaving group, wandering, avoiding responding)

3. Nonsocial seating

- Resistance: self-directed, doing own thing, delay in starting, pretending to conform, refusal

- Distraction: off-task sustained observing of other stimuli or unsustained diversion of attention off task by external stimuli (student either comes back or remains distracted by the stimuli)

4. Centrally blended among self-directed students

- Dependence on approval from adults

- Manipulation: complaining, pouting, crying, using diverting questions

 ## Personal Commitment

How can you improve on your classroom design?

_____

_____

_____

Summary of Parameters for Cooperation

- Parameters are the boundaries that are necessary for the group to feel physically safe and psychologically secure in the school environment

- Assessing your group's level of social skills determines the amount of structure or freedom that you as a leader will provide.

- Planning for the involvement of your students in this process is key to its success.

- Classroom agreements are norms or guidelines for behavior that apply to all activities all the time.

- When designing classroom agreements, keep in mind that the idea behind rules is to make the environment safe and consistent. Dialogue and participation of those who will live by the rules is a prerequisite.

- Critical and observable expectations are created in the trust that the students are capable of demonstrating them.

- Activity procedures are behavior expectations that apply only to certain types of activities but apply every time the activity occurs.

- It is necessary to teach, describe, model, and review the appropriate social behaviors that will be needed for various activities.

- Directions are the specifics of the task that change from day to day.

- Transition is a brief (2- to 5-minute) activity that immediately directs the student's attention to learning at the beginning of class.

- The physical arrangement of the furniture, supplies, and resources within the classroom to facilitate flow of people, learning, and materials is an important parameter tool.

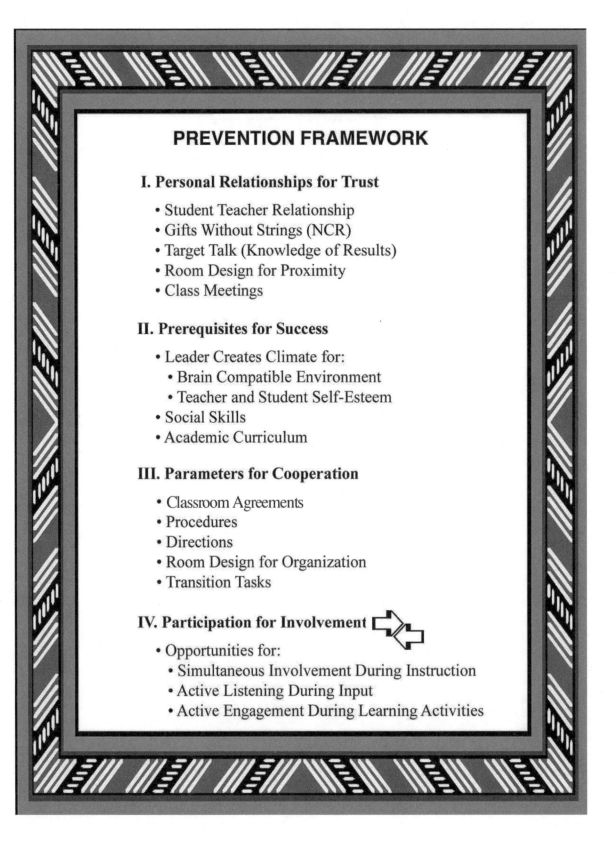

PREVENTION FRAMEWORK

I. Personal Relationships for Trust

- Student Teacher Relationship
- Gifts Without Strings (NCR)
- Target Talk (Knowledge of Results)
- Room Design for Proximity
- Class Meetings

II. Prerequisites for Success

- Leader Creates Climate for:
  - Brain Compatible Environment
  - Teacher and Student Self-Esteem
- Social Skills
- Academic Curriculum

III. Parameters for Cooperation

- Classroom Agreements
- Procedures
- Directions
- Room Design for Organization
- Transition Tasks

IV. Participation for Involvement

- Opportunities for:
  - Simultaneous Involvement During Instruction
  - Active Listening During Input
  - Active Engagement During Learning Activities

Participation for Involvement 6

The Fourth "P" of Prevention

ᔓ

The reason that people drop out of organizations (families and relation-ships too!) is because they do not feel included and of value to others. Most students say they feel isolated, with little sense of importance either to the teacher or to others in the classroom.

Jeanne Gibbs, *Tribes: A New Way of Learning and Being Together*

ᔔ

The fourth and final "P" for preventing problems in the classroom is student participation for involvement. This chapter provides ideas on how we can invite our students to be citizens instead of tourists in our classroom by creating opportunities for *all* students to be actively involved in all classroom activities. The strategies for participation in this chapter are designed to be congruent with any existing curriculum and any grade level of teaching. University professors, corporate trainers, and secondary, middle school, elementary, and kindergarten teachers have used them.

When students don't feel included, they often attempt to gain involvement by asserting influence—sometimes appropriately but often inappropriately. Students need to feel that they play an important part in creating their own educational process rather than being at the mercy of some process created by others. Inappropriate attempts to assert negative influence can be prevented when the classroom environment is designed for students' needs rather than for our convenience. Most classroom management upsets are about who has influence or who should have influence and about how much students feel involved in the classroom process. The following story provides an opening for rethinking how to invite all of your students to be involved in your classrooms.

Classroom Connection

Alex Ghafar taught science at Blanco Middle School. During his instruction/lectures, students often distracted him and others by whispering or making comments to each other. They often did the same thing when he was questioning individual students on some aspect of the lesson. One student would be responding and others would begin to talk. Alex would stop and restate the procedure for "direct instruction" in a limit-setting way by saying firmly and neutrally, "This is a time when one person is talking. Who is supposed to be talking?" The class would say, "You are" or "Marilyn is," and the lesson would resume. Alex's fourth-period class was the worst at this continual interruption. He and his coach reviewed the videotapes and discovered that, for the most part, the students were talking about the lesson content. The next day, before class, Alex gave his students a transition task, asking them to write down answers to the following on small index cards:

1. What do you need from me as your teacher to be good listeners?

2. What do you want me to know about you as learners?

After class, Alex read the cards. He noticed that several students said they would get an idea from something he said that made them think of something else; then they "just had to" say it out loud to someone nearby. Others said that they needed more time to talk and discuss what he was teaching. Some said that they needed him to talk more slowly, show more pictures, or let them talk more. A few said they needed more parties (a typical attempt at humor for this age group). Alex wrote a card too and put his responses on the overhead for all to see. The students said they felt more connected to him and appreciated that he had participated in the activity. Alex told them that he wanted to experiment with some of the brain research on learning and memory with this class and sought their cooperation and feedback. He then described a strategy called "10-2" in which he would teach/talk for only 10 minutes and then give them a minute or two to talk about what he had just taught. Sometimes he might ask them a question; other times he would let them make their own "brain connections" to their experiences and prior knowledge. He asked them to pretend they were piloting a new product or TV show and to give him feedback at the end of the period on how the strategy helped them remember the learning, helped them listen, or got in the way of their learning. He gave one student (a challenging one) the role of timekeeper: the student would hold up, sequentially, six cards numbered 12, 10, 8, 6, 4, and 2 to indicate how many minutes were left in the 12-minute segment. When the student held up the "2" card, Alex would sum up that portion of the lesson and create a question for the class to talk about.

Personal Connection

What do you guess your students might write that they needed from you?

_____

_____

_____

In this section we will focus on instructional strategies to build a sense of inclusion and influence in the classroom. You already know that participation is the key to motivation and provides the arena in which intrinsic motivation can flourish and grow. When students are invited to actively participate in classroom planning, practices, activities, and self-assessment, they begin to feel and experience a sense of influence over their own learning and their own lives. This is the key to critical thinking and citizens who contribute to the classroom and ultimately to society. When students are actively involved in the learning environment, classroom management upsets are happening only in other teachers' classrooms.

Active participation is the opposite of passive participation. Thus all students are actively involved in the learning activity at the same time, rather than just one or two students being actively involved and the rest of the students passively observing. This participation can be verbal, physical or written.

Active participation also includes participation in the classroom decision-making process to determine what is studied and how and when it is studied. This helps develop initiative, problem solving, critical thinking, organization, responsibility, and the life skill of decision making. It is also the key to the development of citizens who contribute to the classroom and ultimately to society.

Active participation fosters and develops a sense of power and influence, which is a critical component of self-esteem. When students are invited to actively participate in classroom planning, practices, activities, and self-assessment, they begin to experience a sense of influence over their own learning and their own lives. This is crucial for intrinsic motivation. The more actively involved learners are, the more "on task" and productive they actually become.

This chapter has three parts, corresponding to the three settings for activities in most classrooms:

1. *Teacher-Directed Settings*: The teacher directly leads the whole class or a small group with a clear objective in mind.

2. *Program-Directed Settings*: Students are assigned practice or review tasks that are directed by the curriculum or text (with the teacher occasionally monitoring, facilitating, and giving feedback) and have a clear objective.

3. *Self-Directed Settings*: Students have a choice about what they work on, where, how, and/or with whom. Examples include the use of centers, individual choice plans, cooperative group work that students are planning, personal activity time, conflict resolution activities, small group meetings, or personal conversation time with the teacher or other students.

■ PARTICIPATION STRATEGIES FOR TEACHER-DIRECTED SETTINGS

ॐ

Being a spectator not only deprives one of participation, but also leaves one's mind free for unrelated activity. If academic learning does not engage students, something else will.

John Goodlad, *A Place Called School*

∾

 ## Classroom Connection

Alex Ghafar's story at the beginning of this chapter provides an example of a teacher-directed setting. Alex was doing direct instruction, and students were struggling to attend. He adjusted his teaching to meet their needs for more participation and used the 10-2 strategy as a solution to their needing more "brain talk" time. In addition, every day for the last 8 to 10 minutes of class during the first few weeks of school, Alex spent personal activity time with his students and played curriculum games with them to build relationships with them and to review prerequisites from prior learning. At the beginning of the year Alex was always the leader, modeling and directing and teaching the class how to play the games. By the second week of school, different students were taking turns leading the games, and after a month they were playing the games independently in small groups around the room.

 ## Personal Connection

Reading this story I connected with . . .

_____

_____

_____

Let's begin with teacher-directed settings, such as the direct instruction that Alex Ghafar was struggling to provide while students were talking. Marilee Sprenger states in her book *Learning and Memory* (1999) that "the number of minutes a student can focus is equal to the student's age plus two" (p. 94). A slightly more conservative rule of thumb for active involvement during direct instruction is that the teacher should not speak for more minutes than the age of the child without providing a few seconds for the students to "interact" with or about the information that was just presented. This response might be a choral response, a partner response, or a response of a three-person group. For example, if in kindergarten the teacher is telling a story or facilitating a sharing time, after 4 or 5 minutes he or she should stop and formulate a question; this allows for simultaneous participation in which every student speaks. Or, as in Alex's classroom, the teacher can experiment with shortening direct teaching time to accommodate his or her students' learning needs.

How often have you sat in a Saturday workshop and planned your dinner menu or shopping list or lesson plans or drifted off to some other topic during a 2-hour lecture? According to Sprenger, even for adult learners prolonged attention to a learning experience is not desirable. Attention span doesn't extend beyond 15 to 20 minutes, no matter what the age of the learner. Eric Jensen has similarly documented in his book *Teaching With the Brain in Mind* (1998) that "generally, the brain does poorly at continuous, high-level attention" (p. 45). Research on brain wave patterns shows that the brain cycles between states of high and low attention and can stay at high attention for only 15 to 20 minutes before it starts to shift downwards. Consequently, Jensen, like Sprenger, recommends that teachers and students take mental breaks of up to 20 minutes several times a day to keep focused and productive. Jensen also points out that the brain requires periods of low attention as "processing time" (pp. 44-45). Conversation can aid this processing. As human beings, our need to talk and share is so intense that when it is denied or stifled, children, and some adults too, will talk about anything or begin to subvocalize inappropriately in an attempt to meet their needs.

Numerous classroom strategies invite participation in teacher-directed settings.

Examples of Classroom Strategies for Participation

- Ten Two (10-2)
- Use of manipulatives
- Brain Gym activities
- Questioning strategies
  - Sampling
  - Signaling
  - Individual private response
  - Think, Pair, Share
  - Numbered Heads Together
  - Group discussion of a question

Each of these will be discussed in detail below.

Ten Two (10-2)

The strategy of 10-2, used by Alex in the story, involves teaching for a certain number of minutes, which will depend on the age of the students, and then stopping and providing a time for the brain to make a connection to the learning. During this time, students can engage in "brain talk" by discussing what they have learned in pairs or in a small group, by writing a response to the learning, or by "mind-mapping" the learning (illustrating with key words and pictures how their minds are making sense of the lesson) or highlighting key ideas with a colored highlighter in the text or on a worksheet. Suggested structures for lesson planning to increase participation are shown in Figure 6.1.

Manipulatives

Manipulatives are any objects, pieces, or parts that students can physically move to help learning or demonstrate understanding. They can use these to figure out math problems, science formulas, patterns, parts of speech, scrambled sentences, letter names, plastic or paper numbers or shapes, parts of speech, parts of the body, and so forth. Using manipulatives (hands-on learning) while teaching will increase involvement and engagement by accessing kinesthetic processing.

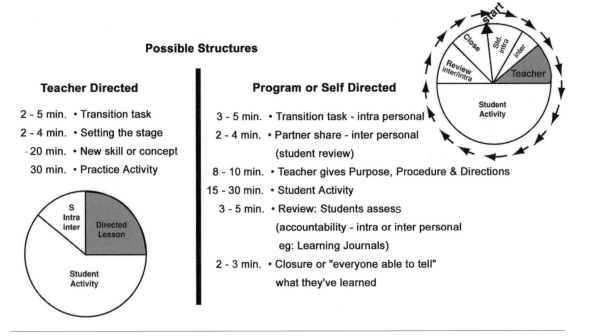

In teacher directed, program directed or self directed settings, the following structures are designed to get the students into the learning activity as soon as possible in order to **maximize** student involvement and **minimize** teacher talk.

Possible Structures

Teacher Directed

2 - 5 min. • Transition task
2 - 4 min. • Setting the stage
· 20 min. • New skill or concept
30 min. • Practice Activity

Program or Self Directed

3 - 5 min. • Transition task - intra personal
2 - 4 min. • Partner share - inter personal
              (student review)
8 - 10 min. • Teacher gives Purpose, Procedure & Directions
15 - 30 min. • Student Activity
3 - 5 min. • Review: Students assess
              (accountability - intra or inter personal
              eg: Learning Journals)
2 - 3 min. • Closure or "everyone able to tell"
              what they've learned

Figure 6.1.   Two Lesson Designs for Active Involvement

Brain Gym Activities

Brain Gym is a trademarked program, created by Gail and Paul Dennison and based on more than 80 years of research, that presents 26 targeted physical activities to improve learning abilities and enhance the retention of information in the brain by integrating brain functions with whole-body movements. Activities include, for example, marching in place while swinging one's arms across the midline of the body, simulating crawling, clasping one's hands together and drawing figure eights in the air. For further information, consult Dennison and Dennison (1989, 1992).

Questioning Strategies

Several questioning strategies can be used to check for understanding as well as increase student participation. Each of these techniques accomplishes a different purpose and offers the student different benefits.

Sampling

Sampling is directing a question to the total group and then calling on one representative group member for a response. For example, one might ask, "Can anyone remember the four characteristics of a metaphor?" or "Who can name three elements of the scientific method?" This technique can be used to determine what one student knows or to sample the group for understanding. It has been the most commonly used strategy over the years, but it is losing popularity as we learn more about the brain and learning. It should be used only if students volunteer an answer and not as a classroom management strategy to frighten students into paying attention. It has some benefits: Students can hear what one student thinks and possibly get more ideas, and the teacher can assess knowledge of the few individual students who responded. But many learners feel put on the spot by sampling and are anxious about sharing and "being wrong." Teachers need to be cautious when using sampling in order to protect the students' sense of security and keep them from "downshifting." It is the least effective questioning strategy because only one student participates while all of the others are passive.

Signaling

Signaling is a questioning technique in which the teacher poses the question to the entire group and every student responds simultaneously. Signaling provides every student a chance to respond and get immediate feedback from peers. It also can be used during the formative stage to practice and recall skills and concepts.

Signaling can take a variety of formats and provides an opportunity for every student to be involved.

- *Choral response*: Students respond in unison out loud. For example, the teacher asks, "What are the four P's of Prevention?" and the students respond in unison with "Personal, Prerequisites, Parameters, and Participation." This is often the safest and most common signaling technique.

- *Response cards*: Students respond by holding up cards with letters, words, or phrases on them. They can create the cards or use commercial prelabeled cards. The teacher says, for example, "Hold up the card labeled 'M' if what I read is a metaphor and the card labeled 'NM' if it is not" or "Hold up the word that means 'more than one.'"

- *Physical signals*: Students respond with a physical signal that the teacher asks them to use. For example, the teacher says, "Stand and clap when you hear the sentence with an exclamation mark," or "Show with thumbs up [or arms across your chest] whether you agree or disagree." By getting students up and moving, the signaling kinesthetically stimulates the brain.

- *Physical objects*: Students actually sort and select from manipulatives, such as science lab materials or art or PE equipment, in response to the teacher's questions or directives. For example, the teacher says, "Hold up the triangle shape," or "Hold up the number that represents another name for 12." This is a way to check for understanding on the use of equipment, and it gives teachers and students immediate feedback.

Individual private response is a variation on signaling in that every student is responding individually without others' seeing their response. This accommodates students who prefer to use their intrapersonal intelligence and work alone. The teacher is usually monitoring, moving about and checking the responses privately. Some teachers have the students hold up their written responses on a whiteboard or card; this would turn the strategy into a signaling strategy. The following are some other variations:

- *Trace*: Have students trace a word or symbol or formula in the air on their desks, or on the floor; have them trace it on a partner's back and see if the partner can guess it.

- *Say in your hand*: The teacher might say, for example, "If you know what type of plant this is, whisper it in your hand." This is a variation on choral response but encourages young children to feel safe responding.

- *Move manipulatives*: Have students privately and individually move numbers, letters, or shapes around—for example, to order them or to form an algorithm.

Signaling benefits students in that it offers opportunities for physical, vocal, and kinesthetic movement, which often anchors the learning in the body as well as the mind. It benefits the teacher in that it allows him or her to quickly assess the entire class by noticing who has to look to peers before responding and provides immediate feedback on how the entire class is understanding the content.

Think, Pair, Share

Developed by Professor Frank Lyman and his associates at the University of Maryland, Think, Pair, Share is a multimodal strategy designed to encourage student participation and create a high degree of student involvement. The directions for it are:

1. The group listens while the teacher poses a question.

2. Students are given time in which to think of a response.

3. Students are then cued to pair with a partner to discuss their responses.

For example, the teacher says, "Let's recall the things we remember about what plants need to grow. Think about it for 30 seconds. . . . Ready, turn to your partner and share." A time limit can be set for each step in the process. The teacher or student uses a signal such as a bell, rain-stick, lights, chime, timer, voice, or hand up to indicate that the time is up. At the end, partners can share their responses with the whole group. Students may also write or "web" their responses with the whole group: that is, show how ideas build on each other by writing a main idea on a board with a circle around it and surrounding it with new ideas that the students come up with, in either words or pictures, that are connected by lines to the central circle.

Think, Pair, Share benefits students by giving them a time to process the teaching, make brain connections to their own prior knowledge, and verbalize their learning with one other person. It also gives them a legitimate time to talk and an opportunity to collaborate with peers and to get peer feedback in a safe setting. It benefits the teacher by reducing the amount of side conversation and by building retention and memory for students to be successful on summative tests.

Numbered Heads Together

Numbered Heads Together is a powerful strategy from Spencer Kagan's *Cooperative Learning* (1994, p. 103) for having students support each other's learning and ensuring that every student knows the information and learns social cooperation.

Only one student represents the group, but the students do not know which one of them will be the group representative. The strategy has four steps:

1. Students number off.

2. Teacher states a question and a time limit: for example, "Make sure everyone in your group knows the five things we are looking for in this lab. You have 75 seconds."

3. Students put their heads together and discuss the answer to ensure that every student can respond correctly.

4. Teacher calls a number. Students with that number raise their hand or stand. Teacher selects one and calls on that student to respond. Alternatively, all students whose number is called record their answers simultaneously on a board, on slates, or on paper or use signaling.

The students benefit in that they are supporting each other in learning the information; they are also learning accountability and practicing social skills. The teacher benefits in that all students are actively involved and the teacher gets immediate feedback. The strategy works well for questions that test knowledge and comprehension, require convergent thinking, and have a brief answer on which there is likely to be high consensus. It is not suited for questions that require application, analysis, synthesis, evaluation, or divergent thinking or that cover low-consensus material.

Group Discussion of a Question

One of the simplest of all the questioning strategies to use with teacher-directed activities is a time-limited small group discussion of a question that the teacher provides. For example, the teacher might say, "You have 8 minutes to discuss, in your groups of four, how teachers can begin to try these questioning strategies out in a safe environment."

Group discussion can encourage higher-level thinking skills and allow for more in-depth, less directed discussion than a whole-class discussion that the teacher facilitates. It is especially useful when the objective is to have students create and exchange novel, unique, set-breaking ideas. It can also be used to process low-consensus questions such as "How might the employment of both parents in most families contribute to the number of children who are dependent on extrinsic motivation?" Group discussion provides an opportunity for application, analysis, synthesis, evaluation, and divergent thinking. Some groups will need the structure of a talking chip or some other device to ensure that everyone gets a chance to discuss and no one person dominates.

After students have discussed the topic, there are a variety of ways to have them share with the whole group. When sharing is done sequentially rather than simultaneously, students often tune out, involvement is minimized, and precious class time is lost. Participation, involvement, and concept development occur during the group discussion time, not the sharing time, so we need to reduce the sharing time or restructure it so there is simultaneous sharing. To reduce sharing time, we can adopt a strategy of "Best Ideas Only": one or two students share a brief synopsis of the best ideas that the group considers really important for the class to hear. To allow for simultaneous sharing, groups can share their best answer with the group adjacent to them, or one representative from each group can record the group's best answers on a board or chart paper at the end of the discussion and then all teams can simultaneously post these. Then the other groups can get up and walk around to read each other's ideas.

Group discussion benefits students by encouraging more open-ended thinking, making learning more fun, actively involving students, helping students retain material, and giving students an opportunity to practice social skills in the context of the curriculum. It benefits teachers by providing immediate feedback on students' understanding, making teaching more fun, and allowing the teacher to check for understanding.

Table 6.1 summarizes guidelines for asking effective questions.

Table 6.1   General Guidelines for Effective Questions

Research has shown that using the following guidelines will promote greater student participation and retention.

1. Ask questions that require conceptual answers.

   ● Avoid yes/no questions; these give students a 50/50 chance of being right or wrong.

   ● Avoid questions that require only one-word responses, as they promote rote learning.

2. Allow for appropriate wait time after the question to give learners an opportunity to process the question and formulate and answer (3 to 5 seconds is how long the brain needs to make connections).

3. Ask specific questions that relate to the key points of the lesson and are not ambiguous.

4. Avoid repeating answers because students quickly learn not to listen to each other. Teacher talk is usually dominant, and we need to talk less. Instead of repeating students' answers, ask the group to repeat or another student to repeat.

5. If you do use sampling, ask the question first and call the student's name last. Once a student's name is called, the rest of the class can take a break from thinking and are off the hook from listening and learning. In addition, the student whose name has been called is now on the spot and may become too nervous to think clearly.

6. Group discussion of a question works for higher-level thinking and more adult social skills. Students are actively involved and engaged rather than talking.

⌐══ Key Criteria for Participation in Teacher–Directed Activities

● Sampling is the weakest strategy because only one student is participating.

● Signaling has many forms and invites all students to participate.

● Think, Pair, Share provides students a chance to collaborate with one other student.

● Numbered Heads Together gives several students who are at different skill levels an opportunity to practice together.

✓ Checking My Understanding

Which questioning strategy has the least amount of student involvement? _____

Answer: sampling.

🏃 Personal Commitment

Which of the questioning strategies feel most compatible for use in my classroom?

_____

_____

_____

■ PARTICIPATION STRATEGIES FOR PROGRAM-DIRECTED SETTINGS

〜

*Teaching is difficult under the best educational conditions
and this failure to take into account the needs of students or teachers
makes what is already a hard job almost impossible.
Any method of teaching that ignores the needs of teachers
or students is bound to fail.*

William Glasser, *The Quality School: Managing Students Without Coercion*

〜

Classroom Connection

Alex Ghafar had solved his problem of kids talking during direct instruction, but he was still totally baffled by their behavior during seatwork times. Most of the students worked on the assignment, but several students asked for lots of help, even though he knew they could do the task. Others got up and down every couple of minutes to sharpen a pencil, get a Kleenex, use the bathroom pass, or borrow an eraser. Others cleaned their desk or organized their binder. A few did homework for another class. Alex knew that these behaviors of delay and inappropriate self-directed tasks were indicative of resistance. So he used a *similar strategy that had been successful for him before. He asked the students at a class meeting what was going on and shared that these behaviors were signs of resistance operating in the classroom. Instead of labeling the students as resistant, which would have provoked them to defend their position, he was careful to identify the problem impersonally, thereby inviting the students to brainstorm ways to deal with it. The class followed the brainstorming directive that all answers would be accepted nonjudgmentally and that selection from the list would take place later. Alex recorded the ideas on chart paper.*

♥ Personal Connection

What have you noticed in your own classroom during program-directed work times?

_____

_____

_____

Program-directed activities can be the most boring and challenging for both teachers and students. Ninety percent of program-directed learning is paper-and-pencil work, copying problems or sentences out of a book, or answering questions from a book. We sometimes call this "drill and kill." These are the activities where students show the most dependence on the teacher and the most off-task delaying, daydreaming, and inappropriate social behaviors. Practically speaking, however, there are times when students need to do program-directed tasks. Building in some participation activities such as those suggested below can provide motivation, interest, and fun, as well as eliminating the traditional classroom management problems that occur during these times.

Alfie Kohn (1998) sums up the keys to motivation in the "three C's": choice, content, and collaboration. The use of all three in planning seatwork activities will prevent most classroom management upsets during those times. To incorporate the first "C," choice, students can be given a menu of practice tasks or learning tasks and they can choose the order in which they will work on them. Or, if they are given an objective, such as "Demonstrate understanding of division of decimals," they can choose how they will demonstrate their skills: for example, with paper and pencil, graphically, creating a song about the formula, or some other way. They can also preview a chapter and select the topics that they are most interested in learning and the ones that they are dreading. This not only incorporates choice but gives personal meaning to the content, the second "C."

The third "C," collaboration, can be incorporated by use of any of the cooperative learning techniques. Giving students the opportunity to work together makes a task more fun and more interesting. Spencer Kagan's book *Cooperative Learning* (1994) provides an abundance of these strategies.

Examples of Cooperative Tasks

Learning Appointments: Program-directed activities can gain more structure if students have a predetermined partner to work with during program-directed times. We have adapted this idea from *Esteem Builders* (Borba, 1994). Students sign up with each other for appointments for the next week or month. The signup sheet can be anything your students will relate to (Figure 6.2). Their appointment schedule is one of the few papers students rarely lose. When it's time for them to do a practice task, the teacher says, "Find your three o'clock appointment." This strategy helps students get to know others and is helpful for those who are shy because the pairing was settled in advance.

Interview: In this strategy from Kagan (1994), students form groups of four, partner up and interview each other, and then return to the group of four to share what their partner shared with them.

Numbered Heads Together/Round Table: A variation on the Numbered Heads Together exercise that was described earlier is to have students contribute to working on one piece of paper that goes around the table. Everyone takes a turn at writing, but the others in the group can help the recorder by giving ideas.

Learning Together
My Appointment Times

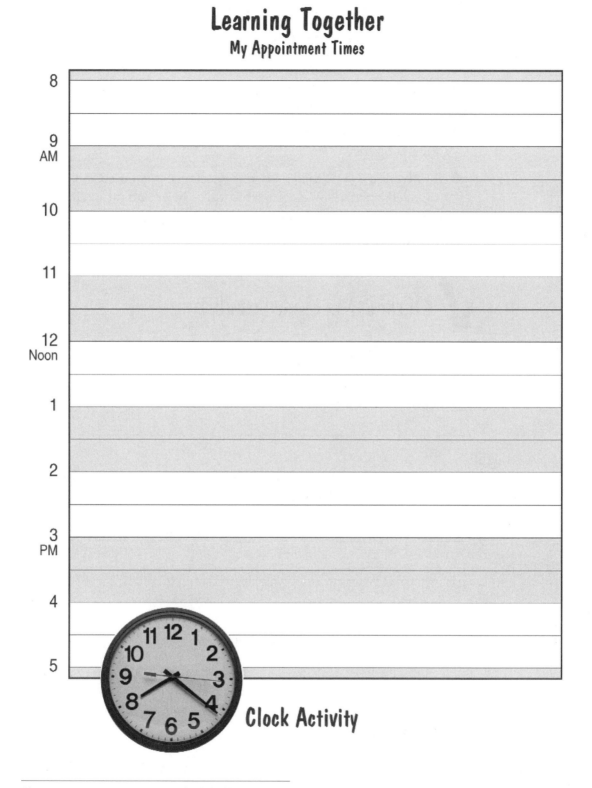

Clock Activity

Figure 6.2.   Appointment Schedule Sheet

🔑 Key Points for Participation During Program–Directed Activities

● Program-directed activities typically invite more off-task behavior than any other activities.

● Give students a choice of how to demonstrate proficiency in a given objective.

● Motivation can be increased and resistance prevented in program-directed activities when students have choices about what to practice and how to practice it.

● Resistance is diminished when students get to collaborate with each other and have some input over the content they are studying.

✔ Checking My Understanding

1. What are the three keys to motivation?

_____

_____

2. Name one strategy/activity that might defuse resistance to program-directed activities.

_____

_____

Answers:

2. Cooperative tasks or partner activities.

1. Choice, Cooperation, Collaboration.

🌟 Personal Commitment

What might you be willing to try to spice up your program-directed activities?

_____

_____

PARTICIPATION STRATEGIES ■
FOR SELF-DIRECTED SETTINGS

ی

*In kindergarten we design our rooms for real work,
not just passive listening. . . . This is, alas, the last time children are
given independence, encouraged to make choices and allowed
to move about on their own steam.*

Deborah Meier, *The Power of Their Ideas*

ى

 ## Classroom Connection

Kimyana Adrin was committed to helping her students learn to make good choices. She designed her middle school core classroom much as she had her kindergarten classroom. She set up learning centers to support and enrich the reading, writing, and social studies that were integrated into her language arts core program. When the students arrived, they had a personal conversation time for 10 minutes to connect with each other and with their teacher. They had signed up the day before, as they left school, for the personal conversation center they wanted. There was a limit of six students per center. Kimyana hosted one where she was present to just visit with the students and listen to them; she called it "Teacher Talk," even though it was really the teacher listening. There was a "Homework Talk" center for students who wanted to share how they did or compare with each other and a "Book Talk" center where students shared about something they were reading that interested them. There were also various special interest centers on such topics as sports, computers, arts and entertainment, and news. The structure was just enough to give the students security, yet there was freedom to choose the topic and group. After a few weeks the students added other topic centers, and by the second month of school they just went in the morning to whichever center they chose, the only criterion being the limit of six per group. So Kimyana provided some structure to the choice initially, then faded to free choice as the students became comfortable and familiar with the process. When the students returned to their tables, they did their transition task. They could choose to write in their journal about their conversation that morning, write a message to the teacher, or write about an experience from the day or night before. So the teacher embedded self-direction and choice in their transition task as well.

💗 Personal Connection

What appealed to you about this story?

_____

_____

_____

Self-directed settings are those in which students are allowed an opportunity to move about the classroom and choose where and when to work, what to work on, and who to work with. The key for determining self-directed activities is the amount of choice students have in directing their learning. When the student directs the learning by choosing which center to go to and what to do, in what order and sequence, the activity is truly self-directed. It is important that there be procedures and directions at each center. Most critical is the number of students allowed at each center at any one time.

Examples of Settings for Self-Directed Activities

- *Personal Conversation Space*: A personal conversation center or space like the one Kimyana set up in the story you just read provides a way for teachers to have time to talk to their students and vice versa. Students can sign up and the teacher can then go and get them individually, or they can come as a small group prepared to share something of importance with their teacher and a few peers.

- *Learning Centers*: These are areas of the room set up to introduce or support your curriculum. They should be graphic, visual, and colorful and with some hands-on activity other than paper and pencil. They are best when they are interactive.

- *Literacy Centers*: These are centers focused on reading and writing activities. They are located around the room, at tables or in nooks and crannies, and can even be just desks pushed together. The activities at each center should be multilevel so students can choose their independent level if they need that. For example, at a writing center, there might be activity suggestions of drawing about an idea or tracing letters, paper for students to write their own stories, story starters, or journals. Other literacy centers might include reading activities, story boards, scrambled letters or sentences, plastic magnetic letters, clipboards that students can carry with them when they are reading the word wall (classroom wall where students put up words they are learning in lessons in alphabetical order for quick reference) and writing down words (e.g., words they know), or computers with writing or reading software.

- *Science Labs*: These could be past labs that students had enjoyed and that could be redone at an enrichment level or to discover new principles or concepts.

- *Free Exploration Centers*: These are areas of the room set up with materials, such as math manipulatives, science equipment, art materials, reading materials, or personal activity games, that will be used later on in a lesson. The objective is for the students to "play with" them and get that out of their system so that when they are used during the lesson, students will be able to use them appropriately. There is quite a body of research supporting this concept (see, e.g., Baratta-Lorton, 1995, p. 2).

- *Computer Research*: Students select topics to study or investigate on the computer/Internet and are given time to do that work at centers.

- *Physical Education Stations*: Various areas of the yard or gym can be set up with activities that students have enjoyed during the year or that build skills for certain sports. Task cards at each station with pictures and directions help students stay focused. Stations might have such activities as bean toss through a target, hula-hoops to develop balance, ball toss at various lengths, jumping rope, frap (a game of paddle ball), or Velcro toss games.

The ideas for centers are endless and allow for creativity for both the teacher and student. They can be designed to support and enrich music programs, art classes, history lessons, or math concepts at any level from K through 12.

Multiple observations over many years have found very little evidence of students showing resistance during self-directed activities (Spaulding, 1980). When you blend the elements of choice, collaboration, and content, intrinsic motivation flows easily (Kohn, 1998).

 *Summary*

- Simultaneous questioning strategies can maximize participation.

- Participation strategies invite students to be "citizens" rather than "tourists" in class.

- They increase motivation when choice, collaboration, and content are considered.

- They encourage the development of a sense of autonomy.

- They increase retention of learning and long-term memory of content.

- They invite decision making, initiative, and problem solving.

Part III

Intervention Techniques and Problem-Solving Strategies

෨

*Most behavioral interventions involve some form of punishment
or negative consequence, a manipulation designed to correct
the offender's actions. Yet, we know that punishment does not work
with many students, particularly those with low self-esteem.*

Evelyn Schneider, "Giving Students a Voice in the Classroom"

෨

This section focuses on temporary intervention techniques and solution-focused problem-solving strategies. Chapter 7 deals with temporary interventions that you may need to stop off-task behavior in order to keep teaching until you have time to review and create a prevention plan. When your prevention strategies are working successfully, you will be able to reduce these interventions to fewer than 2% of daily interactions with students. Chapter 8 presents strategies for addressing and resolving problems in the long term. The Framework for Temporary Interventions and Problem Solving lists both the intervention techniques and the problem-solving strategies you may progress to. By the end of this section, you will be able to restructure inappropriate behavior (social mistakes) while respecting students' self-esteem and preserving a brain-compatible environment. You already know how important it is to keep upsets and stress to a minimum. When you can act on your beliefs rather than your feelings, you can implement options and think through how to prevent upsets in the future. You can also see which prevention strategies may need strengthening and when you will need to move into problem solving. Problem-solving strategies that begin to develop student responsibility and cooperation will be necessary for repeated incidents of inappropriate behavior.

Whether we are doing temporary interventions or problem solving, we need to change our focus from "doing something to" students to "working with" students. This is the strategy of moving from why to what and how: Instead of getting caught up in asking why students are behaving a certain way, we ask what behaviors we are seeing and hearing minus interpretations and how we can assist students to change behavior patterns.

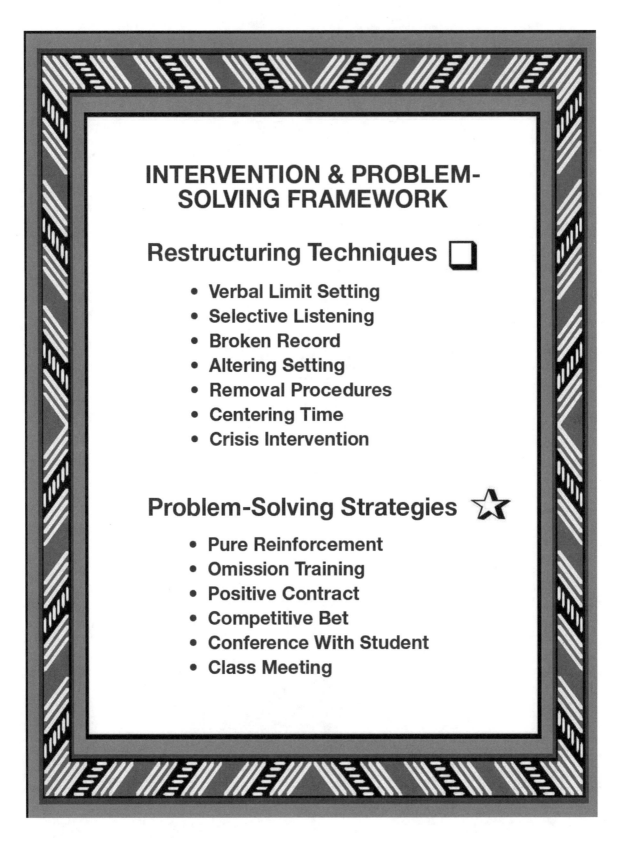

INTERVENTION & PROBLEM-SOLVING FRAMEWORK

Restructuring Techniques

- **Verbal Limit Setting**
- **Selective Listening**
- **Broken Record**
- **Altering Setting**
- **Removal Procedures**
- **Centering Time**
- **Crisis Intervention**

Problem-Solving Strategies

- **Pure Reinforcement**
- **Omission Training**
- **Positive Contract**
- **Competitive Bet**
- **Conference With Student**
- **Class Meeting**

Rethinking Classroom Interventions

7

When students are motivated from within, say experts, all the external
punishments and rewards that many teachers rely upon are not only
unnecessary, they're ineffectual.

Kathy Checkley, "No Room for Control"

 ## Classroom Connection

Lucy Stein had been teaching high school for 10 years. She thought of herself
as a good teacher with an interesting curriculum. Most of the students seemed
to like her, and she had fairly good control of her classroom. After rethinking her
use of classroom management as a leadership tool, she decided to try tackling
some of the problems that surfaced every year and created tension for her and
the students. There was always a looming feeling of disrespect and confusion
that she put up with. Her interpretation was that it went with the territory, and
she had felt hopeless about it in the past. This disrespect and confusion played
out as students talking, whispering, writing and passing notes, blurting out, tattling, teasing, cursing, talking back, getting out of their seats at inappropriate
times, following her around with questions, and losing textbooks, homework,
and papers. She felt a need to be in charge and had used a lot of interventions
to keep things under control.

This year, Lucy wanted to address these behaviors more effectively than she
had in the past. She knew she would need both workable, respectful temporary
intervention techniques and long-term problem-solving strategies that would
foster student responsibility and involvement in finding solutions. She also knew
that she would need to review her prevention strategies to build strong relationships, create a collaborative learning environment, and develop with her class
both a shared vision for the year and realistic agreements and clear procedures
that could be consistently referred to. She was anxious to see if these strategies
could significantly cut down on off-task behavior.

❤ Personal Connection

List three to five common repetitive behavior problems that you continue to encounter on a daily basis. Be sure to include those that create the most stress!

_____

_____

_____

■ # RESEARCH-BASED PHILOSOPHY OF INTERVENTION

Temporary interventions are restructuring techniques to use when there is an upset in the classroom and either the teacher's or the student's brain has downshifted. They are designed to turn inappropriate behavior into appropriate behavior temporarily with the least amount of attention, time, energy, or disruption of class time. They are not intended to be used as punishments because in a brain-compatible classroom the first characteristic is "absence of threat," or what we refer to as a sense of security, both physical and psychological. Rather, they are designed to be respectful toward the students and to achieve the desired end without violating students' sense of security or self-esteem.

It is important to remember that problem solving is inappropriate at the time of the upset because activity in the cerebral cortex shuts down when we are upset (Kovalik, 1993). Therefore, teachers need not only problem-solving strategies but also a range of temporary interventions to deal with upsets as they arise.

■ # PREREQUISITES FOR SUCCESSFUL INTERVENTION

Even temporary intervention requires some groundwork to be laid in advance in terms of attitude change and planning. To do a successful intervention, the teacher needs to do the following:

- Have a bonded relationship with students.
- Make a conscious distinction between inappropriate and unacceptable behavior.
- Escape personalizing motivation of students' behavior.
- Believe in concept of "social mistakes" versus deviancy.

- Value use of discipline rather than punishment.
- Plan for teacher upsets.
- Use the principles of intervention.

Bonded Teacher-Student Relationship

Before restructuring inappropriate behavior, the teacher must be committed to ensuring that all prevention strategies are in place, especially the bonded teacher-student relationship. The success of any restructuring intervention depends upon that relationship. Frequent use of gifts without strings, target talk, and proximity, coupled with an authentic sharing of power, can produce a learning environment where the students are part of a community in which they feel valued. When teachers can show genuine appreciation and support for this community atmosphere, there is a greater probability that internal motivation will be developed and interventions will not be needed.

Distinguishing Between Inappropriate and Unacceptable Behaviors

We all make mistakes, but everyone makes different mistakes.
Ludwig van Beethoven

According to Frederick Jones's Classroom Management Trainers Program, of the specific observable behaviors that can disrupt learning, 80% to 85% are off-task behaviors such as talking, tattling, or passing notes, 10% involve some out-of-seat behavior, and 5% fall in the "other" category. Some of the behaviors in the "other" category will require long-term problem solving, but the rest, along with the off-task behaviors and out-of-seat behaviors, can generally be resolved by temporary interventions.

It is critical to know the difference between behaviors that are inappropriate and those that are unacceptable in order to intervene appropriately. Inappropriate behaviors are disruptive behaviors that are not physically or psychologically harmful—for example:

- Interrupting others
- Whispering
- Bumping someone
- Making noise or running around during a quiet activity

These are the behaviors that temporary interventions are designed to restructure. Unacceptable behaviors are those that are physically or psychologically harmful—for example:

- Derogatory racial name calling

- Poking someone

- Shoving intentionally

- Hitting

These behaviors require immediate action, such as stepping in and protecting the students, separating them, providing a calm place to regroup, and possibly using problem-solving strategies from Chapter 8. If the situation is a crisis—that is, a fight, harassment, taunting, or any kind of struggle between students that is out of control—use the crisis intervention strategies at the end of this chapter.

Personal Connection

What social mistakes occur every year, and how can you use prevention strategies to decrease them?

_____

_____

_____

Escaping Personalizing Motivations: Dancing out of Interpretations

In our opening story, Lucy Stein knew what changes she wanted in her classroom, and she knew she wanted to be positive. In the past, her feeling that the students were being "disrespectful"—a negative interpretation of their motivation—had gotten in her way by encouraging her to see herself as a victim and to focus more on her story about the behaviors than on what could be done about it. Now she was interested in adopting a leader mentality that would focus on how to overcome the situation.

As human beings, we are always trying to make sense of what happens in our lives, and this is an automatic process. But often our attempts to make sense of an upsetting event are dangerous to our relationships because they involve labeling and blaming the other person. One of the first reactions we have as teachers when students violate agreements or norms is to think that the students are doing it on purpose. Our next thought is to interpret their behavior as rude, disrespectful, defiant, thoughtless, or some other negative adjective. Naturally, we then take this behavior personally and feel angry or threatened.

Consider, for example, the instances below:

- *Observable Facts*: A student stops turning in homework.

- *Upsetting Event*: Her grades are deteriorating and her motivation is decreasing.

- *The Interpretation or Story We Think About*: The student is lazy or doesn't care about school or doesn't want to try.

Or again:

- *Observable Facts*: One of your students talks constantly in class.

- *Upsetting Event*: The class is interrupted; you are distracted and doing a lot intervening.

- *The Interpretation or Story We Think About*: The student is thoughtless, rude, and disrespectful.

The problem with such interpretations is that if we think our students are rude, defiant, or disrespectful and we take their behavior personally, we lose our power to be leaders and set the stage for a power struggle. For example, teachers who conclude that their unruly students are deliberately "bad" or plotting against them will be hooked into wanting to control, punish, and get revenge.

As long as we are going to make up a story or interpretation, it is more powerful to make up a positive one. We might think, for example, that a misbehaving student has not learned how to act differently or that his or her old programs and habits are on automatic. Thinking this way frees us up to be supportive and less judgmental.

Using the Concept of "Social Mistakes" Rather Than Deviancy

As Dishon and O'Leary (1984, p. 46) point out, when students make a mistake in math or reading, there isn't a teacher in the world who says, "That's it, pass in your books, you are never doing math again! I am sick and tired of all of your mistakes after all of my explanations. We'll just stop doing math." Yet when students make social mistakes, our reaction is different: We are likely to say, "That's it! No more recess!" or "No more free time!" Why do we treat academic "mistakes" differently from social/behavioral "mistakes"?

In Chapter 2, we discussed how it is useful for teachers to adopt a social learning paradigm and see misbehaviors in terms of social mistakes rather than deviancy. Often children act impulsively or act out of unmet needs. Often they have been taught the wrong behaviors, have not been taught enough of the right behaviors, or have never been taught the right behaviors. A teacher who can help them learn from social mistakes and be responsive in the moment to both the needs of the individual acting out and the needs of the teacher and class can often diffuse potential conflicts.

♥ Personal Connection

How will shifting your thinking help you to respond to classroom upsets from your values and beliefs and not your feelings and help you see these upsets as teachable moments where creativity is called upon to positively model and teach problem-solving skills?

_____

_____

_____

Discipline Versus Punishment

∽

People take time. Dealing with discipline takes time.
Children are not fax machines or credit cards. When they misbehave,
they tell us that they need help learning a better way.
They are telling us that there are basic needs not being met
which are motivating the behavior.

Allen N. Mendler, *What to Do When?*
How to Achieve Discipline With Dignity

∾

As Evelyn Schneider (1996) points out, "You can't have rules without consequences. But responding to an offense should not be about getting revenge but about justice. How do we move from manipulating students with rewards and punishments to helping them make decisions that satisfy their needs without violating those of others?"

The answer lies in the concept of discipline. The word *discipline* comes from the same Latin root as *disciple* and connotes teaching, learning, and instruction. It is training that corrects, molds, or perfects mental or moral character. The delivery of discipline is brain compatible when there is a focus on preventing problems and when the teacher displays respect by using a nonjudgmental, neutral tone and neutral body language. The consequences are natural or logical, and they foster social responsibility and positive alternatives. Thus, for example, an offending student, instead of wasting time in the suspension room, might assess his or her behavior, list alternative choices, practice a more successful behavior during free time, design a restitution, or participate in a conflict resolution process. Some classes create a neutral reflection space where students go to regain self-control. When a student makes a mistake, we want to support reparation done *by* the student rather than doing something *to* the student in the form of punishment (Kohn, 1996) (see Figure 7.1).

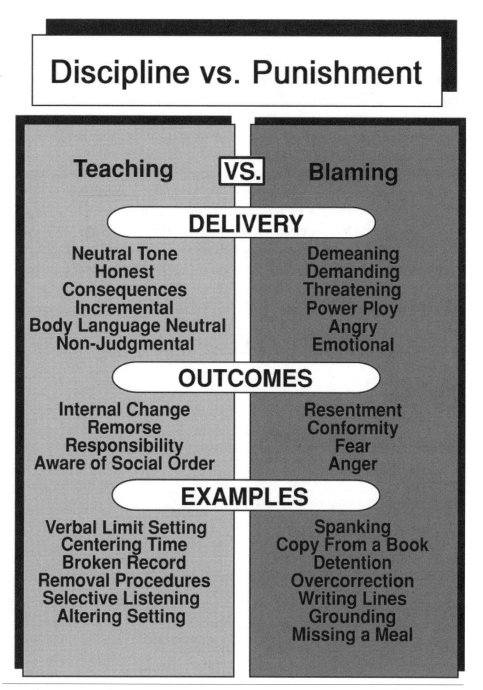

Figure 7.1.   Discipline Versus Punishment

The Caring Menu

❦

But adults also have to offer students a way to make restitution.
We need to give them a chance to heal the relationship
they have with other students.

Diane Chelsom Gossen, "When All Else Fails"

❧

Often when students make a mistake, hurt someone's feelings, or violate a rule, we think of a consequence to teach a lesson when the real goal is to teach them how to make up or repair the damage done to someone's feelings. A "caring menu" is a list of ways to make up for an error that the teacher and the students can create together. It offers students choices in making restitution and teaches the concept of saying "I'm sorry" in an individualistic way rather than a prescriptive way. This encourages moral autonomy and internalization of the value of making amends.

The caring menu is a benefit for the teacher because there is less tattling and dependence. Responsibility is placed on the student to make amends. The following are some list entries you could use, but they are not meant to be "the menu" for your particular students (see also Figures 7.2 and 7.3).

Examples of Caring Menu Possibilities

- Write a note
- Draw a picture
- Share a snack
- Give a gift: flowers, pencil, eraser
- Give up a turn to take out the ball
- Say, "I'm sorry"
- Give a hug
- Help with a chore, project, etc.
- Share a book
- Read a story, play a game
- Make a card

Caring Menu

1. Help them with Something.
2. Give a gift: Candy, Card, note, Picture.
3. Tell them you like them.
4. Compliment them.
5. Do something for them: HW, Chores ___
6. Apologize.
7. Play a game with them.
8. Talk about what happened.

Figure 7.2. A Caring Menu

Most behavioral interventions involve not true discipline, but the imposition of some form of punishment. Punishment is control gained by enforcing obedience and order. It is rarely related to the misbehavior. Punishment is delivered in a reactive way based on feelings in the moment. It demands obedience to an authority figure and external rules. It is demeaning and imposes arbitrary negative consequences.

Figure 7.3.   Elementary Students' Suggestions for Making Restitution

Punishment is a manipulation designed to correct the offender's actions. Yet we know that it does not work with many students. Punishment breeds resentment, fear, conformity, and concealing of mistakes. Student offenders hurt others because they cannot adequately meet their psychological needs, and their teachers are burning out from trying to coerce them into obedience.

✓ Checking My Understanding

Discipline or punishment? For each item below, mark "P" for punishment or "D" for discipline.[1]

_____ 1.   Someone has been stealing things in the classroom. The teacher engages the class in a discussion about ways to make their room safe and how to re-create a trusting community. Students are asked to share how they feel when incidents like this occur and to brainstorm ideas about how to reestablish trust and honor in the classroom. They pick two ideas to try, and everyone writes his or her thoughts anonymously on a card. At the end of the day, the teacher finds a note on her desk from a student who says he/she is sorry that she/he has been taking stuff.

_____ 2. Johnny comes into the room at the beginning of the school day in a foul mood. He knocks over books on Shirley's desk and makes rude comments to two other girls as he continues on to his seat. When the teacher starts instructing the class, he blurts out incorrect answers without regard to the class procedures. The teacher goes over to Johnny and privately suggests in a firm and even tone that he go outside and get a breath of air, think about his actions, and then come back in to restart his day appropriately.

_____ 3. When students in Mr. Jones's class misbehave in class, they are required to publicly apologize to either the teacher or the student, whichever is appropriate. Students comply with this by usually saying "I'm sorry" with little meaning.

_____ 4. Vickie is arguing about the assignment and when it is due. Mr. Jasim simply repeats back to her what he hears her saying and then simply repeats his deadline. He then asks someone in class to share with Vickie the process the class used to meet and agree on it.

_____ 5. Cheryl is in a second-grade class and constantly complains about doing her work. When the teacher asks to see her work, she always responds with "I can't do it," "I did my best," or "I really tried hard but I didn't know how to do it." She always seems to be trying to manipulate the teacher with her remarks and body language. The teacher responds, "Cheryl, I'm not going to accept any more of your excuses. If you don't understand something, you need to ask for help so you can finish the assignment. If you do not ask for help and the assignment remains uncompleted, you will have to miss recess or stay after school to show what you can do and get help to finish the assignment."

_____ 6. Mrs. Constraint has a procedure for any type of misconduct. She uses a wall chart that lists students' names. Alongside each name is an envelope or library pocket into which Mrs. Constraint places a colored card. That card may be green, yellow, orange, or red. The green card means you are conforming, the yellow card is a first warning card, the orange card is a second warning card, and the big red card means you are out of the classroom or your parents are called or some other scary consequence. When a student misbehaves, his or her card is turned over, and a list of consequences for each color is followed.

Answers: 1D, 2D, 3P, 4D, 5P, 6P

Planning for Upsets

When there is an upset, the goal is to build a climate of respect and a spirit of cooperation. The first step is to arrange for cooldown time for teacher and/or students.

- Breathing

- Grounding yourself in your body

- Looking at a poster in the room to remind you of your desire to respond rather than react

- Turning your back on the class for a moment

- Visualizing a calming scene

- Walking it off

- Referring to a plan you made for this kind of upset

- Remembering your reasoning for coming from a calm place

The second step is to directly communicate the problem in terms of the actual behaviors and facts that are seen. An example would be "The pens are dry and without caps."

The next step is to share your feelings in an honest way without being hurtful. An example would be "It bothers me when you are out of your seat and interacting with students." It is an option to write a note to share your feelings.

When you have moved through the initial emotions of the upset, you are ready for a short-term intervention. Plan to follow the intervention with an examination of what preventions need to be increased and what issues may need problem solving.

General Principles of Intervention

Before implementing any of the temporary intervention strategies described in this chapter, you should be familiar with some general principles of conducting those interventions (Figure 7.4):

1. *Use of body language*: Since body language is 80% of any message, your body language—both body posture and facial expression—should be neutral and nonthreatening. This does not mean that you don't have feelings but that you are intervening from your values and beliefs rather than your feelings. You should maintain direct eye contact with your students when making a request and expecting a response. You should make no eye contact when attention would serve to reinforce the negative behavior, as in techniques of low-level verbal limit setting or selective ignoring (described in next section).

2. *Use of spoken language*: When you speak, not only your body language but your tone of voice should be emotionally neutral in

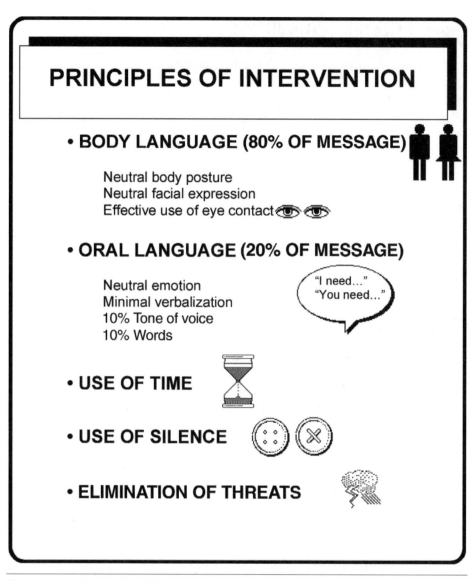

Figure 7.4. Principles of Intervention

order to give the same message—that you are operating from your beliefs not your feelings. Use as few words as possible, since the actual words convey only 10% of the message.

3. *Use of time*: When you begin an intervention, move deliberately, calmly, and slowly: "Ooze rather than pounce." Do not rush to get back to your lesson. The students need to get the message that your stopping to restructure is important, so take your time to send this message.

4. *Use of silence*: When students push your buttons, do not respond. Stay focused on the objective of your intervention. You do not want to become reactive and respond like a yo-yo to each one of their comments. Hit the pause button and wait.

5. *Elimination of threats*: Threats only escalate the problem to a power struggle and give the message that you are desperate.

Personal Commitment

How will you remember to stay neutral? How will you anchor your-self?

_____

_____

_____

_____

■ GUIDELINES FOR TEMPORARY INTERVENTION TECHNIQUES

When you have laid the groundwork to be able to shift out of upset into a responsive mode of discipline, you can intervene successfully. Temporary restructuring interventions can be used to help students build new programs for how they will behave in the classroom community. They establish a climate that promotes fairness and respect while maintaining standards for student behavior. These are proactive strategies resulting from beliefs.

 Benefits of Temporary Interventions

- Maintain a brain-compatible environment
- Support respectful relationships
- Uphold group agreements

The rest of this chapter describes some specific temporary interventions, with guidelines on how and when to use them.

Verbal Limit Setting and "Excuse Me" Technique

Classroom Connection

In Lucy Stein's 11th-grade English class, there was a problem with three girls talking and passing notes to each other. One of the girls, Patty, was also out of her seat quite often and delivering notes for her friends Mina and Yolanda. In the past, Lucy had oscillated between ignoring this kind of behavior because of not wanting to disrupt the class with interventions and repeatedly telling the girls to stop talking. This year she had committed to a clearer plan for interventions.

The first time she noticed the girls talking at an inappropriate time, she said, "Everyone's focused on page 32 and our discussion of the theme of this piece." When the talking set in again, Lucy said, "I need everyone's attention to how the characters are woven into the theme of this story." Later that day, Lucy has a chance to reflect on how she could use seating, proximity, target talk, class meeting discussion, and building more of a relationship with these three girls to decrease her need for verbal limit setting. She decided to change the seating arrangement to get Patty closer to the front of the class where she couldn't see her girlfriends. She also made an attempt to get to know Patty better by talking with her before class a few times a week. She put the topic of "talking during class" on the class meeting agenda to include the group in brainstorming the question "When would be appropriate talking times?"

Personal Connection

How do you feel when students are talking while you or another student is talking?

_____

_____

_____

When to Use Verbal Limit Setting: Verbal limit setting can be used when, after receiving directions, students are

- Resisting work
- Daydreaming
- Talking
- Writing notes
- Wandering in the classroom
- Delaying

Verbal limit setting involves stating the appropriate behavior to the student or students who are behaving inappropriately by violating classroom agreements or procedures. This message is delivered with a neutral body posture and tone of voice. The student's name is not used. To use this technique, the teacher first decides which level of verbal limit setting is appropriate: the question, which is the least assertive; the hint; or the "I message," which is the most assertive. Often teachers will start with the question format, then use the hint, and finally, if necessary, use the "I message."

Formats for Verbal Limit Setting

● Question: "Everyone has their math book open?" (stated declaratively with questioning intonation).

● Hint: "Everyone should be in their seat with their math book open" (stated with globally inclusive phrasing).

● Excuse Me: "Excuse me Carol, we can't hear you because someone else is speaking."

● I Message: "I [or 'We'] need everyone to open your math book" (stronger, more assertive than question or hint; stated with "I/We need" or "I/We want").

Examples of Questions, by Grade Level

1. Elementary

   • "The math group has its area cleaned up?"
   • "All books are back on the shelf?"
   • "Our chair legs are all flat on the floor?"

2. Secondary

   • "Everyone in the back of the room is ready to begin?"
   • "Everyone has their book out?"
   • "We're ready for the test?"

Note that questions should be prompts, not real questions. A common mistake is to put them in grammatical question form: for example, "Are we ready for the test?" But if they are delivered in this way, they are likely to get answered! Instead, put them in a declarative form and just give them a questioning tone.

 Examples of Hints, by Grade Level

1. Elementary

   - "Everyone should be seated and ready for lunch."
   - "All chairs should be flat on the floor."
   - "Everyone has their pencil down and their eyes up here."

2. Secondary
   - "Everything should be off your desks."
   - "Everyone should be seated and ready for the discussion."
   - "All students have their eyes on their own paper."

 Examples of "I" Messages, by Grade Level

1. Elementary

   - "We want everyone to have the floor under their desk cleaned up."
   - "I need the room quiet so I can hear Sue read."
   - "We want the math group to work silently."

2. Secondary

   - "I need the students in the back of the room to look up here."
   - "We want your eyes on your own paper during this test."
   - "I need everyone to sit down."

Key Criteria for Verbal Limit Setting

- Body Language

    – Bland, calm facial expression

    – Direct, unbroken eye contact

    – Neutral, audible tone of voice

    – Body directly facing student(s)

- Minimal Verbalization

    – Omit student's name

    – Limit language to verbal limit setting format

- Delivery

    – Tell student(s) what to do

    – State acceptable behaviors

✓ Checking My Understanding

Choose the best example from each of the two choices below.
Behavioral Situation: Class not ready.

1. Question:

    a) Are your books and materials ready yet?

    b) Everyone's got their books and materials ready?

2. Hint:

    a) You all have your books and materials ready.

    b) Everyone has got their books and materials out?

3. "I" message:

    a) We need to have all books and materials ready.

    b) I think everyone needs their books and materials ready.

Answers: b, a, a

The "Excuse Me" technique is a still higher level of verbal limit setting that is kinesthetic as well. It is often helpful to use to break a pattern of interrupting: for example, when students are sharing or reporting and you want to focus attention on the student who is speaking in turn versus students who might be speaking out of turn. Suppose that one student is asking a question or responding and two or three others are whispering to each other. The teacher says, "Excuse me, Kent, I can't hear your question," and then, in a neutral tone to the whole group, "Class, who is speaking now? Point to [or 'look at'] the person who is speaking." The class says, "Kent" and looks at Kent or points. The teacher then says, "Excuse us, Kent, we forgot our agreements. Let's try again."

Make sure this technique is used with care. It should be delivered in a respectful way that does not feel threatening or punitive.

☀ Personal Commitment

Pick one of the following situations or think up one of your own:

1. Three students are talking in the back of the room instead of doing their math.

2. Class is watching students going by outside the classroom window.

3. Class is not ready to begin lesson (books and other materials are not out).

4. Students are misusing the art supplies at the art center.

5. Students are possibly cheating during quiz.

6. Three students are not listening to teacher's directions.

7. A small group of students don't have their work area cleaned up.

8. Part of the class is distracted by students working in back of the classroom.

Write three types of verbal limit setting statements for a behavioral situation.

Behavioral situation:

_____

_____

Question:

_____

_____

Hint:

_____

_____

"I" message:

_____

_____

How would you use the "Excuse Me" technique respectfully in this situation?

_____

_____

_____

_____

Selective Listening

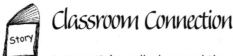 Classroom Connection

As Lucy Stein walked around the classroom, Thomas called out, "My paper is finished." Lucy ignored Thomas by not looking at him or responding. She said to another student, "Lisa, you're right on target with responsibility. When you finished, you set your paper on the corner of your desk and began your reading assignment." When Thomas was quiet and on task, Lucy went to his desk and delivered the same type of positive reinforcement.

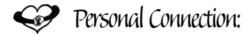 Personal Connection:

For which behaviors do you want to withhold reinforcement?

_____

_____

_____

When to Use Selective Listening:

1. Any attempts to manipulate the teacher (make teacher give up his or her agenda and attend to student's agenda)

   - Calling out to teacher for help
   - Following the teacher around classroom
   - Making attention-getting comments or noises so teacher will comment
   - Tattling in order to get the teacher to do something to another student

2. Dependent, submissive conformity

   - Hanging onto teacher's arm
   - Trying to get teacher to make decision for student
   - Trying to get teacher to do the hard problem by complaining, "I don't know how to" or "I can't do this"

3. Resistant behavior or comments

   - "I won't do this!"
   - "I don't give a darn!"
   - "You can't make me!"
   - Taking extra time to get into class and sit down in hopes of being confronted by teacher

With the intervention of selective listening, you purposefully and consistently ignore behaviors that you determine to be manipulative. In other words, you refrain from reinforcing the behaviors that you wish would disappear. The students should be aware that this technique will be used, and role plays can be used to demonstrate and practice. Lucy's class discussed this early in the year. It took Lucy's consistency for them to see over time that certain expectations would be upheld and that inappropriate behaviors would be consistently ignored.

When Not to Use Selective Listening:

1. For behavior that cannot be tolerated temporarily (e.g., physical aggression, verbal abuse, safety issues)

2. For behavior that is being imitated by the other students beyond a tolerable level

3. For behaviors that have their own built-in reinforcer (e.g., cheating, stealing, eating, drugs)

4. For behaviors where escalation cannot be permitted (e.g., student is calling out, then begins to scream, then cry, then fall on the floor and crawl around the room)

Key Criteria for Selective Listening

● Teacher must be sole source of reinforcement.

● Students should be prepared to have the teacher ignore them when they show certain behaviors. Model how selective listening will look when used and role-play as a demonstration. (The younger the students, the more modeling they will need.)

● Behavior is likely to get worse before it gets better.

● Effects of selective listening are gradual.

● Behavior must be temporarily tolerable.

● Combine with positive reinforcement.

Checking My Understanding

Place a check mark by the behaviors where it would be appropriate to use selective listening.

_____ 1. Susie frequently tells the teacher what other students are doing wrong.

_____ 2. Beth taps her pencil nervously on the desk while she works.

_____ 3. Jim climbs the 20-foot fence to leave the school grounds.

_____ 4. Bill reminds the teacher that he has finished his work and deserves a check mark.

_____ 5. Theresa rarely turns in her homework on time.

_____ 6. Jake constantly complains about his other teachers.

_____ 7. Jim leaves the campus during class time.

_____ 8. Bill reminds the teacher that his parent is on the school board and the teacher better have interesting lessons.

Answers:

1. Yes.

2. Because this is done nervously without intent, use proximity.

3. Unacceptable behavior is never ignored.

4. Yes, if in the context where an established procedure is being ignored.

5. Problem-solve with this student.

6. May use selective listening or actively listen to Jake's feelings.

7. Unacceptable behavior is never ignored.

8. Ignore at this time and decide if there should be a conversation later.

Personal Commitment

List the behaviors you will purposely ignore as an effective way of extinguishing manipulative behavior. Also indicate how and when you will positively reinforce the student.

_____

_____

_____

The Broken Record

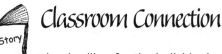

Classroom Connection

The deadline for the individual reports is approaching in Lucy Stein's 11th-grade social studies class. The students are begging for an extra week. The due date was a group decision, and Lucy has given a segment of the paper as homework to support the students in chunking the assignment over time. She has also made herself available to help during extended office hours. She will not change the due date. As the class pesters her and chants "One more week," she calmly states, *"The paper is due on Friday."* They continue chanting, but she remains solidly focused and repeats, *"The paper is due on Friday."* A few students try to keep the chant going, and she says the third time, *"The paper is due on Friday."* After a few moments of silence, she says, *"Turn to page 76 and do the practice task for our transition today."*

❤ Personal Connection

How do you stay focused and respond from your beliefs?

_____

_____

_____

When to Use the Broken Record Technique: This technique can be used in specific private interactions with individual students when they

● Delay in owning responsibility for their behavior

● Resist responding to a request

● Persist in responding inappropriately to teacher directives or class procedures

For the whole class, it can be used when the teacher is committed to something.

The broken record technique is a proactive technique from assertiveness training adapted to meet the needs of the brain-compatible classroom. To use it, the teacher keeps stating again and again what he or she wants, sounding like a broken or stuck record. Often selective listening is used first; then, if it fails, broken record may be appropriate. It gives the message that the teacher is firm and consistent with respectful "absence of threat." The teacher often has to think through whether the student understands the prerequisites of the situation before using this intervention.

Here is how the technique works:

1. Make your "statement of want."

2. Respond to student comments by repeating your statement of want neutrally.

3. Repeat a maximum of three times.

4. Respond with silence and wait for conformity.

One caution: When a student feels backed into a corner and publicly reprimanded or confronted, this technique will escalate to a power struggle, and although you may win the battle, your victory may weaken the relationship you have established with the student. Think about how you would feel if a workshop leader did this to you in a training session. Sometimes it can be very effective, but at times it will create a disaster. The key ingredient is respect and privacy of the individual.

Examples of Use of the Broken Record Technique

Situation: A student is out of his seat.

> **Teacher (privately to student):** Joe, you need to be in your seat.
>
> **Student:** My pencil keeps breaking.
>
> **Teacher:** You need to be in your seat.
>
> **Student:** I needed to tell Bob something.
>
> **Teacher:** You need to be in your seat.

Note that the teacher does not respond to the content of what the student says. The body language and tone of voice of the teacher is critical.

Situation: A student is trying to engage the teacher in conversation so he won't have to do the assignment.

> **Paul:** Hey, Mr. Roberts, what did you think of the Giants game Sunday?
>
> **Teacher:** I'll chat with you about it after class. It's time for the writing assignment now.
>
> **Paul:** I just wanted to know whether you thought that call at third was a fair call.
>
> **Teacher:** I'll chat with you about it after class. It's time for the writing assignment now.
>
> **Paul:** You're tight, Teach!

Here the teacher uses the technique in such a way as to be responsive to the student's request while still staying focused on the task at hand.

Key Criteria for the Broken Record Technique

- Ignore attempts to manipulate; free yourself from power struggle.
- Remain calm, focused, and respectful.
- Limit response to broken record format (not content).
- De-escalate and avoid confronting.
- Say your statement no more than three times.

✓ Checking My Understanding

Find the positive example for each choice of teacher statements.

A student is creating a drawing for a rally.

Teacher:

a) Susan, you need to be working on the transition task.

b) Susan, why are you continuing to draw?

Student: We need this drawing for our noon rally.

Teacher:

a) You know the procedure.

b) I understand, but you need to be working on the transition task.

Student: It will only take another minute and then I'll get started.

Teacher:

a) I understand, but you need to be working on the transition task.

b) You can finish your drawing later.

Answers: a, b, a

♡ Personal Commitment

Select one of the behavioral situations as a practice for using the broken record technique.

a) A student is tattling after recess and not standing in line with the rest of the class as expected.

b) A student delays starting the daily transition task and gives excuses instead.

c) A student is misusing art or lab supplies and giving excuses to the teacher.

d) A student is not following the teacher's request and is giving excuses as to why.

e) A student is asking the teacher digressing questions in an apparent attempt to delay the teacher from handing out an exam.

Then supply the following:

1. Behavioral situation:

_____

_____

2. Teacher's "statement of want":

_____

_____

3. Student comment:

_____

_____

4. Teacher statement of want repeated:

_____

_____

5. Student comment:

_____

_____

6. Teacher statement of want repeated:

_____

_____

7. Student comment:
(Teacher responds with silence and waits for conformity.)

_____

_____

_____

Altering the Setting

When to Use Altering the Setting: Altering the setting is an inexpensive strategy to use for the following:

- A student is talking or a class is falling apart

- A student is disturbing another student or a class is drifting into space

- A student is distracted by his or her environment or a class is brain dead

- A student is too far away from the teacher or a class is sleepy/bored

- A student is causing a general class disruption while the teacher is teaching

In this intervention, the teacher identifies and alters events that seem to stimulate undesirable behavior. This may involve moving furniture or changing the mode of instruction, place of instruction, or materials. For example, a teacher altered the setting one day when her students were reading out loud from the text and making note of key words. They were bored by this activity, and many of them were drifting. She decided to have them break into groups and read the text, picking out key words as they went for a group list.

 ## Examples of Altering the Setting

- Taking the whole class outside for a reading activity

- Moving desks around, having students all come stand around overhead

- Changing the materials students are using

- Varying the classroom routine (e.g., by going for a walk or changing the agenda)

- Varying the method of instruction (e.g., changing from direct instruction to putting students into small groups for discussion [divide and conquer]

Once you decide to alter the setting, you should tell the class neutrally and without blame:

- "Something's amiss today. Let's try coming up here and standing around the overhead to finish this lesson, then recording the key points with a partner."

- "Let's switch gears and try and get back on track. Everyone leave your books on your desks and let's move outside for 10 minutes and get some fresh air while we are finishing up this lesson."

Removal Procedures

Classroom Connection

One day in Lucy Stein's class, Yolanda was passing a note to Mina. Lucy had already tried a hint and then an "I message" to focus on the class discussion of the material. She had moved close to Mina and was standing in the area. When the note went by, she calmly put out her hand and gently took the note. After 3 minutes, she gave the note back to Yolanda with a gentle, positive glance. Yolanda stuck the note in her bag.

When to Use Removal Procedures: Removal procedures should be used when students are doing the following:

- Playing
- Disturbing a group activity
- Misusing materials
- Abusing privileges of an activity

In this intervention, a teacher removes a student or materials that are distracting from the lesson. The removal lasts 2 to 3 minutes, and then an opportunity is given for the student to act appropriately or for the materials to be used appropriately. The teacher looks at the student in a way that conveys positive expectation. This technique can be considered after verbal limit setting and proximity have been tried. The teacher is objective and uses a gentle neutral approach.

Examples of Removal for Grades K–12

- Taking materials away from a student who is not using them correctly.

- Sending students back to their desks when they are disturbing a group or area.

The following are examples of removal that can be used for grades K-3:

- Pulling a chair back when a student is talking or not attending in a group setting

- Pulling a chair back when student is disturbing others in a group

Centering Time

Centering time can be used for any serious unacceptable disruptive behavior, such as hitting or name calling. The teacher facilitates the student's isolating of him- or herself to eliminate dangerous or severely disruptive behavior. Procedures are developed for centering time, with options of places to go, things to do, and ways to track the time. This is a strategy to teach students anger management and to give them an opportunity to get over an upset and go back to thinking clearly.

Examples of Format Options for Centering Time

1. Preplan and set up an area with timer or egg timer in an unstimulating area of room. Have a picture of the brain in the area.

2. Have a spot set up with headphones where student can listen to classical music for calming.

3. In lower grades, the centering spot can have a tent to climb into or a name, such as "Australia."

4. Decide on a nonverbal signal to suggest that the student take some centering time. You may need to physically escort the student to the centering spot if he or she is too upset.

5. Avoid verbal interactions other than acknowledging feelings.

6. Plan positive reinforcement 10 to 15 seconds after student returns from centering time and begins appropriate task.

■ CRISIS INTERVENTION

Classroom Connection

Reggie was a student who occasionally went beyond the acceptable limits of the classroom. He began poking his pencil into the head and back of the student in front of him. This is an abusive and dangerous act, which creates an unsafe environment for learning. It calls for immediate crisis intervention. After several rounds of removing the pencil and one centering time, Lucy Stein placed Reggie's seat where he could not poke people. A problem-solving session was planned for working with Reggie to get a clear focus and a plan for eliminating his aggressive behavior.

As stated earlier, crisis intervention is an intervention used during a fight, harassment, taunting, or any kind of a struggle between students that is out of control, where anger is running the situation and physical or psychological harm is imminent. It should be used as follows:

● Only if preventive strategies are exhausted and after all other interventions have failed

● Only for extremely unacceptable behavior

● Sparingly and infrequently

It should be preplanned proactively with an objective resource person.

What to do in a crisis? It can be helpful to anticipate the common unacceptable behaviors and have a basic plan of action for dealing with them. Your district's student conduct policy and your state's education code can help clarify some of the gray areas.

In a crisis, it is extremely important to give the message that the teacher, as leader in the classroom, has personal power and is in charge. Once we publicly go outside of the classroom for help with a behavior problem—for example, by sending a child to the office—we are giving the message that we have lost or given away our power and that we are not in charge. (Seeking private guidance or counsel from an administrator, resource person, counselor, or peer is not included.)

In many cases, a crisis can be dealt with solely by the teacher, without recourse to outside help.

Examples of Crisis Strategies Contained Inside the Classroom

● Move the student to a different seat.

- Impose a content-equivalent consequence: Have the student reverse damage done, substituting use for abuse of property and restoring the environment to its previous condition (e.g., cleaning a desk that he or she wrote on).

- Employ overcorrection: Have the student restore what was damaged to a better condition than it was in before it was damaged (e.g., if the student wrote on one desk, have him or her clean all desks).

- Detain the student for a problem-solving conversation after school. Although detention used as a punishment tends to be ineffective in producing behavior change, detention used for collaborative problem solving can be very effective.

However, there are some exceptional times when we should enlist outside help, such as an administrator, parents, or another teacher.

Examples of Crisis Strategies That Involve Going Outside the Classroom

- Send the student to the office when he or she engages in more serious threatening behaviors or behaviors that are illegal or violate educational codes (e.g., fights, weapons, or drugs).

- Phone the student's home.

- Send a note home.

- Give the student a time-out in a peer teacher's classroom (sometimes necessary when the teacher needs to downshift).

- For a student fight:

  1. Send three or four bystanders for specific help.

  2. Move closer and ask who is losing the fight.

  3. Loudly address the losing student: "Fighting is against the rules. Move away now."

  4. Move in and deal with other student (hopefully, help is now arriving).

  5. If none of this works, have a loud distracting sound prepared (Mendler, 1997).

Such interventions can be followed by a solution-focused problem-solving session.

Summary of Temporary Interventions

- When your preventive strategies are working successfully, interventions can be reduced to less than 2% of daily interactions with students.

- Temporary interventions are restructuring techniques to use when there is an upset in the classroom and either the teacher or the student is not thinking clearly.

- Interventions are used to turn inappropriate behavior into appropriate behavior temporarily with the least amount of attention, time, energy, or disruption of class time.

- Teachers can maintain a leadership role when they avoid negative, blaming interpretations or stories that personalize student motivation.

- Interventions establish a climate that promotes fairness and respect while maintaining standards for student behavior.

- Interventions are proactive strategies resulting from the teacher's beliefs.

NOTE

1. This exercise was developed with Linda Smith, Coordinator of Special Projects for Hollister Elementary School District.

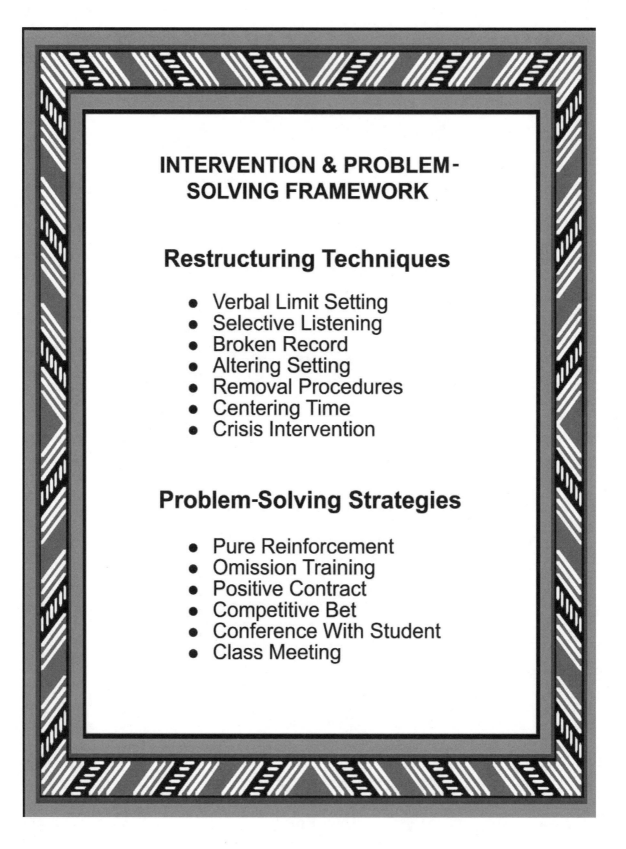

INTERVENTION & PROBLEM-SOLVING FRAMEWORK

Restructuring Techniques

- Verbal Limit Setting
- Selective Listening
- Broken Record
- Altering Setting
- Removal Procedures
- Centering Time
- Crisis Intervention

Problem-Solving Strategies

- Pure Reinforcement
- Omission Training
- Positive Contract
- Competitive Bet
- Conference With Student
- Class Meeting

Solution-Focused, Problem-Solving Strategies 8

$\sim$

The benefits gained from learning how to manage conflict constructively far [outweigh] the costs of learning time lost by students being upset and angry. . . . One of the soundest investments educators and students can make in classroom and school productivity is teaching how to manage conflict constructively.

David Johnson and Roger Johnson, *Teaching Students to Be Peacemakers*

$\sim$

In recent workshops where large groups of teachers were asked to choose whether they would prefer to work with teachers who were exactly like them or with teachers who were varied and different, over 90% chose to work in teams of people who had styles different from their own. What they were in fact choosing was conflict. Conflict is inherent in all human interactions, personally, professionally, nationally, and internationally, where people hold differing beliefs, backgrounds, and standards for behavior.

Problem solving is an ongoing and essential element in all human relationships as long as individual differences exist. Cooperative teamwork among individuals who hold different standards, beliefs, and cultures will require leaders who are able to solve problems in a collaborative and collegial spirit in the classroom; in their neighborhoods, cities, states, and nations; and in the world at large.

In this final chapter, we will explore a "no-blame," solution-focused conflict resolution approach that can be used in three types of problem solving (we have named them to resemble an orchestra because effective leaders are literally orchestrating a process for decision making and student responsibility):

1. Solo: The teacher problem-solves intrapersonally and then seeks counsel from one or more objective colleagues to affirm and guide her plan of action regarding an individual student.

2. Duet: The teacher decides to meet with that student to collaborate with him or her, using a "no-blame" problem-solving model for resolving conflicts.

3. Ensemble: The teacher facilitates problem solving with a small group or the entire class in a class meeting using the brainstorming conflict resolution model.

By the end of this chapter, you will be able to do the following:

● Use a process model for problem solving with two other colleagues at your site.

● Problem-solve for a target student using a conflict resolution model.

● Use a solution-focused, "no-blame" problem-solving model for conferencing with that target student.

● Facilitate class meetings to problem-solve group upsets.

Initially, the teacher assumes the role of leader and facilitator. The goal is to model effective problem solving and then teach the students to assume this role and to initiate and use proactive problem solving to resolve personal and group conflicts.

Classroom Connection

The students in Carol Rasul's history class were quietly working in groups around the classroom on presentations about the underlying versus the immediate causes of various wars that different groups had chosen. Some were working on skits, some on videos, some on murals and verbal presentations; one group was out in the patio area creating a song. Carol was sitting with the group working on the murals and was guiding them in their thinking by asking them questions. Suddenly, above the working hum in the classroom, came two voices raised in anger from the video-recording group. Carol looked up to see Rachel and Reuben, both students known for angry outbursts, having a tug of war with the videotape in the camcorder that their group was using. Carol stood quietly, moved in their direction, looked at them firmly and assertively said, "Rachel, Reuben, put the tape back in the camcorder." Reuben promptly relinquished his hold on Rachel and the tape. Rachel lifted the tape over her head and hurled it to the floor, screaming, "This is the most boring group I've worked with, they're unfair, they're uncreative, and they hate me, and I hate this tape." The tape lay on the floor in pieces. Carol felt the blood rush to her head, her muscles tighten, her body tense. She was angry, and her first impulse was to strike out and send Rachel to the office. Instead, in a very strained voice she asked Reuben and Rachel to sit at opposite ends of a discussion table that was behind the video group. "I'm too upset to talk to you now. Wait here until we are all thinking clearly again and can talk rationally about this!" She then went back to the mural group she had been guiding. As she walked, she took a few deep breaths and reminded herself of Rachel's struggles with anger and her lack of self-esteem and impulse control. Instead of thinking of her as aggressive and difficult, she thought of her as needy and not knowing how to get her needs met. She also thought about how she and Reuben should never have been in the same group. All of the prevention ideas flooded her mind as she searched for how she would problem-solve with them and how she would model for the class a nonviolent model of responding to frustration.

More than 5 minutes passed before Carol was ready to return to Rachel and Reuben. As she moved around the classroom, she gave some "target talk" to the group that was nearby. "You were very focused on your work during the upset with Rachel and Ruben. Because you had self-control and ignored them, they were able to calm down sooner. How did you keep your focus?" One of the team replied, "We just kept remembering what you taught us about the brain being unable to think when we are upset." "Great," said Carol, "that helps me think more positively too."

She then approached Rachel and Ruben. "Reuben, go ahead and return to your group, and we can talk after Rachel and I have had a chance to talk."

Turning toward Rachel, she said, "What happened?" "Nothin'," Rachel said, looking away from her teacher. In a soft voice, with a private tone, Carol said, "Well, this is what it looked like, you and Reuben were in a tug of war over the tape, and then the anger got in the way and you threw the tape on the floor and broke it. Now the group can't complete their project without the tape."

"The group was being difficult, and Reuben wouldn't let me rewind the tape and start over," Rachel sidetracked and blamed. Carol stayed focused on the observable facts and repeated the problem. "Okay. That's what the group and Reuben did, and I'll be talking with him in a moment. Let's focus on what you could have done differently." Rachel looked away sullenly but acted resigned to the situation. After a brief pause, she said, "I could have made a request or taken some time away from the group to pull myself together or put our group's name up on the board for you to come and facilitate our conflict."

"Right, so we've got two problems. First, the videotape is broken and your group can't work without it. Second, the anger took over and interfered with other students' working, right?" Rachel nodded.

"Let's tackle one problem at a time. What can we do about the broken tape?"

"I could get it fixed."

"Okay, so you have one idea, are there any other solutions?"

"I could take it to a video store and have them transfer it to a new tape or ask one of the kids in the computer photo class to help me." The ideas were coming more quickly as Rachel felt free to solve the problem.

"Do you have any more ideas, Rachel?"

"No."

Carol summed up the three ideas and asked Rachel which one she thought would work best. Rachel concluded that she would take the tape to the video store first and see what it would cost to have it transferred and spliced.

Carol then asked, "How do you want to handle sharing this with your folks? Remember that one of our classroom agreements is that when equipment is broken the student's parents are informed."

Rachel replied, "Well, I'll talk to them when I get home. Shall I have them call you or are you going to call them?"

Carol smiled and said, "Which would you prefer?"

"If you call them after 8:00 p.m." Rachel smiled faintly.

"Okay, that still leaves the problem of the angry outburst. Let's talk about that one tomorrow after you've had time to think tonight about a plan for how you are going to manage the anger in the future."

(Story to be continued)

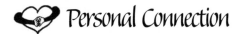 Personal Connection

What decisions and choices did Carol make?

_____

_____

What did Carol do to uphold the four dimensions of self-esteem for herself, Reuben, Rachel, and the class?

	Security	Connectedness	Competence	Power
Teacher				
Reuben				
Rachel				
Class				

You already know that the prevention strategies need to be integrated smoothly before problem solving, as they form the foundation for the solution. Carol clearly had a bonded relationship with Rachel and Reuben and knew how to use her body language to send a firm, neutral message. The rest of the class had procedures in place and were able to manage themselves during the upset. If Rachel and Reuben had felt blamed, they would have been defensive, and possibly more aggression would have resulted. This was defused by the teacher's calm, neutral, nonjudgmental approach. So let's begin exploring the "no-blame" thinking that is the core of successful solution-focused problem solving.

RETHINKING PROBLEM SOLVING FOR SOLUTIONS WITHOUT BLAME ■

൭

*Blaming never helps. When you plant lettuce
if it does not grow well, you don't blame the lettuce.*

Thich Nhat Hanh, *Peace Is in Every Step*

൭

Classroom Connection

(The story continues . . .)

On the following day, Carol met with Rachel during her prep period after clearing this with the other teacher. Rachel missed 15 minutes of another class to do this, but it was better than her spending time in the counselor's or vice-principal's office where the teacher would not have been a participant in the solution. Carol asked Rachel if she could recall a time when she had felt frustrated and angry and had been able to use her words rather than let the anger take over her whole body. Rachel said that she couldn't remember. Carol probed by asking her about the last time she had worked with a group on a project. Rachel recalled that she had been easier with the group's decisions and had participated more and helped everyone reach consensus when they disagreed but thought that it was because the group members were more patient. Carol asked her how she stayed focused on the solutions in the other group and asked her how she might try that in any group. Rachel wasn't sure she could do it in another group but agreed to try. Carol asked her what she could do if "anger took her by surprise." They brainstormed some ideas: Count to 10; walk over to the door and breathe, then walk back; go to her own desk and write or draw her feelings; go to the conflict resolution table and fill out a form; tell the group she needed a break. Carol asked Rachel which of these ideas she thought might really work for her. Rachel picked leaving the group and going to her desk or walking to the door and breathing. After school that day, Carol wrote Rachel a note:

Dear Rachel,

I really admired your willingness to problem-solve ideas for working better in groups. You stuck with it, even when it was tough. I hope you will remember the times that you have been in charge of yourself when you worked in groups and overcome the feelings to let the anger loose on the group. I want you to try what worked for you before, tomorrow when you finish the video project. I look forward to your sharing how it went for you with your new strategies.

Ms. Rasul[1]

❤ Personal Connection

What was unique about the problem solving between Carol and Rachel in this part of the story?

_____

_____

_____

Some of the thinking currently popularized in the media encourages us to see our students as people who are lacking, weak, or deficient in some way. This kind of thinking leads us to believe that we should explore their past, fix their weaknesses, and mediate or remediate their deficits. Many teachers who begin to internalize this "pop psychology" approach are feeling that they need to give more and more and are feeling increasingly overwhelmed and hopeless. The only viable solution seems to be to do more or to give up or hang on until retirement. This is a dreadful way to live a life as a caring professional.

Carol Rasul had done that in the past, but now she was committed to working with this challenging group of sophomores differently. She realized that much of what happened to them in their lives was outside her circle of influence or theirs. So she focused on the observable behaviors of Rachel and Reuben that were within her circle of influence, her classroom. Many teachers would have kicked Rachel out of class. But because Carol thought differently about Rachel's behavior, she was able to keep her within the community of learners rather than isolating her once again. She recalled from the self-esteem chapter how important a sense of connection and a sense of power are during adolescence. Her direct, firm, caring, solution-focused approach invited Rachel to participate in finding a solution and modeled for the rest of the class "conflict resolution" in action. Rachel was invited to be a citizen in the classroom rather than a tourist.

Many conflict resolution models such as those of pop psychology are based on finding fault or blame. They tend to have us either blame ourselves for not doing more or blame others such as the family or the system or the school. These models tend to recycle doom and gloom and don't get us very far along the path to a solution. We are spending too much time trying to "figure out" what is wrong and why and who is at fault. It is not a particularly helpful way of thinking because you, I, and 500 psychologists will never agree on who is to blame or why a particular child—or adult, for that matter—is doing what he or she is doing. And even if we did "figure it all out," we would have lost all our focus on the solution. Trying to ascribe motivation to others' behavior is a dangerous and costly game. It colors our thinking. If our interpretation is negative, it leads us to take negative action, which almost always destroys the relationship.

Although insight and understanding promote empathy and caring, they rarely change behavior.

There is another way to think about the "problem" that will actually free us up to solve it and avoid the blame. It is called the "no-blame" approach. It is quite simple: "The problem is the problem." Anger is the problem, aggression is the problem, resistance is the problem, and "it," the problem, has effects on the student, child, parent, and/or teacher and keeps him or her from acting in a way that is helpful and solution focused. Did you notice how Carol did not label Rachel with the adjective *angry* but rather talked about the noun *anger* as something outside her as a person? This new way of thinking has been referred to as the narrative model, the competency-based model, or the solution-focused brief therapy model. This way of rethinking is freeing up therapists, counselors, teachers, and parents to stop labeling everyone and instead focus on solutions that will be helpful. Thinking differently means looking beyond the negative behaviors and noticing times when the negative behaviors are not dominating the student. It also means speaking differently: "The anger outburst is in control again, Jaime, how can you take over now?" rather than "Jaime, you're having a temper outburst again." This new way of thinking dissolves resistance and opens the door for information to reach students. The psychologist Bradford Keeney says that "diagnoses are like barbed wire fences" in that the labels we often place on people keep them "stuck" (quoted in Metcalf, 1995, p. 4). Many of us feel that labels are for jelly jars, and all of us know that discouraging labels will discourage possibilities. When no one is to blame and no one is labeled, everyone's task is simply to solve the problem, and the problem becomes the enemy for everyone— parents, teachers, and students. Everyone is freed up to join forces and rally together to defeat "the problem" (Zimmerman & Dickerson, 1996)!

ELEMENTS OF SOLUTION-FOCUSED PROBLEM SOLVING

Solution-focused problem solving has several important elements:

- Focusing on the solution
- Agreeing on the goal
- Agreeing on what maintains the problem
- Identifying exceptions to the problem
- Agreeing on a single task

The story that opens this chapter illustrates how all these elements of solution-focused problem solving might be used in a particular situation.

Examples of Use of the Elements of Solution-Focused Problem Solving

- *Focus on the Solution*: Carol helped the individual (Rachel) see what she needed to do to change the pattern rather than focusing on how others (Reuben, the group) needed to change. Notice that Carol's questions were simple, no-blame questions. She never asked Rachel why she threw the tape or why she got angry. "Why" questions tend to focus on the problem, provide an arena for excuses, and lead away from solutions. She only focused on how to recover from the upset and how to prevent it from happening again.

- *Agree on the Goal*: Using brainstorming and the no-blame approach, both teacher and student could agree on the goal, which was to repair or replace the tape. The focus is on how to make amends and reparation for the upset and on how to escape being at the effect of "the problem"—in this case, "the anger."

- *Agree on What Maintains the Problem*: Rachel was easily guided to reflect on how anger got triggered and to think about how to avoid and escape the problem of anger the next time, because without blame, resistance and defensiveness are less likely to get in the way.

- *Identify Exceptions to the Problem*: When the teacher helped Rachel identify times when she was able to work cooperatively with a group and have control over her frustrations, Rachel could access her strengths. Those exceptions provide clues for solutions/ empowerment.

- *Agree on a Single Task*: Carol focused on one task at a time and on only one task for Rachel to accomplish. The rule of thumb here is to never ask anyone to do something that he or she has never done before because the ability to do the task must be based on a prior success, even if that success is only a successive approximation. (Adapted from Metcalf, 1995)

Benefits of Solution-Focused Problem Solving

- Produces paradigm shifts
- Students become responsible for the solution
- Without blame, resistance is reduced
- Teacher and student model conflict resolution
- Takes less effort than trying to figure out motivations

SOLO PROBLEM SOLVING   ■

ᔆ

There is nothing new under the sun. So when faced with a problem it is best not to wait for inspiration. Chances are the solution lies not in new ideas, but in a new look at an old one.

Albert Einstein

ᔆ

In solo problem solving, the teacher problem-solves intrapersonally regarding an individual student and then seeks counsel from an objective colleague or two to help assess which prevention strategies are working and to create, on the basis of that assessment, a plan of action for working with that student.

Classroom Connection

Donyal was a new student in Kathie Houseman and Lee Belvedere's fourth-grade classroom. The two teachers shared a teaching assignment: one taught in the morning and one in the afternoon. Donyal had been transferred from another school; this was his fifth transfer in 4 years. He had never completed an assignment and rarely even started one. When the principal approached the two teachers about Donyal, they agreed to accept this challenging student as an opportunity to apply what they were learning in their staff development program about solution-focused problem solving. They would use their district coach 1 day a week for support. The rest of their class was very self-directed, and things were running smoothly. They had decided not to read his "cumulative" folder so as not to have negative thinking color their actions. The prevailing story was that Donyal was resistant and had a very disrupted home life, with divorced parents and no consistent ties.

Kathie and Lee both knew that the rule of thumb for "resistance" was to provide choice and avoid confrontations, and they committed to planning with that in mind. They met with Donyal and his mother before school the first morning and invited Donyal to simply observe and take notes the first few days on what he saw other students doing, what he liked about the classroom, and what he didn't like. They gave him a journal in which to keep his notes. "You are welcome to participate in any of the activities that interest you. Our class is divided into tribes, and we have included you in one we think you will like. We will meet with you again at the end of the week to see how it is going." Donyal was a good observer but made no notes in his journal. He entered into some of the "Personal Activity Games" in small groups and was interested in the math manipulatives and any opportunity to "play with stuff." He was great at PE but did not return to the classroom after recess; rather, he stayed out to play with the tetherballs. The challenge was on!

Lee taught in the mornings and was responsible for the language arts and PE *and personal activity time. Donyal observed and wandered around the room while other students worked on writing stories, reading stories, or meeting with their teacher. He listened to the stories and would join in the skill groups that were teacher directed, but he did no writing. In the afternoons, he was very engaged in the math lessons and the math manipulatives with Kathie, seemed to understand the concepts, and would help record answers on the overhead or whiteboard, but again no paper-and-pencil recording was happening. Science and social studies was pretty much the same. He engaged in teacher-directed or group-directed activities but did no paper-and-pencil work other than illustrating or drawing. Within 3 weeks, he was fully participating in the afternoons with Kathie but doing no written work at all in the mornings with Lee.*

Lee and Kathie met to compare notes. Lee shared that she thought Donyal liked Kathie better because she was younger and blonde. They both laughed but realized that Lee's thinking was becoming more negative and that her ability to escape being dominated by her feelings was weakening. It was clear that Donyal had a bonded personal relationship with Kathie and enjoyed the afternoon curriculum better than the morning one. All of this indicated that there were times when resistance wasn't dominant. The two teachers decided to ask the third-grade teacher next door to sit with them and their district coach to problem-solve the morning issues.

♥ Personal Connection

Describe the student in your classroom who is the most difficult to be positive with. Remember to just write observable behaviors, no interpretations. For example, "throws objects on floor" is an observable behavior. "Is defiant" (or "rude" or "lazy") is an interpretation.

_____

_____

_____

_____

What is your biggest challenge to maintaining a climate for your target student like Carol Rasul did for Rachel or Kathie did for Donyal?

_____

_____

_____

_____

Prerequisite Concepts and Their Applications to Problem Solving

As we begin to plan for our introspective problem solving with objective colleagues, we need to review three important prerequisite concepts for problem solving and to use these in the assessment process.

1. The principles of power struggles

2. The concepts of pure reinforcement and shaping

3. The criteria for intrinsic motivation

The Principles of Power Struggles

෨

The first step to effectively and positively deal with power struggles is to side-step the power struggle—in other words, refuse to pick up the other end of the rope.

Karan Sims, "Dealing With Power Struggles"

෨

". . . Big Circle/Little Circle" Dynamics

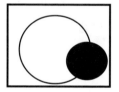

Several years ago, Dr. Eric Berne, founder of Transactional Analysis, introduced the metaphor of "Big Circles" and "Little Circles" as a way of thinking about who has the power in relationships. It can be helpful to teachers and adults today as a way of visualizing the power plays that can develop. Adults are naturally bigger physically and also hold more power than students. It is a common feeling for students to see the teacher as the Big Circle and themselves as Little Circles. What happens to you in situations where you are the Little Circle in the relationship dynamic and power flows down from the Big Circle person (e.g., the administrator or boss)? Most teachers say that resistance, anger, frustration, helplessness, aggression, and passive resistance are natural responses to feeling that one is on the bottom in a power dynamic. As teachers, we want to prevent power struggles. However, even with the best of intentions, they will happen. Our goal is to recognize power struggles quickly and dance out of them with grace and flexibility to prevent them from becoming all-out wars. Donyal and Lee were in the early stages of a power struggle. He felt like the Little Circle, and when Lee tried to encourage him to write his responses to questions, he felt as if she was the Big Circle imposing directives on him.

Aggression or resistance is a warning sign that a power struggle is looming: "Little Circle" feels very little and wants "Big Circle" to be smaller.

Examples of Signs That Aggression Is Dominating a Student's Activity

- *Physical Aggression:* Student hits, pokes, bites, kicks, jumps on, spits, trips, pinches, slaps, elbows, or shoves others; writes on desks; destroys property; throws objects; tears materials; steals.

- *Verbal Aggression:* Student disrupts the classroom by making inappropriate comments to teacher or students, swearing, calling others names, making smart-mouth remarks, saying putdowns, using abusive language, criticizing teacher or peers, or threatening others.

- *Physical Negative Attention Getting:* Student taps pencil/object, falls out of chair, makes body gestures, blows bubble gum, makes faces, rocks in chair, drops objects intentionally.

- *Verbal Negative Attention Getting:* Student makes noises, talks loudly, yawns loudly, burps or makes other bodily noises, makes ridiculous comments to get a laugh, whistles.

- *Manipulation:* Student demands that teacher stops doing what she is doing and helps student, calls out of turn, tattles, complains, cries, pouts, whines, makes excuses, has temper tantrums, gets others to join in ganging up on teacher (e.g., "Let's all drop a book at the same time") (Spaulding, 1980).

A good rule of thumb to use when aggression is dominating a student's activity is to provide more structure and an extra amount of teacher supervision and proximity.

Examples of Signs That Resistance Is Dominating a Student's Activity

- *Inappropriate Self-Directed Activity:* Instead of doing class work, student does other tasks that are of more interest but at the wrong time, such as drawing, reading a library book, sewing, doing homework for another class, playing with a game, or writing notes to friends.

- *Inappropriate Social Activity:* Student engages in social interactions at the wrong time, such as talking with peers, passing notes, visiting with classmates, interacting with peers via sign language or gestures, playing cards or games with friends, or planning a rally during class time.

- *Resisting Requests:* Student does the opposite of a request or refuses to do work, violates classroom norms, states, "I won't," "I don't want to," or "Make me," either verbally or nonverbally with body language.

- *Delaying Tasks:* Student finds other things to do that are not purposeful: sharpens pencil, turns in late assignments, asks questions to stall, walks around room looking at others, stalls with materials, hunts in desk, gets up 10 times to get a Kleenex, cleans desk or backpack, doodles, scribbles, all in an attempt to stall getting to work. He or she often withdraws from participating with the group by being passive.

- *Pretending to Conform:* Student works quickly and carelessly, reads without reading, watches teacher and conforms only while being watched, engages in defensive checking. This is often called "yo-yoing the teacher" because when the teacher walks over, the student gets on task, and when the teacher leaves, the student resumes the delay (adapted from Spaulding, 1980).

A good rule of thumb to use when resistance is dominating a student's activity is to provide more choice and resist the urge to confront. For example, Kathie Houseman offers Donyal choices of how he wants to demonstrate understanding in social studies, other than paper-and-pencil tasks, such as a mural, a group project, a song, a mind map, or a skit. She also offers choices and options in math and uses strategies such as round table (see "Questioning Strategies" section in Chapter 6, "The Fourth 'P' of Prevention: Participation for Involvement") and partner work for practice math tasks. These choices defuse resistance and increase motivation, so she has fewer issues than Lee Belvedere, who wants Donyal to write down his daily language arts stories with pen or pencil. Kathie also resists the urge to confront Donyal and call attention to him publicly when he is off task or delaying. Instead, she walks over to him privately and asks him questions like "How's the project going?" or "How long will you need to finish up?"

Three Choices in a Power Struggle

When "Big Circles" get into power struggles with "Little Circles," there are three choices for the "Big Circle" to consider.

1. *Strengthen the Relationship Bond*: Provide more opportunities for connecting, increase the use of gifts without strings, make more deposits in the student's emotional bank account. When Lee noticed an increase in delay behaviors with Donyal, she had to shift

her thinking in order to keep the relationship. She had to think of herself as the adult and remember that she was someone that he wanted to be connected with but didn't know how to express his needs. This freed her up to ask him questions about his sports games, his running shoes, and his new Game Boy.

2. *Increase Negative Interventions*: Lee was tempted to act out of her feelings by increasing the consequences for "resisting work" and coming up with punishments to try to shape him up. She knew that this was contrary to all research and that it would increase the power struggle. On the other hand, when "anger" was dominating her, it was a kneejerk reaction. Her brain fired to this old program of "getting tough."

3. *Do Collaborative Problem Solving*: Lee knew the principle of tug of war. If she could "drop the rope, let go of it," there would be no resistance to pull against. She knew that the answer for Donyal was in Donyal and that meeting with him so that they could create a plan together was the only way for an intrinsic shift to happen. She needed her colleagues to support her new way of thinking and help her learn to use the positive interventions that are based on pure reinforcement theory and shaping, such as omission training, competitive bet, or positive contract.

Key Points of the Principles of Power Struggles

- When power flows down, resentment flows up.
- Power struggles are a "no win" situation.
- Separate the student from the problem.
- Make decisions based on values and beliefs.
- Teacher needs time to "upshift."
- Goal is to avoid and escape power struggles, "drop the rope."

Checking My Understanding of Power Struggles

1. Why is it so hard to strengthen our relationship during these upsets with students? What gets in our way?

_____

_____

2. When students delay or do the opposite of a request, is it resistance or aggression that is operating?

_____

_____

3. What is the rule of thumb for defusing aggression?

_____

_____

4. What is the rule of thumb for defusing resistance?

_____

_____

Answers:

1. Usually our feelings get in the way, or we begin to take it personally or interpret the motivation for the student's behavior.
2. Resistance.
3. Provide structure and lots of supervision and support.
4. Provide choice and avoid confrontations and public comments.

 Personal Commitment

How will I use the principles of problem solving with my target student? How might I neutralize the effect of being the "Big Circle," given that I am bigger and do have more power than my students?

_____

_____

_____

_____

The Concepts of Pure Reinforcement and Shaping

ی

In general, it is cheaper to use mild social discipline
with the least provocative students, a mixture of reinforcement
(and consequences) with more disruptive students
and pure reinforcement with the most disruptive students.

Frederic Jones, *Positive Discipline*

ى

Pure reinforcement is positive reinforcement given only when the student is successful. It focuses solely on success; there is no negative consequence to reinforce the student's thinking that he or she can't do the desired behavior. As Jones says above, consequences and punishment don't work with "the most disruptive students" because they support students' negative thinking about their lack of success. Experienced teachers don't need research to prove this theory correct: The same students who were in detention in September are still there in May. Many of the citizens incarcerated in our prisons were "the most disruptive students" in their classrooms. We know that the rate of recidivism is very high when prisoners are released back into society after their years of punishment. Donyal is a perfect example of a student who had been kicked out of four schools and thought of himself as someone who never did written work. All the consequences and threats and contracts that were tried in his other schools only reinforced his negative concept of himself as someone who would not succeed in school.

Pure reinforcement means that when there is a mistake or regression to old habits, we simply start over with compassion and forgiveness, knowing that new behaviors take time to build into an established program. It's the same concept as in Alcoholics Anonymous, Weight Watchers, and other change programs, where if you fall down, make a mistake, or break your word, you forgive yourself and start over. It is based on the belief that every day is a new day and new "programs" take time to build into our brain. Pure reinforcement is different from the notion of having students sign contracts, which implies that the contract will hold the behavior and that it's all a matter of choice. Contracts ignore the fact that the brain has stored a program and all the desire in the world will not change it. Contracts seem to be a quick-fix technique that puts all the responsibility on the student, but the brain research and behavior change research show that this kind of change takes time and support from the entire learning community. Behavior change comes about when an individual thinks about him- or herself as someone who can accomplish the challenge.

Many pure reinforcement strategies involve the principles of shaping. Shaping is based on learning theory and is the backbone of many reading, language and math programs, as well as training for other skills such as athletic skills, musical skills, and typing. It involves teaching a new behavior by beginning with a behavior as it exists and reinforcing slight changes as the learner gradually approaches the goal behavior. We identify the goal—the big picture—and then break it into very small manageable steps and reward successive approximations as well as actual success. The goal must be within our sphere of influence: For example, behaviors must happen within my classroom so that I can support and reinforce them.

The most familiar experience of shaping that most of us have had is learning to ride a bike. Whether we learned by the old "catch hold" method of someone running alongside of us and letting go of the handlebars and then the seat in various stages as we got the feel of it or whether we learned with training wheels, shaping was the key principle employed.

Shaping can be used for any of the classroom behaviors students need to learn to function successfully.

Examples of Classroom Behaviors for Which Shaping Can Be Used

- Participating in a discussion
- Following along in the book
- Beginning transition tasks independently
- Bringing materials to class

We will discuss three strategies of pure reinforcement that involve shaping of the new behavior:

1. Omission training
2. Competitive bet
3. Positive contracts

Omission Training. Omission training is a pure reinforcement strategy adapted from Frederic Jones's book *Positive Discipline* (1987). It uses the principles of shaping, a timer, and a system for marking successes to help students omit an inappropriate behavior and develop a new program for the appropriate behavior.

When to Use Omission Training: Omission training should be used after all other strategies have failed, for students like Rachel, Reuben, or Donyal who need a concrete, visual plan and are showing signs of

● Resistance

● Aggression

● Commenting out loud

● Talking repetitively

Before implementing omission training, you must draw up a plan for presenting your goal, positively phrased, to the student that will include the following:

1. State acceptable behavior(s) as you would explain it to the student.

2. State unacceptable behavior(s) as you would explain it to the student.

3. Get input from student on the following:

   a) A reasonable time interval during which the student will demonstrate the behavior

   b) A marking system: that is, a system the student can use to mark/tally when he or she is successful

   c) What setting will be best for the training

   d) What reward will be chosen and whether it will involve only the individual or others as well

   e) How you will deal with the others in the class

4. Decide how you will fade the omission program as success increases.

The example below shows how these steps would work in a particular case.

Example of an Omission Training Program Plan for a Student

Goal for Eduardo: "Eduardo will raise his hand and be called upon before answering questions orally."

1. *State acceptable behavior(s)* as you would explain it to the student.

   a) Remain in seat.

   b) Quietly raise hand.

   c) Be silent while another student answers.

   d) When called upon, answer with classroom voice.

2. *State unacceptable behavior(s)* as you would explain it to the student.

   a) Being out of seat

   b) Calling out answers out of turn

   c) Interrupting teacher or students

3. *Get input from student* on the following:

   a) *A reasonable time interval* during which the student will demonstrate the behavior. For Eduardo, this time interval will initially be 5 minutes.

   b) *A marking system.* For Eduardo, this will be tallying on a card at his desk every time he wants to call out and doesn't.

   c) *What setting will be best for the training.* Eduardo has the most difficulty in teacher-directed settings, so the training program will focus on those.

   d) *What reward will be chosen and whether it will involve only the individual or others as well.* Eduardo and I will make these decisions together. I will suggest that he will earn bonus time for the class to watch a PBS video or extra time for curriculum games or a popcorn party for the class.

   e) *How you will deal with the others in the class.* Eduardo and I will talk about when and how and what he wants the class to know. I will encourage him to wait until he has earned something before sharing with them to reduce the risk of failure.

4. *Decide how to fade the omission program as success increases.*

   a) I will increase the time gradually from 5 minutes to 8, then to 10.

   b) I will remove the visual prompt of the timer and note card.

   c) I will sever the contingency in stages. After a week of success, I will state that the class will still get the bonus time or video but that I won't keep tracking time.

5. The last step is to say that this tool is no longer needed because Eduardo has gotten in charge of himself and the bonus time is just a gift to the class from both of us.

Once the plan is worked out, it is time to implement:

1. Set timer.

2. State acceptable/unacceptable behavior.

3. Reset timer if student fails.

4. Tally points and give reinforcer (reward).

To fade omission training:

1. Extend time interval.

2. Remove visual prompt (points).

3. Extend to other settings.

4. Sever contingency: that is, give the reinforcer unconditionally.

Personal Commitment

If you have a target student who might benefit from omission training, you can create a plan like the one in the example as a way of preparing for your meeting with your student.

1. Your goal (stated positively) regarding one student's observable behavior:

   _____

   _____

   a) State acceptable behavior(s) as you would explain it to the student.

   _____

   _____

   b) State unacceptable behavior(s) as you would explain it to the student.

   _____

   _____

2. Reasonable time intervals and a tally system will begin with:

   _____

   _____

3. How will reward(s) be chosen, and will it involve only the individual student or the entire class?

_____

_____

4. How will you deal with the others in the class?

_____

_____

5. How will you fade omission program as success increases?

_____

_____

Positive Contract. Positive contract is a private use of omission training, set up on intervals of time, without a timer, to omit or establish a desired behavior. It can be used after all other strategies have failed and student continues to

- Resist working
- Withdraw
- Forget homework
- Interrupt
- Talk repetitively
- Turn in incomplete assignments

An example of a positive contract would be: "For every 15 minutes that you remember to raise your hand, you will receive a point. Five points and you will earn 5 minutes of free drawing time."

Here is how to structure a positive contract:

1. Discuss plan with the student.

2. Contract can be formal or informal.

3. State acceptable/unacceptable behavior.

4. Structure reasonable time intervals.

5. Give points when student succeeds.

6. Begin again when student fails.

7. Fade as success increases:

   a) Remove visual prompts.

   b) Sever contingency in stages.

Competitive Bet. A competitive bet is a challenge issued to a capable student who has a competitive nature and needs to diminish an unacceptable behavior. Paradoxically, you offer to bet that the student *cannot* diminish the behavior. This can be used when all other strategies have failed for a competitive student who continues to

● Be disruptive

● Comment out loud

● Physically wander

Here is how to structure a competitive bet:

1. Preplan bet.

2. Tell student that you are making a bet that he or she cannot (whatever the behavior is) less than (number of times) during a specified time interval (one period, before lunch, the entire day).

3. Tell student you will keep points inconspicuously on the board. His or her challenge is to get no more than or less than a specified number of points.

4. Agree on reward.

🔑 Key Criteria for Pure Reinforcement Strategies (Omission Training, Competitive Bet, Positive Contracts)

● Use pure reinforcement.

● Involve student in planning.

● Keep plan flexible.

● Use principles of shaping.

● Fade when success is stable.

● Maintain neutral body language.

Benefits of Pure Reinforcement Strategies

- Diminish resistance

- Strengthen relationship with teacher

- Eliminate arena for a power struggle

- Strengthen teacher-student bonded relationship

- Change student's agenda

- Promote social interaction

- Provide opportunity to succeed

- Foster self-esteem

- Provide teacher with more flexibility

- Build student decision making

Motivation Theory

*Leadership is the art of getting someone else to do something
you want done because he wants to do it.*

Dwight D. Eisenhower

Motivation as defined by Webster is the stir to action, the stimulation of an active interest in something. It is important for us as teachers to understand the principles of motivation and to choose motivational strategies that are congruent with our beliefs and sound research.

Alfie Kohn (1998) identifies "three C's" of intrinsic motivation. The first is *choice*, learners' power to choose whom they work with, what they work on, and how they demonstrate their competence. The second is *collaboration*, the ability to work with others and generate ideas and projects. The third is the *curriculum*, which needs to be relevant and meaningful to the learners. All three of these requirements were discussed in the section "The Six Elements of a Brain-Compatible Classroom" in Chapter 4. When the environment is brain compatible, intrinsic motivation flourishes.

Consulting With Colleagues:
Triad Activity for Target Student Problem Solving

ร

Seek first to understand and then be understood.
Stephen Covey, *Seven Habits of Highly Effective People*

๛

Once you have considered your problem introspectively, the Triad Activity described below will enable you to consult with colleagues.

Directions: Find two objective colleagues who might also have target students for whom they want some help problem solving. Set aside 20 to 25 minutes per teacher, and follow the format below. Make a copy of the form shown in Figure 8.1 to write your notes on. You will then have a prevention plan of action for your target student. It is very important to set a timer and stick to the time frames. In the figure on the right, "A" is the teacher presenting the problem and "B" and "C" are the two colleagues. The three triangles in the picture indicate that the three people will take turns playing the three roles discussed below.

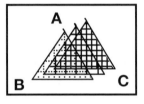

The Triad Activity has three stages:

1. Describing the Problem (2 minutes)

    "A" describes the problem regarding the target student (focusing on the effects of the problem rather than the "why" of the problem—that is, the motivations of the target student).

    "B" listens, using active listening skills.

    "C" observes and takes notes.

2. Assessing the Prevention Factors (10 minutes)

    "B" asks "how," "what," and "when" questions, using the "Questions to Rethink Prevention Strategies for a Target Student" (Table 8.1) as a guide.

    "C" records "A's" responses on plan of action.

    "A" responds to questions.

3. Brainstorming Solutions (10 minutes)

    "B" and "C" offer suggestions to resolve/dissolve problem.

    "A" records suggestions on plan of action.

Rotate twice so each person has an opportunity to share.

Table 8.1   Questions for Rethinking Prevention Strategies for a Target Student

A.   Personal Relationships for Trust
- How do you maintain a positive relationship with this student?
- What is the ratio of noncontingent reinforcement (gifts without strings) to contingent reinforcement (gifts with strings)?
- When do you consciously connect with this student?
- How often do you use target talk or focus on this student's strengths?
- What is your first thought about this student?

Gauging your responses: If your answers to these questions indicate that your relationship with this student is weak, then this is where you should begin to plan your strategies to strengthen them. Move immediately to Stage 3 of the Triad Activity process, "Brainstorming Solutions." If, on the other hand, your responses led you to think that your relationship was strong, proceed to Area B of these questions, "Prerequisites for Success."

B.   Prerequisites for Success
- Which dimension of self-esteem is strongest for this student? Which is weakest?
- How have you verified your perceptions?
- What specific steps have you taken to ensure that the classroom environment is brain compatible for this student?
- Where does this student sit in the classroom?
- What was your rationale for the placement?
- What is his/her level of social skills?
- How do you ensure that the activity is appropriate to this student's learning style/seven intelligences?
- Give an example of how you've adapted the learning to ensure that this student will experience 80% success.
- What resources did you use to determine that the curriculum is both age-level and developmentally appropriate?
- How do you know that the student sees the learning as relevant to his/her personal life?
- Give an example of how you provide the student with opportunities for intrinsic motivation by constructing tasks so that the activity itself is rewarding and by delivering some positive feedback for the portion of the task accomplished.

Gauging your responses: If your answers to these questions indicate that the classroom environment does not support the student's self-esteem or is not brain compatible or that the student is missing either social skills or academic skills, then this is where you should begin to plan your strategies to strengthen them. Move immediately to Stage 3 of the Triad Activity process, "Brainstorming Solutions." If, on the other hand, your responses led you to think that your relationship was strong, proceed to assess Area C of these questions, "Parameters for Cooperation."

C.   Parameters for Cooperation
- Where does the student fit on the structure/freedom scale?
- How have you ensured that he/she remembers the procedures for various activities?
- What strategies have you used to determine he/she knows the directions for the task?

Gauging your responses: If your answers to these questions indicate that the classroom environment does not invite cooperation or that the student needs more structure or freedom, then this is where you should begin to plan your strategies to strengthen them. Move immediately to Stage 3 of the Triad Activity process, "Brainstorming Solutions." If, on the other hand, your responses lead you to think that parameters are in place for the student, proceed to assess Area D of these questions, "Participation for Involvement."

D.   Participation for Involvement
- Which questioning strategies invite this student to participate during directed lessons and keep him or her actively involved?
- Which instructional strategies (cooperative learning, direct instruction, concept attainment, inquiry, role play) work best for this student?
- How do you monitor and support active engagement for him/her during the learning activities?

Gauging your responses: If your answers to these questions indicate that the classroom environment needs more opportunities for this student to participate, brainstorm those now. If not, review your notes and brainstorm accordingly.

Name: **Date:**
Problem Behavior: (Coping Style)
Desired Behavior:

PERSONAL:	Student-Teacher Relationship • Gifts Without Strings • Target Talk • Proximity	
PREREQUISITES:	**PARAMETERS:**	**PARTICIPATION:**
Brain Compatible Environment Self-Esteem Social Skills Powerful Curriculum	Ground Rules Procedures Directions	Environment provides for: Involvement Active Listening Active Engagement
PROBLEM-SOLVING STRATEGIES: Positive Interventions		

Figure 8.1.   Classroom Plan of Action for Student Success

Key Criteria for Problem Solving With Colleagues

- Stay objective.
- Use outside resource for objectivity.
- Begin with your circle of influence.
- Focus on the problem as the problem.

When you are problem solving with a target student, it is important to have other students realize that this is a student who has a broken arm and needs a cast. This is an opportunity to teach your students about teaching to individual needs. You can ask them how old they were when they rode their bike or how many of them went to the doctor recently when they had a cold. Ask various students what their doctor prescribed. Ask how many of them called the doctor to ask why they didn't get what their friends got for their prescription. Sometimes the doctor prescribes chicken soup with rice, and sometimes the doctor tells them to go home and take decongestants and drink lots of liquids. The doctor's been to school many years to know what their body needs to heal. As a teacher you've been to school for many years, and you know what different students need both academically and socially. You will prescribe on the basis of what you know each student needs. This is called teaching to individual differences.

What Will The Other Students Say?

ఒ

*There is nothing so unequal as the equal treatment
of students of unequal ability.*

Plato, *The Republic*

ఞ

DUET PROBLEM SOLVING   ■

ఒ

*When students are involved in finding a solution to a problem,
they tend to accept responsibility for making the solution work.*

Jeanne Gibbs, *Tribes: A New Way of Learning and Being Together*

ఞ

Meeting With the Student

After meeting with two colleagues, Lee Belvedere decided she needed to meet with Donyal to include him in the problem solving about the resistance. The purpose of meeting with the student is to collaborate, using a no-blame, solution-focused problem-solving model for resolving conflicts. Before this meeting, Lee needs to review the difference between her role as teacher and the role of a facilitator. Conflict resolution meetings like this will require the teacher to put on a new hat in order to have a more equal conversation with the student. The facilitator role is similar to the teacher role in that its purpose is to maintain safety for the group or the individual. However, there are some distinct differences.

The facilitator also needs to be able to rephrase or reframe contributions to ensure that everyone feels heard. Because body language is 80% of the message, it is important to stay in touch with our beliefs rather than get caught up in our feelings so that we can paraphrase and validate for the individual or the group. Much as in teaching, the teacher-facilitator will define the purpose of the conversation or the meeting. The facilitator also needs to be able to clarify with questions that are open ended and maintain a sense of humor to stay connected with the student. (Eventually some of these skills can be taught to various students, who can take turns with the teacher being the facilitator.)

Key Criteria for Teacher as Facilitator

1. Maintains safety

   - Is nonjudgmental

   - Protects norms

   - Makes sure everyone feels heard

2. Rephrases (reframes)

   - Has neutral body language

   - Paraphrases

     "Are you saying that . . . ?"

   - Validates

3. Defines purpose

   - Focuses

   - Paces

   - Structures

4. Clarifies with open-ended questions

   - "When have you used "what," "how," and "when" words?

   - "How would you feel about that . . . ?"

5. Maintains relationship

- Focuses on strengths
- Uses humor

✓ Checking My Understanding of Facilitation Skills

In the account below, Lee Belvedere uses the facilitation skills just described with Donyal to address the problem of his language arts participation and skills. Where blanks are inserted in parentheses in the story, mark the number(s) of the facilitation skill(s) in the "Key Criteria for Teacher as Facilitator" that are being used. Answers are at the end of the story.

1. T.L.C. (Setting the Emotional Tone, Length, and Concern of Meeting)

Lee begins by writing a note to Donyal inviting him to meet with her to problem-solve ways for him to be in charge of himself in the classroom in order to get up to grade level in language arts. She offers him a choice of meeting on a bench on the baseball field, in the library, or on the park adjacent to school. (This information can be communicated verbally or in a letter, depending on the teacher or student.)

Dear Donyal,

When would be a good time to meet to talk about ways for you to be more in charge of yourself in our classroom and what you need from me for that to happen? I've put down some times that would work for me. Circle the time that would be best for you. Please put this on my desk at the end of school today.

Tuesday during activity time

Wednesday after school

Tuesday while the class is doing math

Monday at lunch

Pick a place and know that this will take about 20 minutes.

Bench at the baseball field

The library

Park adjacent to the school

The following is a dialogue between Donyal and his teacher that took place on the bench at the baseball field Wednesday afternoon.

2. O.K.S. (Outlining Kid's Strengths)

> **Teacher:** You know, Donyal, you're someone we can always count on to be helpful. If there's a job to do, you are often the first one to offer to help. You're thoughtful with your social studies group and you're a team player, you often help them illustrate their mission projects. How did you learn to be so thoughtful? (a. _____)
>
> **Student:** I like to help, it's fun, it's better than boring writing.

3. CAN/CAN'T (Deciding Where to Begin and What the Student Can and Can't Do in the Situation)

> **Teacher:** What's going on for you that gets in the way of your being in charge and fighting off resistance during reading and language arts? (b. _____)
>
> **Student:** I don't know. I feel it's boring work. And there's too much of it.
>
> **Teacher:** So you feel it's not interesting, it's overwhelming, and there's too much to do? (c. _____)
>
> **Student:** Yeh.
>
> **Teacher:** Do you feel I understand how you feel about the language arts assignments?
>
> **Student:** I guess.
>
> **Teacher:** It's important that you know that I hear how you feel overwhelmed and bored.
>
> **Student:** Okay, I guess you get it.
>
> **Teacher:** I'm feeling frustrated and helpless in trying to get your language arts skills up to grade level. Can you tell me how I'm feeling?
>
> **Student:** Well, you said you were helpless and frustrated.
>
> **Teacher:** And I also realize it's really your problem and you need to be the one to come up with a solution. I can only help you. Has there ever been a time, Donyal, that you escaped resistance and did something that you felt was boring? (d. _____)
>
> **Student:** Maybe baseball practice drills—they're boring.
>
> **Teacher:** How did you do that?
>
> **Student:** I had to, I wanted to play baseball.

4. M.A.P. (Making a Plan)

Teacher: So you have an experience where you can take charge? Let's brainstorm some ideas for how you could get your language arts skills up to grade level without feeling bored or overwhelmed. Brainstorming means we write down all our ideas without judging whether they're good or bad. And at the end you pick the idea that you think works best for you, okay? Willing to try it?

Student: Okay.

Teacher: Okay, I'll write that down. I have an idea. You could work with a partner and you write half and they write half.

Student: Yeah, I'll try that.

Teacher: Remember we're brainstorming now, not picking now. Let's write all the ideas down and then you can pick. Any more ideas? (e. _____)

Student: Okay, how about if I dictate my work to someone else to write for me, or I could go back a grade. (Teacher records but doesn't say anything.)

Teacher: You could type them on the computer.

Student: I could dictate my stories into the tape recorder.

Teacher: You could cut the writing assignments in half or you could write three sentences yourself and dictate the rest. I have another idea, Donyal, you could proof and correct other students' writing until you are ready to write your own. (Teacher records all of these ideas.) (f. _____)

Student: Do we have enough ideas?

Teacher: If you think so, let's go through them and see which ones we both like. First, is there anything you don't like that you'd want to cross out? (Teacher hands him a colored pen.)

Student: Type on the computer. I can't type.

Teacher: Go ahead, cross it off. (He does.) Well, there's one I'll get to cross off too. (She crosses off dictating for someone else to write.) So is there one here you really like?

Student: I like proofing and correcting other kids' writing.

Teacher: Well, that will help you in your language arts skills by finding their grammar and punctuation errors. Let's try that and see how it goes. What do you think?

Student: Well, okay.

Teacher: Yes, and maybe you can help them illustrate their story. (g. _____)

Student: Can I start illustrating tomorrow?

Teacher: You can start proofing their stories and then illustrating.

5. A.S.K. (Anticipate Some Kinks)

Teacher: So what do you like about the plan?

Student: That I don't have to write my own stories.

Teacher: I bet that was really getting us all off base. (Teacher laughs.) Any possible roadblocks or problems that might get in the way of this working? (h. _____)

Student: Only if I have to write.

6. R.A.R. (Review, Anticipate, Reconnect)

Teacher: Let's write down our agreements. You'll proof and correct two to three stories written by peers in your group and help them with their illustrations. Let's check in Friday during lunch to see how it's going and if you feel in charge of making progress in language arts. (i. _____)

Answers:

a) F-5, Maintains relationship (by focusing on strengths).

b) F-4, Clarifies with open-ended questions.

c) F-2, Rephrases/reframes.

d) F-3 and F-4, Defines purpose and clarifies with open-ended questions.

e) F-3 and F-4, Defines purpose and clarifies with open-ended questions.

f) F-1, Maintains safety (by being nonjudgmental).

g) F-5, Maintains relationship (by focusing on strengths).

h) F-5, Maintains relationship (by humor).

i) F-1, Maintains safety, by reiterating what has been decided.

Table 8.2 summarizes the steps of the model for problem solving with a target student that Lee Belvedere used with Donyal.

Table 8.2   Model for Problem Solving With a Target Student

1. T.L.C. (Setting Tone, Length, Concern of Meeting)
   a) Allow student choice of where to meet.
   b) Agree on length of time.
   c) Tell purpose and reason for meeting.

2. O.K.S. (Outlining Student's Strengths)
   a) Tell student what he/she does well.

3. CAN/CAN'T (Deciding Where to Begin and What the Student Can and Can't Do in the Situation)
   a) State problem (without blame) and goal.
   b) Ask student about his feelings and needs.
   c) Share your (teacher's) feelings and needs.
   d) Help student see where/when he/she has "escaped the problem."

4. M.A.P. (Making a Plan)
   a) Restate goal.
   b) Brainstorm and record all ideas on how to achieve goal without evaluating them.
   c) Select mutually agreeable ideas to start.
   d) Allow student to cross off one that he doesn't like, and you do the same.
   e) Have the student mark which suggestions he/she likes and doesn't like and pick one to try.
   f) Write it down.

5. A.S.K. (Anticipate Some Kinks)
   a) Have student tell what he/she likes about plan.
   b) Have student tell any possible roadblocks.

6. R.A.R. (Review, Anticipate, Reconnect)
   a) Review strategy and record agreements.
   b) Agree on follow-up meeting time to check in.[1]

SOURCE: This format for problem solving with a student was adapted from a model created by Dr. Vicki Dickerson.

ENSEMBLE PROBLEM SOLVING ■

ॐ

If children learn to participate in a problem solving group when they enter school and continue to do so with a variety of teachers throughout six years of elementary school they learn that the world may be difficult but they can use their brains individually and as a group to solve problems of living in their school world.

William Glasser, *The Quality School: Managing Students Without Coercion*

ॐ

In ensemble problem solving, the teacher facilitates problem solving with a small group or the entire class in a class meeting, using the brainstorming conflict resolution model.

Class Meetings for Problem Solving

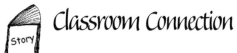 *Classroom Connection*

Kristin Daniels has used class meetings with her third/fourth-grade combination class since the beginning of the year for planning curriculum projects and field trips, building community, and helping students learn how to listen to each other's feelings and give each other target talk. She has decided that now, in October, the time is right to introduce the concept of conflict resolution and problem solving. The students have been taught to use the form shown in Figure 8.2 to write down problems that they have been unable to solve on their own. The procedure is that the students are given 2 days to solve the problem on their own before asking the class to help.

Ms. Daniels calls the class to the circle for a class meeting and brings the problem box with student forms to the circle. She begins by complimenting the class on their teamwork during last week's social studies project. The class takes turns giving each other target talk about other social skills they have been working on during the past week.

Ms. Daniels opens the box and begins to pull out the five problem forms. "Kelly, is this still a problem for you, or did you solve it on your own?"

Kelly responds, "I've taken care of it."

Ms. Daniels asks Muriel, "Is yours still a problem?"

Muriel answers, "It's not a problem anymore."

Ms. Daniels asks Andrew: "How about you, Andrew, is this still a problem?"

Andrew says, "Yes, I need the class to help me."

Ms. Daniels reads the problem. "Someone is bothering you during work time, and you have tried to solve it by asking the person to stop and by asking someone else in the class to help you. So how do you feel?"

Andrew says, "I'm frustrated and angry because I can't get my work done, Ms. Daniels."

"So which dimension of self-esteem is missing for you, Andrew?"

"Well, I guess security because I am worried that I won't have time to get my work done."

Ms. Daniels then asks the class how many of the class have felt that way and over three fourths of the class raise their hands. "So you can see, Andrew, that a lot of the class has had the same problem and feels the same as you do. So class, what have some of you done to solve the same problem that Andrew had? Let's brainstorm ideas for Andrew." (Teacher or student records ideas on easel.)

Raymond raises his hand. "I ignored them when they did that."

Ms. Daniels says, "And how did that work for you?"

Raymond says, "It worked, but it was hard. It took them a long time to get tired of bothering me."

Ms. Daniels asks, "Michelle, what worked for you?"

Michelle says, "I went and stood by your desk and pretended I was waiting to ask you a question. They followed me to your desk but finally went back to their desk since it was taking so long."

Ms. Daniels says, "So you used the 'remove' strategy from our conflict resolution IRRR [Ignore, Request, Remove, Report] model? You have your hand up, Isabel, what have you tried?"

Isabel says, "I tried to ignore them too, I just didn't even look at them. And that finally worked."

Puneet raises his hand and says, "I wrote a note and requested that they quit bothering me."

Ms. Daniels responds, "So you used the 'request' part of our IRRR conflict resolution model. How did that work for you, Puneet?"

He says, "They quit bothering me."

Ms. Daniels says, "Okay, Andrew, you've heard five people give ideas. Is there one that you want to try?"

Andrew says, "I want to try 'ignore' and 'remove.'"

"Ok, 'ignore' is the most powerful and the hardest to do. Let's role-play how 'ignore' would look if someone were bothering you during work time. Who is really good at ignoring and wants to model for Andrew?"

Solution Form

Name: _____ Date: _____

Did you try our conflict resolution recipe? Which one did you try? Circle it.

IGNORE　　　　　**REQUEST**　　　　　**REMOVE**　　　　　**REPORT**

* Describe what happened (remember, no names)

_____

_____

How did you feel?

_____

_____

What way(s) did you try to solve it?

_____

_____

Figure 8.2.　　Problem-Solving Form

Class meetings can be held to help those who have problems find solutions. In addition, such meetings foster the following in students:

● Involvement/sense of power

● Value judgment

● Commitment

● Social responsibility

● Facilitation skills (when these are taught to students, they can take turns with the teacher at being the facilitator)

Key Criteria for Class Problem–Solving Meetings

- Meetings are always directed toward constructive solutions.

- All problems relate to class as a group or to any individuals who need the class to help with school solution.

- Fault finding or punishments are unacceptable.

- Students sit in a tight circle for 10 to 30 minutes.

- Agenda is created by students.

- The meeting also serves as a forum for compliments to the students.

- On issues where the class as a whole makes a decision, such as where to go on a field trip or what project to do or what game to play, consensus is used rather than voting.

Refer to Chapter 3 for guidelines for class meetings, which are the same for prevention as for problem solving.

Example of a Format for a Class Meeting

1. Begin with ritual, such as target talk compliments or celebrations.

2. Prioritize agenda or go item by item.

3. Think about how the meeting can incorporate the four dimensions of self-esteem: making the students feel safe and secure, providing time for fostering a sense of connectedness, building competence (e.g., through target talk compliments), and fostering a sense of power or influence by enabling students to make their own choices. You have the role of ensuring that all of these are happening. Feel free to add fun as a fifth dimension.

4. Use the four dimensions of self-esteem as a framework for problem solving. Students can be taught to recognize how the dimensions of self-esteem are affected by how they and everyone else in the classroom acts.

5. Problem-solve what the students need next time to be more successful.

6. Close with a ritual: a song, chant, poem, reading, etc.

Benefits of Class Problem–Solving Meetings

- Decrease tattling and fault finding

- Students become competent at problem solving

- Increase self-esteem: build security, connectedness, competence, power

- Teach model for conflict resolution

Conflict Resolution Strategies to Teach Your Class

The following lists are conflict resolution strategies that may be taught to your class in the context of a class meeting using role play and group practice.

Twelve Ways to Solve Problems

Take cooldown time to upshift, then:

1. Talk about it (negotiate).

2. Take turns.

3. Both give up something (compromise).

4. Flip a coin.

5. See a funny side (use humor).

6. Share the blame.

7. Say you're sorry (apologize).

8. Ask for help (see Chapter 7, "Rethinking Classroom Interventions").

9. Wait for another time to talk (postpone).

10. Forget the whole thing (abandon).

11. Agree to disagree.

12. Do "Paper, rock, scissors."

The following are anger management strategies to teach for individual students to use when they feel anger. They also can be taught and modeled at a class meeting. These ideas were generated by teachers in various schools as some options for appropriately releasing angry feelings. They will fit different cultures, different grade levels, and different styles of teaching.

Twelve Ways to Blow off Anger

1. Run screaming to the fence.

2. Write your upset and put it into a paper bag and throw it away.

3. Draw on and jump up and down on a bag.

4. Create a class earthquake (kids stand up and jump and try to rock the floor).

5. Write a fantasy letter.

6. Shoot hoops.

7. Walk around a path.

8. Kick a ball.

9. Throw a ball at the wall.

10. Go to "Australia"/"Antarctica" for centering time, listen to music, read.

11. Pound a pillow.

12. Tear up phone books or rip old scrap paper.

Summary of Problem-Solving Strategies

- Focus on solutions rather than blame.

- "Drop the rope" in power struggles.

- The problem is the problem, not the person.

- Leader seeks objective counsel about student.

- Pure reinforcement is positive reinforcement that is given only when the student is successful.

- Shaping is focused on successive approximations, not all or nothing.

- Omission training shifts students' thinking to successes.

- Those who have the problem have the conference (i.e., teacher/student).

- Teacher uses facilitation skills.

- For intrinsic motivation, offer the "three C's": choice, collaboration, (meaningful) curriculum.

NOTE

1. This story was inspired by Alfie Kohn and adapted from his story of "Tanya's Tantrum" in his *Beyond Discipline: From Compliance to Community* (1996).

Suggested Readings

Benoit, R. B., & Mayer, G. R. (1974). Extinction: Guidelines for its selection and use. *Personal and Guidance Journal, 52,* 290-295.

Berne, Eric. (1972). *I'm O.K.—you're O.K.* New York: Bantam.

Brendtro, Larry K., Brokenleg, Martin, & Van Bockern, Steve. (1990). *Reclaiming youth at risk, our hope for the future.* Bloomington, IN: National Educational Service.

Dalton, Joan, & Boyd, Julie. (1992). *I teach: A guide to inspiriting classroom leadership.* Portsmouth, NH: Heinemann.

Dalton, Joan, & Watson, Marilyn. (1997). *Among friends: Classrooms where caring and learning prevail.* Oakland, CA: Developmental Studies Center.

Faber, Adele, & Mazlish, Elaine. (1995). *How to talk so kids will learn.* New York: Simon & Schuster.

Gootman, Marilyn E. (1997). *The caring teacher's guide to discipline.* Thousand Oaks, CA: Corwin.

Harmin, Merrill. (1994). *Inspiring active learning: A handbook for teachers.* Alexandria, VA: Association for Supervision and Curriculum Development.

Hendricks, Gay, & Wills, Russell. (1975). *The centering book: Awareness activities for children, parents and teachers.* New York: Prentice Hall.

Howell, J. C., Krisberg, B., Hawkins, J. D., & Wilson, J. J. (Eds.). (1995). *A sourcebook: Serious, violent, and chronic juvenile offenders.* Thousand Oaks, CA: Sage.

Jones, Elizabeth. (1990, October). Playing is my job. *Educational Leadership,* pp. 10-13.

Karns, Michelle. (1994). *How to create positive relationships with students.* Champaign, IL: Research Press.

Kohn, Alfie. (1991, March). Teaching children to care: The role of the schools. *Phi Delta Kappan, 2*(7), 496-506.

Leeds, Dorothy. (2000). *The seven powers of questions: Secrets to successful communication in life and at work.* New York: Berkley.

Loomans, Diane, & Kolberg, Karen. (1993). *The laughing classroom.* Tiburon, CA: H. J. Kramer.

Ruiz, Don Miguel. (1997). *The four agreements.* San Rafael, CA: Amber-Allen.

Teolis, Beth. (1998). *Ready-to-use conflict-resolution activities for elementary students.* West Nyack, NY: Center for Applied Research in Education.

Tracy, Louise Felton. (1994). *Grounded for life?!* Seattle, WA: Parenting Press.

References

Ames, Louise Bates, & Haber, Carol Chase. (1989). *Your eight-year-old: Lively and outgoing.* New York: Delacorte.

Ames, Louise Bates, & Haber, Carol Chase. (1990). *Your nine-year-old: Thoughtful and mysterious.* New York: Delacorte.

Ames, Louise Bates, Ilg, Frances L., & Baker, Sidney M. (1988). *Your ten- to fourteen-year-old.* New York: Delacorte.

Armstrong, Thomas. (1994). *Multiple intelligences in the classroom.* Alexandria, VA: Association for Supervision and Curriculum Development.

Baratta-Lorton, Mary. (1995). *Mathematics their way.* Menlo Park, CA: Addison-Wesley.

Benard, Bonnie. (1993). Fostering resiliency in kids. *Educational Leadership, 51*(3), 44-48.

Benson, Peter. (1997). *Report on Wisconsin Youth at Risk Behavior Survey.* Atlanta, GA: Centers for Disease Control and Prevention.

Borba, Michelle. (1994). *Esteem builders.* Torrance, CA: Jalmar.

Botvin, G. J., & Griffin, K. W. (1999). Preventing drug abuse. In A. J. Reynolds, R. P. Weissberg, & H. J. Walberg (Eds.), *Positive outcomes in children and youth: Promotion and evaluation* (pp. 197-228). Thousand Oaks, CA: Sage.

Bridges, William. (1980). *Transitions: Making sense of life's changes.* Reading, MA: Addison-Wesley.

Brophy, J. E., & Good, T. L. (1970). Teachers' communication of differential expectation for children's classroom performance: Some behavioral data. *Journal of Educational Psychology, 61,* 365-374.

Brophy, J., & Good, T. (1974). *Teacher-student relationships: Causes and consequences.* New York: Holt, Rinehart, & Winston.

Buzan, Tony. (1974). *Use both sides of your brain.* New York: E. P. Dutton.

Caine, Renate Numella, & Caine, Geoffrey. (1991). *Making connections: Teaching and the human brain.* Alexandria, VA: Association for Supervision and Curriculum Development.

California Task Force on Self Esteem. (1990). *Toward a state of esteem.* Sacramento: California State Department of Education, Office of State Printing.

Cami, Constance (1991). Toward autonomy: The importance of critical thinking and choice making. *School Psychology Review, 20,* 387.

Carnevale, Anthony P., Gainer, Leila J., & Meltzer, Ann S. (1989). *Workplace basics: The skills employers want.* Alexandria, VA: American Society for Training and Development and U.S. Department of Labor.

Checkley, Kathy. (1998). No room for control. *Education Update, 40*(6), 4-7.

Covey, Stephen. (1989). *Seven habits of highly effective people.* New York: Simon & Schuster.

Crane, Thomas G. (1998). *The heart of coaching.* San Diego, CA: FTA Press.

Deci, Edward L., Koestner, Richard, & Ryan, Richard M. (2001, Spring). Extrinsic rewards and intrinsic motivation in education: Reconsidered once again. *Review of Educational Research, 71,* 1-27.

Dennison, Gail E., & Dennison, Paul E. (1992). *Brain Gym activities: Simple activities for whole brain learning.* Ventura, CA: Edu-Kinesthetics, Inc.

Dennison, Gail E., & Dennison, Paul E. (1989). *Brain Gym, Teachers' edition* (Rev. ed.). Ventura, CA: Edu-Kinesthetics, Inc.

Dinkmeyer, Don, & McKay, Gary. (1982). *The parent's handbook: Systematic training for effective parenting (STEP).* Circle Pines, MN: American Guidance Service.

Dishon, Dee, & O'Leary, Pat Wilson. (1984). *A guidebook for cooperative learning: A technique for creating more effective schools.* Holmes Beach, FL: Learning Publications.

Dreikurs, Rudolf. (1990). *Children: The challenge.* New York: Plume.

Evertson, Carolyn, & Randolph, Catherine. (1995). *Classroom management in the learning-centered classroom.* Englewood Cliffs, NJ: Prentice Hall.

Freiburg, Jerome H. (1996, September). From tourists to citizens in the classroom. *Educational Leadership,* p. 34.

Gajewski, Nancy, Hirn, Polly, & Mayo, Patty. (1998). *Social skill strategies: A social-emotional curriculum for adolescents.* Eau Claire, WI: Thinking Publications.

Gibbs, Jeanne. (2000). *Tribes: A new way of learning and being together.* Windsor, CA: Center-Source.

Ginott, Haim. (1972). *Teacher and child.* New York: Macmillan.

Glasser, William. (1968). *Schools without failure.* New York: Harper & Row.

Glasser, William. (1986). *Control theory in the classroom.* New York: Harper & Row.

Glasser, William. (1990). *The quality school: Managing students without coercion.* New York: Harper & Row.

Goodlad, John. (1984). *A place called school.* New York: McGraw-Hill.

Gossen, Diane Chelsom. (1998). When all else fails. *Education Update, 40*(6), 7.

Hanh, Thich Nhat. (1992). *Peace is in every step: The path of mindfulness in everyday life.* New York: Bantam.

Hart, Leslie A. (1983). *Human brain and human learning.* New York: Longman.

Hawkins, David J., Lishner, D. M., & Catalano, R. F. (1998). Childhood predictors and the prevention of adolescent substance abuse. In C. L. Jones & R. J. Battjes (Eds.), *Etiology of drug abuse: Implications for prevention.* Washington, DC: National Institute on Drug Abuse.

Herbert, Ann. (1992). *Random acts of kindness.* Berkeley, CA: Conari Press.

Herrick, Jeanne Horan. (1980). *Basic instructional course: Behavior management.* Milpitas, CA: Milpitas Unified School District.

Hord, Rutherford, & Huling-Austin, Hall. (1989). *Taking charge of change: Teacher education, University of Texas in Austin.* Alexandria, VA: Association for Supervision and Curriculum Development.

Howell, J. C., & Gleason, D. K. (1998). *Youth gangs, drugs, and crime: Results from the 1996 National Youth Gang Survey.* Unpublished report. Tallahassee, FL: National Youth Gang Center.

Hunter, Madeline. (1989, January). *Teaching as decision making.* Paper presented at the Santa Clara Office of Education, Santa Clara, CA.

Hunter, Madeline. (1995a). *Retention theory for teachers.* Thousand Oaks, CA: Corwin.

Hunter, Madeline. (1995b). *Teach more—faster!* Thousand Oaks, CA: Corwin.

Jensen, Eric. (1998). *Teaching with the brain in mind.* Alexandria, VA: Association for Supervision and Curriculum Development.

Johnson, David, & Johnson, Roger. (1991). *Teaching students to be peacemakers.* Edina, MN: Interaction.

Jones, Frederic H. (1987). *Positive discipline.* New York: McGraw-Hill.

Jones, Vernon F., & Jones, Louise S. (1998). *Comprehensive classroom management.* Newton, MA: Allyn and Bacon.

Joyce, Bruce, & Weil, Marsha. (1992). *Models of teaching.* Needham Heights, MA: Allyn & Bacon.

Kagan, Spencer. (1994). *Cooperative Learning.* San Clemente, CA: Kagan Cooperative Learning.

Kaufeldt, Martha. (1999). *Begin with the brain: Orchestrating the learner-centered classroom.* Tucson, AZ: Zephyr.

Kohn, Alfie. (1993). *Punished by rewards.* Boston: Houghton Mifflin.

Kohn, Alfie. (1996). *Beyond discipline: From compliance to community.* Alexandria, VA: Association for Supervision and Curriculum Development.

Kohn, Alfie. (1998). *What to look for in the classroom.* San Francisco: Jossey-Bass.

Kounin, Jacob. (1970). *Discipline and group management in classrooms.* New York: Holt, Reinhart, & Winston.

Kovalik, Susan. (1993). *ITI: The Model.* Oak Creek, AZ: Susan Kovalik & Associates.

Krovetz, Martin L. (1999). *Fostering resiliency: Expecting all students to use their minds and hearts well.* Thousand Oaks, CA: Corwin.

Lewis, Catherine, Schaps, Eric, & Watson, Marilyn. (1996, September). The caring classroom's academic edge. *Educational Leadership,* p. 19.

Lowery, L. F. (1989). *Thinking and learning: Matching developmental stages with curriculum and instruction.,* Pacific Grove, CA: Midwest Press.

MacLean, P. D. (1990). A mind of three minds: Educating the triune brain. In National Society for the Study of Education (Ed.), *77th Yearbook of the National Society for the Study Of Education* (pp. 308-342). Chicago: University of Chicago Press.

Maslow, Abraham. (1999). *Toward a psychology of being* (3rd ed). New York: John Wiley.

Meier, Deborah. (1995). *The power of their ideas*. Boston: Beacon.

Mendler, Allen. (1992). *What to do when? How to achieve discipline with dignity*. Bloomington, IN: National Education Service.

Metcalf, Linda. (1995). *Counseling toward solutions*. West Nyack, NY: Center for Applied Research in Education.

Olson, Karen D. (1989). *The mentor teacher role: Owner's manual* (5th ed.). Oak Creek, AZ: Books for Educators.

Palmer, Parker J. (1998). *The courage to teach*. San Francisco: Jossey-Bass.

Phelan, P., Davidson, A., & Cao, H. (1973). Speaking up: Students' perspectives on school. *Phi Delta Kappan*, 695-704.

Piaget, J. (1969). *Psychology of intelligence*. Totowa, NJ: Littlefield, Adams.

Poplin, M., & Weeres, J. (1992). *Voices from the inside: A Report on schooling from inside the classroom*. Claremont, CA: Claremont Graduate School.

Reasoner, Robert. (1982). *Building self-esteem*. Palo Alto, CA: Consulting Psychologists Press.

Rich, Dorothy. (1988). *MegaSkills*. Boston: Houghton Mifflin.

Rogers, Carl. (1961). *On becoming a person*. Boston: Houghton Mifflin.

Rogers, Spence, & Renard, Lisa. (1999, September). Relationship-driven teaching. *Educational Leadership*, pp. 34-37.

Rosenshine, B. (1971). Teaching behaviors and student achievement. Slough, UK: National Federation for Educational Research.

Schneider, Evelyn. (1996). Giving students a voice in the classroom. *Educational Leadership, 54*(1), 22-26.

Sims, Karan. (2002). Dealing with power struggles. Positive Parenting On-Line. Retrieved May 7, 2002, from www.positiveparenting.com/power.html.

Smith, Frank. (1986). *Insult to intelligence*. Portsmouth, NH: Heinemann.

Spaulding, Robert L. (1980). *Cases manual*. San Jose, CA: Robert L. Spaulding Press & San Jose State University.

Sprenger, Marilee. (1999). *Learning and memory*. Alexandria, VA: Association for Supervision and Curriculum Development.

Standing, E. M. (1962). *Maria Montessori: Her life and work*. New York: New American Library.

Sylwester, Robert. (1995). *A celebration of neurons: An educator's guide to the brain*. Alexandria, VA: Association for Supervision and Curriculum Development.

Sylwester, Robert. (1998). *The downshifting dilemma*. Unpublished paper.

Weil, Marsha. (1990). *School Effectiveness Study*. Santa Clara, CA: Santa Clara County Office of Education, Educational Development Center.

Werner, Emmy. (1996). How kids become resilient: Observations and cautions. *Resiliency in Action, 1*(1), 18-28.

Zimmerman, Jeffrey L., & Dickerson, Victoria C. (1996). *If problems talked: Narrative therapy in action*. New York: Guilford.

■ ■ ■

Index

**CORWIN
PRESS**

The Corwin Press logo--a raven striding across an open book--represents the happy union of courage and learning. We are a professional-level publisher of books and journals for K-12 educators, and we are committed to creating and providing resources that embody these qualities. Corwin's motto is "Success for All Learners."